CAPITAL PUNISHMENT

CRUEL AND UNUSUAL?

ISSN 1538-6678

CAPITAL PUNISHMENT
CRUEL AND UNUSUAL?

John W. Weier

INFORMATION PLUS® REFERENCE SERIES
Formerly Published by Information Plus, Wylie, Texas

THOMSON

GALE

Detroit • New York • San Francisco • San Diego • New Haven, Conn. • Waterville, Maine • London • Munich

THOMSON

GALE

CAPITAL PUNISHMENT: CRUEL AND UNUSUAL?
John W. Weier
Paula Kepos, Series Editor

Project Editor
John McCoy

Permissions
Margaret Abendroth, Edna Hedblad,
Emma Hull

Composition and Electronic Prepress
Evi Seoud

Manufacturing
Drew Kalasky

ISBN 0-7876-5103-6 (set)
ISBN 1-4144-0407-7
ISSN 1538-6678

This title is also available as an e-book.
ISBN 1-4144-1043-3 (set)
Contact your Thomson Gale sales representative for ordering information.

Printed in the United States of America
10 9 8 7 6 5 4 3 2 1

TABLE OF CONTENTS

This chapter presents an overview of capital punishment in the United States from the colonial period to the present day. Federal death penalty legislation, crimes punishable by death, constitutional legality of the death penalty, and worldwide trends are also covered.

This chapter presents court cases and legal decisions regarding the constitutionality of the death penalty. Also discussed are judgments concerning the proper imposition of the death penalty; guidelines for judges and jurors, including consideration of lesser charges; the jury selection process in capital cases; the admissibility of parole information; and sentencing procedures.

CHAPTER 3

This chapter presents U.S. Supreme Court capital punishment cases and legal decisions regarding rape and kidnapping; criminal intent; the right to counsel; prosecution errors (including coerced confessions and presumption of malice); types of evidence on which appeals may be based; and court challenges to execution methods.

This chapter investigates court cases and legal decisions regarding mitigating factors, minors and the death sentence, the role of psychiatrists (including validity of testimony, a prisoner's right to an examination, and proving insanity), and the competency standard. Information about cases considering the execution of insane and mentally retarded persons is also included, along with racial issues in capital cases.

As of 2005, thirty-eight states authorized the death penalty. The first section of the chapter defines the different types of capital offenses and discusses statutory changes to state death penalty laws since 2001. The second section discusses statutes regarding minimum age for execution, the execution of mentally retarded persons, and death penalty methods. The chapter also includes information on witnesses at executions, challenges to state death penalty statutes, and state moratoriums on the death penalty.

From 1930 to 2003 approximately 4,744 executions were conducted under civil authority in the United States. This chapter supplies statistics on the number and location of executions; the gender, race, and ethnicity of those executed; the crimes that had led to the executions; and methods of execution.

From 1973 to 2003 approximately 7,403 people had received the death sentence. The first part of the chapter discusses the death sentence in terms of geographic distribution, race, gender, and characteristics of death row inmates. The second section provides information about getting off death row, the capital appeals process, legal resources, and exoneration. The last section covers execution moratoriums, DNA testing, studies of racial and ethnic bias, state studies of their death penalty systems, and costs of administering the death penalty.

This chapter presents public opinion surveys regarding capital punishment. Areas covered include support for the death penalty, acceptable penalties for murder, crimes deserving the death penalty, death penalty versus life imprisonment without parole, reasons for supporting capital punishment, rate of imposition, and the death penalty as a deterrent.

PREFACE

Capital Punishment: Cruel and Unusual? is part of the *Information Plus Reference Series*. The purpose of each volume of the series is to present the latest facts on a topic of pressing concern in modern American life. These topics include today's most controversial and most studied social issues: abortion, capital punishment, care for the elderly, crime, the environment, health care, immigration, minorities, national security, social welfare, women, youth, and many more. Although written especially for the high school and undergraduate student, this series is an excellent resource for anyone in need of factual information on current affairs.

By presenting the facts, it is Thomson Gale's intention to provide its readers with everything they need to reach an informed opinion on current issues. To that end, there is a particular emphasis in this series on the presentation of scientific studies, surveys, and statistics. These data are generally presented in the form of tables, charts, and other graphics placed within the text of each book. Every graphic is directly referred to and carefully explained in the text. The source of each graphic is presented within the graphic itself. The data used in these graphics are drawn from the most reputable and reliable sources, in particular from the various branches of the U.S. government and from major independent polling organizations. Every effort has been made to secure the most recent information available. The reader should bear in mind that many major studies take years to conduct, and that additional years often pass before the data from these studies are made available to the public. Therefore, in many cases the most recent information available in 2006 dated from 2003 or 2004. Older statistics are sometimes presented as well if they are of particular interest and no more recent information exists.

Although statistics are a major focus of the *Information Plus Reference Series*, they are by no means its only content. Each book also presents the widely held positions and important ideas that shape how the book's subject is discussed in the United States. These positions are explained in detail and, where possible, in the words of their proponents. Some of the other material to be found in these books includes: historical background; descriptions of major events related to the subject; relevant laws and court cases; and examples of how these issues play out in American life. Some books also feature primary documents or have pro and con debate sections giving the words and opinions of prominent Americans on both sides of a controversial topic. All material is presented in an even-handed and unbiased manner; the reader will never be encouraged to accept one view of an issue over another.

HOW TO USE THIS BOOK

Few topics are as controversial as capital punishment. Capital punishment has been debated since the colonial period in America and is currently a worldwide issue. This book includes the history of capital punishment plus discussions of numerous court cases, legal decisions, and historical statistics. Also included is information about execution methods, minors and the death penalty, public attitudes, and capital punishment around the world.

Capital Punishment: Cruel and Unusual? consists of eleven chapters and three appendices. Each of the chapters is devoted to a particular aspect of capital punishment. For a summary of the information covered in each chapter, please see the synopses provided in the Table of Contents at the front of the book. Chapters generally begin with an overview of the basic facts and background information on the chapter's topic, then proceed to examine subtopics of particular interest. For example, Chapter 7, Under Sentence of Death, begins with a discussion of the number of prisoners on death row, their race, gender, and other characteristics. This is followed by a discussion of the automatic appeals process and other methods of getting off death row, such as moratoriums and DNA testing. A series of sections examine the fairness of the death penalty by presenting studies on regional, racial, and other variations in how the death penalty is imposed. The chapter concludes with studies on the cost of implementing the death penalty. Readers can find their way through a chapter by looking for the section and subsection headings, which are clearly set off from the text. They can also refer to the book's extensive Index if they already know what they are looking for.

Statistical Information

The tables and figures featured throughout *Capital Punishment: Cruel and Unusual?* will be of particular use to the reader in learning about this issue. These tables and figures represent an extensive collection of the most recent and important statistics on capital punishment and related issues—for example, graphics in the book cover capital offenses; federal laws providing for the death penalty; methods of execution; number of prisoners executed; number of persons under sentence of death; support for capital punishment; and countries retaining the death penalty. Thomson Gale believes that making this information available to the reader is the most important way in which we fulfill the goal of this book: to help readers to understand the issues and controversies surrounding capital punishment in the United States and reach their own conclusions.

Each table or figure has a unique identifier appearing above it for ease of identification and reference. Titles for the tables and figures explain their purpose. At the end of each table or figure, the original source of the data is provided.

In order to help readers understand these often complicated statistics, all tables and figures are explained in the text. References in the text direct the reader to the relevant statistics. Furthermore, the contents of all tables and figures are fully indexed. Please see the opening section of the Index at the back of this volume for a description of how to find tables and figures within it.

Appendices

In addition to the main body text and images, *Capital Punishment: Cruel and Unusual?* has three appendices. The first is the Important Names and Addresses directory.

Here the reader will find contact information for a number of government and private organizations that can provide information on capital punishment. The second appendix is the Resources section, which can also assist the reader in conducting his or her own research. In this section the author and editors of *Capital Punishment: Cruel and Unusual?* describe some of the sources that were most useful during the compilation of this book. The final appendix is the detailed Index, which facilitates reader access to specific topics in this book.

ADVISORY BOARD CONTRIBUTIONS

The staff of Information Plus would like to extend its heartfelt appreciation to the Information Plus Advisory Board. This dedicated group of media professionals provides feedback on the series on an ongoing basis. Their comments allow the editorial staff who work on the project to make the series better and more user-friendly. Our top priority is to produce the highest-quality and most useful books possible, and the Advisory Board's contributions to this process are invaluable.

The members of the Information Plus Advisory Board are:

- Kathleen R. Bonn, Librarian, Newbury Park High School, Newbury Park, California

- Madelyn Garner, Librarian, San Jacinto College—North Campus, Houston, Texas

- Anne Oxenrider, Media Specialist, Dundee High School, Dundee, Michigan

- Charles R. Rodgers, Director of Libraries, Pasco–Hernando Community College, Dade City, Florida

- James N. Zitzelsberger, Library Media Department Chairman, Oshkosh West High School, Oshkosh, Wisconsin

COMMENTS AND SUGGESTIONS

The editors of the *Information Plus Reference Series* welcome your feedback on *Capital Punishment: Cruel and Unusual?* Please direct all correspondence to:

Editors
Information Plus Reference Series
27500 Drake Rd.
Farmington Hills, MI 48331-3535

CHAPTER 1
A CONTINUING CONFLICT—A HISTORY OF CAPITAL PUNISHMENT IN AMERICA

THE COLONIAL PERIOD

Since the first European settlers arrived in America, the death penalty has been accepted as just punishment for a variety of offenses. In fact, the earliest recorded execution occurred in 1608, only a year after the English constructed their first settlement in Jamestown, Virginia. Captain George Kendall, one of the original leaders of the Virginia colony, was convicted of mutiny (some historians say he was also convicted of being a Spanish spy) by a jury of his peers and sentenced to death by shooting in Jamestown. In 1632 Jane Champion, a slave, became the first woman to be put to death in the new colonies. She was hanged in James City, Virginia, for the murders of her master's children.

The English Penal Code applied to the British colonies from the beginning and listed fourteen capital offenses. Actual practice, however, varied from colony to colony. In the early days of the Massachusetts Bay Colony, twelve crimes warranted the death penalty— idolatry, witchcraft, blasphemy, rape, statutory rape, kidnapping, perjury in a trial involving a possible death sentence, rebellion, murder, assault in sudden anger, adultery, and buggery (sodomy). In the statute each crime was accompanied by a quotation justifying capital punishment from the Old Testament of the Bible. Later arson, treason, and grand larceny were added.

Virginia's early statutes were even stricter, based on biblical morality and military laws developed in the Netherlands. First enacted by Jamestown governor Sir Thomas Gates in 1610, the *Lawes Divine, Morall and Martiall* were expanded in 1612 by Sir Thomas Dale. Life in the colony was hard, and many of the laws were enacted in response to harsh necessities. Capital offenses included unauthorized trading with Native Americans, gathering vegetables or fruits from a garden without permission, and giving false testimony under oath. In addition, the laws held that "he that shall rob the store of any commodities therein, of what quality soever, whether provisions of victuals, or of Arms, Trucking stuffe, Apparrell, Linnen, or Wollen, Hose or Shooes, Hats or Caps, Instruments or Tooles of Steeles, Iron, & c. or shall rob from his fellow souldier, or neighbour, any thing that is his, victuals, apparell, household stuffe, toole, or what necessary else soever, by water or land, out of boate, house, or knapsack, shall bee punished with death."

The Quakers, who settled in the mid-Atlantic region, initially adopted much milder laws than those who settled in the Massachusetts, New York, and Virginia colonies. The Royal Charter for South Jersey (1646) did not permit capital punishment for any crime, and there was no execution until 1691. In Pennsylvania, William Penn's Great Act of 1682 limited the death penalty to treason and murder.

The methods of execution in the fledgling American colonies could be especially brutal. While hanging was the preferred method, some criminals were burned alive or pressed to death by heavy stones. Probably the cruelest punishment was known as "breaking at the wheel," wherein the executioner would snap all the offender's arm and leg joints with a chisel and then weave their extremities through the spokes of a large wheel like meaty ribbons. The prisoner would then be left outside to die of blood loss and exposure (M. Watt Espy and John Ortiz Smykla, "Executions in the United States, 1608–2002: The ESPY File," the Inter-University Consortium for Political and Social Research, 2004).

These executions were held in public as a warning to others, and often a festival atmosphere prevailed. Crowds of onlookers gathered near the gallows, and merchants sold souvenirs. Some spectators got drunk, turning unruly and sometimes violent. After the execution, the body of the convict was on some occasions left hanging above the square in a metal cage.

David G. Chardavoyne described a typical nineteenth-century execution scene in *A Hanging in Detroit: Stephen Gifford Simmons and the Last Execution under Michigan Law* (Detroit: Wayne State University Press, 2003). One of only two executions in Michigan before the death penalty was outlawed there in 1846, Simmons was hanged in September 1830 for murdering his pregnant wife. At the time, according to Chardavoyne, "public executions owed much of their continuing legitimacy to the use of ritual." The associated rituals could last for hours and included parading the condemned prisoner through the crowd with a coffin by his side and a noose around his neck, speeches by public officials and religious leaders denouncing the crime, and in some cases a repentance speech by the prisoner.

Over time, the colonies phased out the crueler methods of execution, and almost all death sentences were carried out by hanging. The colonies also rewrote their death penalty statutes to cover only serious crimes involving willful acts of violence or thievery. By the late 1700s, typical death penalty crimes included arson, piracy, treason, murder, and horse stealing. Southern colonies executed people for slave stealing or aiding in a slave revolt. After the American Revolution, some states went further, adopting death penalty statutes similar to Pennsylvania's. New York built its first penitentiary in 1796. With a place to house burglars and nonviolent criminals, the state reduced its capital offenses from thirteen to two. Maryland, Vermont, Virginia, Kentucky, Ohio, and New Hampshire all followed suit by constructing large jails and cutting their capital offenses to just a few of the worst crimes.

THE DEATH PENALTY ABOLITION MOVEMENT

Although the founders of the United States generally accepted the death penalty, many early Americans did oppose capital punishment. In the late eighteenth century, Dr. Benjamin Rush (1745–1813), a physician who helped establish the slavery abolition movement, decried capital punishment. He attracted the support of Benjamin Franklin (1706–90), and it was at Franklin's home in Philadelphia that Rush became one of the first Americans to propose a "House of Reform," a prison where criminals could be detained until they changed their antisocial behavior. Consequently, in 1790 the Walnut Street Jail, the primitive seed from which the American penal system grew, was built in Philadelphia.

Dr. Rush published numerous pamphlets, the most notable of which was *Inquiry into the Justice and Policy of Punishing Murder by Death* (1792). Rush argued that the biblical support given to capital punishment was questionable and that the threat of hanging did not deter crime. Influenced by the philosophy of the Enlightenment (the Age of Reason in the mid- to-late 1700s), Rush believed the state exceeded its granted powers when it executed a citizen. In addition to Franklin, Rush attracted many other Pennsylvanians to his cause, including William Bradford (1755–95), Pennsylvania's attorney general. Bradford suggested the idea of different degrees of murder, some of which did not warrant the death penalty. As a result, in 1794 Pennsylvania repealed the death penalty for all crimes except first-degree murder, defined as "willful, deliberate, and premeditated killing or murder committed during arson, rape, robbery, or burglary."

The Nineteenth Century

Dr. Rush's proposals attracted many followers, and petitions aiming to abolish all capital punishment were presented in New Jersey, New York, Massachusetts, and Ohio. No state reversed its laws, but the number of crimes punishable by death was often reduced.

The second quarter of the nineteenth century was a time of reform in America. Capital punishment opponents rode the tide of righteousness and indignation created by antisaloon and antislavery advocates. Abolitionist societies sprang up, especially along the Atlantic coast. In 1845 the American Society for the Abolition of Capital Punishment was founded.

EARLY SUCCESSES FOR DEATH PENALTY OPPONENTS. The anti–death penalty movement first strove to put an end to public executions. They largely succeeded. In 1828 the State of New York passed a law allowing county sheriffs to hold executions in private. The law, however, was not mandatory, and no sheriff took advantage of it. In 1835 the New York legislature passed another law requiring that all executions be held within the prison walls. The law further required that twelve respectable citizens be chosen to witness the hanging and report on the execution through the state newspaper. In 1830 Connecticut became the first state to pass a law prohibiting all public executions. The Pennsylvania, Rhode Island, New Jersey, and Massachusetts legislatures all followed suit. Maine outlawed public executions and put a temporary moratorium in place in 1835 after one public execution brought in 10,000 people, many of whom became violent after the execution and had to be restrained by the police.

In the late 1840s Horace Greeley (1811–72), the editor and founder of the *New York Tribune* and a leading advocate of most abolitionist causes, led the crusade against the death penalty. In 1846 Michigan became the first state to abolish the death penalty for all crimes except treason (until 1963), making it the first English-speaking jurisdiction in the world to abolish the death penalty for common crimes. Common crimes, also called ordinary crimes, are crimes committed during peacetime. Ordinary crimes that could lead to the death penalty include murder, rape, and, in some countries, robbery or embezzlement of very large sums of money. In comparison, exceptional crimes are military crimes committed during exceptional times, mainly wartime. Examples are treason, spying, or desertion (leaving the armed services without permission). The Michigan law took effect on March 1, 1847. In 1852 and 1853 Rhode Island and Wisconsin, respectively, became the first two states to outlaw the death penalty for all crimes. Most states began limiting the number of capital crimes. Outside the South, murder and treason became the only acts punishable by death.

Opponents of the death penalty initially benefited from abolitionist sentiment, but as the Civil War (1861–65) neared, concern about the death penalty was lost amid the growing antislavery movement. It was not until after the Civil War that Maine and Iowa abolished the death penalty. Almost immediately, however, their legislatures reversed themselves and reinstated the death penalty. In 1887 Maine again reversed itself and abolished capital punishment. It has remained an abolitionist state ever since. Colorado abolished capital punishment in 1897, a decision apparently against the will of many of its citizens. At least twice, Coloradans lynched convicted murderers. In response, the state restored the death penalty in 1901.

Meanwhile, the federal government, following considerable debate in the U.S. Congress, reduced the number of federal crimes punishable by death to treason, murder, and rape. In no instance was capital punishment to be mandatory.

INTRODUCTION OF ELECTROCUTION AS A METHOD OF EXECUTION. Electricity had become widespread by the end of the nineteenth century. As a demonstration of how dangerous alternating current (AC) electricity could be, the Edison Company electrocuted animals in public demonstrations. The Edison Company, which manufactured direct current (DC) electrical systems, wanted to discredit Westinghouse Company, the manufacturer of AC electrical systems. However, instead of steering people away from AC systems, the effective demonstrations only served to inspire state executioners. New York became the first state to tear down its gallows and erect an electric chair in 1890. The chair was first used on William Kemmler in 1890. Other states soon followed.

ANTI–DEATH PENALTY MOVEMENT DECLINES

At the start of the twentieth century, death penalty abolitionists again benefited from American reformism as the Progressives (liberal reformers) worked to correct perceived problems in the American system. Between 1907 and 1917 nine states (Arizona, Kansas, Minnesota, Missouri, North Dakota, Oregon, South Dakota, Tennessee, and Washington) and Puerto Rico, a U.S. territory, abolished capital punishment. However, the momentum

did not last. By 1921, of the nine states, just Minnesota and North Dakota remained abolitionist. The Prohibition Era (1920–33), characterized by frequent disdain for law and order, almost destroyed the abolitionist movement, as many Americans began to believe that the death penalty was the only proper punishment for gangsters who committed murder.

The movement's complete collapse was only prevented by the determined efforts of the famed Clarence Darrow (1857–1938), the "attorney for the damned"; Lewis E. Lawes (1883–1947), the abolitionist warden of Sing Sing Prison in New York; and the American League to Abolish Capital Punishment (founded in 1927). Nonetheless, of the sixteen states and jurisdictions that outlawed capital punishment between 1845 and 1917, only seven—Maine, Michigan, Minnesota, North Dakota, Rhode Island, Wisconsin, and Puerto Rico—had no major death penalty statute at the beginning of the 1950s. Between 1917 and 1957 no state abolished the death penalty.

The abolitionist movement made a mild comeback in the mid-1950s, and the issue was discussed in several state legislatures. In 1957 the U.S. territories of Alaska and Hawaii abolished the death penalty. In the states, however, the movement's singular success in Delaware (1958) was reversed three years later (1961), a major disappointment for death penalty opponents.

Modest Gains in the 1960s

The abolitionists were able to recover during the civil rights movement of the 1960s. In 1963 Michigan, which in 1847 had abolished capital punishment for all crimes except treason, finally outlawed the death penalty for that crime as well. Oregon (1964), Iowa (1965), and West Virginia (1965) all abolished capital punishment, while many other states sharply reduced the number of crimes punishable by death.

RESOLVING THE CONSTITUTIONAL ISSUES

Until the middle of the twentieth century there was legally no question that the death penalty was acceptable under the U.S. Constitution. In 1958, however, the U.S. Supreme Court opened up the death penalty for reinterpretation when it ruled in *Trop v. Dulles* (356 U.S. 86) that the language of the Eighth Amendment (the amendment that states that criminals could not be subjected to "cruel and unusual" punishment) held "an evolving standard of decency that marked the progress of a maturing society." Opponents of capital punishment believed the death penalty should be declared unconstitutional in light of the *Trop* decision (which did not specifically address capital punishment). The abolitionists claimed that society had evolved to a point where the death penalty was "cruel and unusual" by the established "standards of decency." As such, the death penalty violated the Eighth Amendment of the U.S. Constitution.

In 1963 U.S. Supreme Court Justice Arthur J. Goldberg, joined by Justices William O. Douglas and William J. Brennan, dissenting from a rape case in which the defendant had been sentenced to death (*Rudolph v. Alabama*, 375 U.S. 889), raised the question of the legality of the death penalty. The filing of a large number of lawsuits in the late 1960s led to an implied moratorium (a temporary suspension) on executions until the Supreme Court could decide whether the death penalty was constitutional.

In 1972 the high court finally handed down a landmark decision in *Furman v. Georgia* (408 U.S. 238), when it ruled that the death penalty violated the Eighth and Fourteenth Amendments (the right to due process) due to the arbitrary nature with which the death penalty was administered across the United States. The Court also laid down some guidelines for states to follow, declaring that a punishment was "cruel and unusual" if it was too severe, arbitrary, or offended society's sense of justice.

Prior to the late 1960s, death penalty laws in the United States varied considerably from state to state and from region to region. Few national standards existed on how a murder trial should be conducted or which types of crimes deserved the death penalty. Specifically, *Furman* brought into question the laws of Georgia and a number of other states that allowed juries complete discretion in delivering a sentence. In these states, juries could declare a person guilty of a capital crime and then assign any punishment ranging from less than a month in jail to the penalty of death. Though verdicts were swift, the punishments such juries meted out were frequently arbitrary and at times discriminatory against minorities.

CREATING A UNIFORM DEATH PENALTY SYSTEM ACROSS THE UNITED STATES

Within a year of the U.S. Supreme Court's ruling in *Furman* thirty-five states had updated their laws regarding the death penalty. Many of these new statutes were brought before the high court in the mid-1970s. By issuing rulings on the constitutionality of these state statutes, the U.S. Supreme Court created a uniform death penalty system for the United States.

In *Coker v. Georgia* (433 U.S. 584, 1977) and *Eberheart v. Georgia* (433 U.S. 917, 1977) the Court ruled that the death sentence cannot be given to criminals who commit rape. In *Gregg v. Georgia* (428 U.S. 153, 1976), *Jurek v. Texas* (428 U.S. 262, 1976), and *Proffitt v. Florida* (428 U.S. 242), which are collectively known as the *Gregg* decision, the Court established that states

must employ a bifurcated (two-part) trial system in death penalty cases. In this system, a trial is used to determine a defendant's guilt, which must be beyond a reasonable doubt if the defendant is found guilty. A second trial is then held to determine the sentence of a guilty defendant. If a defendant is convicted of a capital crime, the jurors or judges in the sentencing trial cannot sentence the defendant arbitrarily. They must choose between set punishments, one of which has to be a punishment less severe than the death penalty (*Woodson v. North Carolina* [428 U.S. 280, 1976]). In most states this second option is life in prison without parole.

Gregg also established that juries must consider both the mitigating and aggravating circumstances surrounding the crime and then convict and sentence a defendant based on these factors. A mitigating factor is a factor that may lessen the defendant's responsibility for the crime, such as a deeply troubled childhood. An aggravating factor, on the other hand, is a factor that adds to the severity and depravity of the crime, such as raping a victim before murdering him or her. Just as with the crime itself, any aggravating factor must be proven beyond a reasonable doubt before it can be applied.

States amended their laws once again after the Supreme Court issued the new rulings. Every state switched to a bifurcated trial system. Generally, only those convicted of first-degree murder were eligible for the death penalty. (See Table 1.1.) Most states also required the jury or judge in the sentencing phase of the trial to identify one or more aggravating factors beyond a reasonable doubt before they could sentence a person to death. State legislatures drafted lists of aggravating factors that could result in a penalty of death. Typical aggravating factors included: murders committed during robberies, the murder of a pregnant woman, murder committed after a rape, and the murder of an on-duty firefighter or police officer.

With the Supreme Court–approved laws in place, the states resumed executions. In January 1977 the nationwide moratorium ended when the state of Utah executed Gary Gilmore. Gilmore had been convicted of killing Ben Bushnell, a motel manager in Provo, Utah, on July 20, 1976. Authorities had also charged him with the July 19 murder of Max Jensen, a gas station attendant, in Orem, Utah. Gilmore received the death penalty for the Bushnell murder. He refused to appeal his case, demanding that his sentence be carried out swiftly. Gilmore requested the state supreme court to grant his wish because he did not want to spend his life on death row. The court granted his wish, but interventions by his mother, as well as by anti–death penalty organizations, resulted in several stays of execution. These organizations were concerned that the defendant's refusal to

TABLE 1.1

Capital offenses, by state, 2003

Alabama. Intentional murder with 18 aggravating factors (Ala. Stat. Ann. 13A-5-40(a)(1)-(18)).

Arizona*. First-degree murder accompanied by at least 1 of 10 aggravating factors (A.R.S. 13-703(F)).

Arkansas*. Capital murder (Ark. Code Ann. 5-10-101) with a finding of at least 1 of 10 aggravating circumstances; treason.

California. First-degree murder with special circumstances; train wrecking; treason; perjury causing execution.

Colorado*. First-degree murder with at least 1 of 17 aggravating factors; treason.

Connecticut*. Capital felony with 8 forms of aggravated homicide (C.G.S. 53a-54b).

Delaware*. First-degree murder with aggravating circumstances.

Florida*. First-degree murder; felony murder; capital drug trafficking; capital sexual battery.

Georgia*. Murder; kidnaping with bodily injury or ransom when the victim dies; aircraft hijacking; treason.

Idaho*. First-degree murder with aggravating factors; aggravated kidnaping.

Illinois*. First-degree murder with 1 of 21 aggravating circumstances.

Indiana*. Murder with 16 aggravating circumstances (IC 35-50-2-9).

Kansas*. Capital murder with 8 aggravating circumstances (KSA 21-3439).

Kentucky*. Murder with aggravating factors; kidnaping with aggravating factors (KRS 532.025).

Louisiana*. First-degree murder; aggravated rape of victim under age 12; treason (La. R.S. 14:30, 14:42, and 14:113).

Maryland*. First-degree murder, either premeditated or during the commission of a felony, provided that certain death eligibility requirements are satisfied.

Mississippi. Capital murder (97-3-19(2) MCA); aircraft piracy (97-25-55(1) MCA).

Missouri*. First-degree murder (565.020 RSMO 2000).

Montana. Capital murder with 1 of 9 aggravating circumstances (46-18-303 MCA); capital sexual assault (45-5-503 MCA).

Nebraska*. First-degree murder with a finding of at least 1 statutorily-defined aggravating circumstance.

Nevada*. First-degree murder with at least 1 of 14 aggravating circumstances (NRS 200.030, 200.033, 200.035).

New Hampshire. Six categories of capital murder (RSA 630:1, RSA 630:5).

New Jersey. Murder by one's own conduct, by, committed in furtherance of a narcotics conspiracy, or during the commission of the crime of terrorism (NJSA 2C:11-3c).

New Mexico*. First-degree murder with at least 1 of 7 statutorily-defined aggravating circumstances (Section 30-2-1 A, NMSA).

New York*. First-degree murder with 1 of 13 aggravating factors (NY Penal Law §125.27).

North Carolina*. First-degree murder (NCGS §14-17).

Ohio. Aggravated murder with at least 1 of 10 aggravating circumstances (O.R.C. secs. 2903.01, 2929.02, and 2929.04).

Oklahoma. First-degree murder in conjunction with a finding of at least 1 of 8 statutorily defined aggravating circumstances.

Oregon. Aggravated murder (ORS 163.095).

Pennsylvania. First-degree murder with 18 aggravating circumstances.

South Carolina*. Murder with 1 of 10 aggravating circumstances (§ 16-3-20(C)(a)).

South Dakota*. First-degree murder with 1 of 10 aggravating circumstances; aggravated kidnaping.

Tennessee*. First-degree murder with 1 of 15 aggravating circumstances (Tenn. Code Ann. § 39-13-204).

Texas. Criminal homicide with 1 of 8 aggravating circumstances (TX Penal Code 19.03).

Utah*. Aggravated murder (76-5-202, Utah Code Annotated).

Virginia*. First-degree murder with 1 of 13 aggravating circumstances (VA Code § 18.2-31).

Washington*. Aggravated first-degree murder.

Wyoming. First-degree murder.

*Twenty-five States excluded mentally retarded persons from capital sentencing as of December 31, 2003: Arizona, Arkansas, Colorado, Connecticut, Delaware, Florida, Georgia, Idaho, Illinois, Indiana, Kansas, Kentucky, Louisiana, Maryland, Missouri, Nebraska, Nevada, New Mexico, New York, North Carolina, South Dakota, Tennessee, Utah, Virginia, and Washington. Mental retardation is a mitigating factor in South Carolina.

SOURCE: Thomas P. Bonczar and Tracy L. Snell, "Table 1. Capital Offenses, by State, 2003," in *Capital Punishment, 2003*, U.S. Department of Justice, Bureau of Justice Statistics, November 2004, http://www.ojp.usdoj.gov/bjs/pub/pdf/cp03.pdf (accessed June 1, 2005)

appeal his case and the court's agreement to carry out his wish might establish a precedent that would hurt the causes of other inmates. After several suicide attempts, Gilmore finally got his wish and died by firing squad on January 17, 1977.

THE APPEALS PROCESS IN CAPITAL CASES

In the mid-1970s, the lengthy appeals process for capital cases was also established. The appeals process in capital cases varies slightly from state to state but generally consists of similar procedures.

The appeals process begins with the direct appeal. In the *Gregg* decision, the U.S. Supreme Court ruled that any death sentence must be appealed from the trial court directly to the highest court in the state with criminal jurisdiction. The highest court of the state may be either the state supreme court or the highest court of criminal appeals. The state high court evaluates the trial court records for constitutional or legal errors. If the high court upholds the conviction and sentence, the defendant can appeal directly to the U.S. Supreme Court using a *writ of certiorari*. The *writ of certiorari* is a petition to the Supreme Court to review only the issues brought up in the direct appeal in the state's high court. If the Supreme Court denies *certiorari*, the trial court's ruling stands.

If the first round of direct appeals is denied, the inmate may then seek state *habeas corpus* appeals, starting with the trial judge. *Habeas corpus* review, which affords state and federal prisoners the chance to challenge the constitutionality of their convictions or sentences, has long been considered an important safeguard in all criminal trials, especially those involving the death penalty. If turned down by the trial judge, the convict may petition the first level of state appellate courts and finally the state's highest court. This second round of appeals differs from the direct appeal in that the condemned may raise issues that were not and could not have been raised during the direct appeal. These issues include the incompetence of the defense lawyer, jury bias, or the suppression of evidence by police or prosecution. If the state review is denied, the condemned can again appeal directly to the U.S. Supreme Court.

A death row inmate who has exhausted all state appeals can then file a petition for a federal *habeas corpus* review on grounds of violation of his or her constitutional rights. The right may involve a violation of the Eighth Amendment to the Constitution (the ban against cruel and unusual punishment), the Fourteenth Amendment (the right to due process), or the Sixth Amendment (the right to have the assistance of counsel for defense). The inmate files the appeal with the U.S. District Court in the state in which he or she was convicted. If the district court denies the appeal, the inmate can proceed to the U.S. Circuit Court of Appeals in their region. (As of 2005, eleven U.S. Circuit Courts of Appeal existed across the country, each holding jurisdiction over a number of states.) Lastly, if the circuit court denies the appeal, the condemned can for a third time ask the U.S. Supreme Court for a *certiorari* review.

If a convict comes to the end of all appeals and is still on death row, the only way the sentence can be altered is through the power of clemency. The power of clemency may rest solely with a state's governor, with a clemency board, or with the governor and a board of advisers. In federal cases the president alone has clemency power. All states provide for clemency, which may take the form of a reprieve, a commutation, or a pardon. A reprieve, which typically involves a stay of execution, is just a temporary measure to allow further investigation of a case. A commutation involves the reduction of a criminal sentence after a criminal conviction. In the context of capital punishment, a commutation typically means replacing the death sentence with a lesser sentence, such as life without parole. Neither a reprieve nor a commutation removes a person's responsibility for the crime. A pardon, however, frees from punishment a person convicted of a crime, as well as removes his or her criminal record as if the conviction never happened. Pardons are generally only given if investigators can prove beyond any doubt that a death row inmate did not commit the crime of which he or she was convicted.

THE NUMBER OF EXECUTIONS INCREASE WITH THE END OF THE MORATORIUM

Several states reinstated the death penalty after the U.S Supreme Court declared it constitutional. Oregon brought back the death penalty in 1978. In 1995 New York became the thirty-eighth state to reinstate the death penalty, ending its eighteen-year ban on capital punishment. At year-end 2005 the death penalty was approved by the statutes of thirty-eight states, the federal government, and the U.S. military.

Since the end of the moratorium in 1976, the number of executions carried out in the United States has generally been on the rise. Executions hit the double digits in 1984, when twenty-one people were put to death in the United States, and peaked in 1999, when ninety-eight inmates were executed. The number of criminals put to death then dipped to fifty-nine in 2004. Overall, between 1976 and mid-2005, 970 persons were put to death. Of course, these numbers were much smaller than the number of executions that occurred in the early part of the twentieth century. In 1938, for instance, some 190 people were executed. Figure 1.1 shows the number of executions in the United States between 1930 and 2003.

FIGURE 1.1

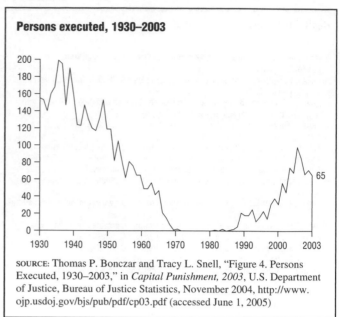

Persons executed, 1930–2003

SOURCE: Thomas P. Bonczar and Tracy L. Snell, "Figure 4. Persons Executed, 1930–2003," in *Capital Punishment, 2003*, U.S. Department of Justice, Bureau of Justice Statistics, November 2004, http://www. ojp.usdoj.gov/bjs/pub/pdf/cp03.pdf (accessed June 1, 2005)

MAJOR CHANGES IN CAPITAL PUNISHMENT IN THE UNITED STATES SINCE *FURMAN* AND *GREGG*

Since 1972, with *Furman v. Georgia* and the accompanying cases, the Supreme Court has been defining and refining what is and is not acceptable under the U.S. Constitution. With the replacement of Chief Justice Earl Warren by Chief Justice Warren Burger, and his later replacement by Chief Justice William Rehnquist, the Court majority generally interpreted the death penalty as worthy of extra attention because of the seriousness of the consequences.

New Rules on How States Impose Death Sentences

U.S. Supreme Court decisions continued to redefine state death penalty laws well after the *Gregg* opinions. In *Ford v. Wainwright* (477 U.S. 399, 1986), the nation's highest court ruled that executing an insane person constituted "cruel and unusual" punishment and was thus in violation of the Eighth Amendment. Since a precedent did not exist in American legal history with regards to executing the insane, the justices looked to English common law to make this ruling. English law expressly forbade the execution of insane people. The English jurist Sir Edward Coke (1552–1634) observed that, while the execution of a criminal was to serve as an example, the execution of a madman was considered "of extreme inhumanity and cruelty, and can be no example to others."

In *Atkins v. Virginia* (536 U.S. 304, 2002), the Court held that executing mentally retarded persons violates the Eighth Amendment's ban on cruel and unusual punishment. The Court, however, did not define mental retardation but left it to each state to formulate its own definition.

In *Ring v. Arizona* (No. 01-488, 536 U.S. 584, 2002), the Court ruled that a death sentence violates the Sixth Amendment right to a trial by jury when a judge and not a jury determines the facts required for imposing the death penalty. The *Ring* decision immediately affected Arizona, Idaho, and Montana, where a single judge made the final decision to impose a death sentence. Since *Ring*, these three states have passed legislation requiring jury sentencing in capital cases. Colorado and Nebraska, which used three-judge panels to determine death sentences, also amended their laws to allow for jury sentencing. Prior to the *Ring* ruling, judges in Alabama, Delaware, Florida, and Indiana also determined the punishment after juries made a recommendation.

The Supreme Court, in two jointly considered cases, *Stanford v. Kentucky* and *Wilkins v. Missouri* (492 U.S. 361, 1989), ruled that people who committed their crimes at ages sixteen or seventeen could be executed for murder. Fifteen years later the Court reversed this decision in *Roper v. Simmons* (543 U.S. 633, 2005), when it decided that executing Donald Roper was "cruel and unusual" based on the fact that Roper was younger than eighteen when he committed murder. The majority reasoned that adolescents do not have the emotional maturity or understanding of lasting consequences that adults have and therefore should not be held to an adult standard or punished with a sentence of death.

Limiting Federal Appeals

Congress passed and President Bill Clinton signed the Antiterrorism and Effective Death Penalty Act (AEDPA; P.L. 104-132) in 1996. The law restricts death row inmates' use of *habeas corpus* petitions, federal appeals by which state and federal inmates request a federal Court to determine whether they are being held in violation of their constitutional rights. The law requires death row inmates to file their *habeas corpus* petitions in the appropriate district courts within six months of the final state appeal. Prior to the enactment of this law, no filing deadline existed. Under the 1996 law, a defendant who fails to challenge his or her conviction or sentence within the time specified cannot file another petition unless approved by a three-judge appellate court. The AEDPA further dictates that federal judges must defer to the rulings of the state courts, unless the rulings violate the Constitution or the laws of the United States or contradict "the Supreme Court's recognition of a new federal right that is made retroactively applicable."

Some opponents feared that the limitations on federal *habeas corpus* petitions required by AEDPA would contribute to the execution of innocent people. In addition, they believed that the unclear language of the AEDPA allowed for varying interpretations in federal appeals courts. For the first time, in 2000, in *(Terry) Williams v. Taylor* (529 U.S. 362) and *(Michael) Williams v. Taylor* (529 U.S. 420), the U.S. Supreme Court addressed the lower courts' interpretation of the AEDPA, ultimately ruling that AEDPA was valid as long as the state appellate courts did not uphold rulings contrary to the precedents laid down by the U.S. Supreme Court.

DNA TAKES THE STAND

In the 1980s and 1990s DNA testing procedures advanced to the point where such evidence could be used in criminal cases. Across the United States, police suddenly had the ability to identify a suspect and place him or her squarely at the scene of a crime with a small sample of hair, blood, or other biological material. Due to the accuracy of DNA testing, DNA evidence could hold as much sway in a courtroom as an eyewitness or camera footage. States started collecting biological samples, such as blood and saliva, from criminal offenders and storing these DNA profiles in databases.

In 1994 Virginia became the first state to execute a person who was convicted as a result of DNA evidence. The defendant, Timothy Spencer, was convicted in 1988 for several rapes and murders he committed starting in 1984. Virginia also became the first state to execute someone based on a DNA "cold hit" when it executed James Earl Patterson in March 2002. (A "cold hit" is when DNA evidence collected at a crime scene matches a DNA sample already in a database.) In 1999 Patterson was in prison on a rape conviction when DNA from the 1987 rape and murder of Joyce Aldridge was found to match his DNA in the database. He confessed to the Aldridge crime in 2000 and was sentenced to death. Patterson waived his appeals in order to let his execution proceed as scheduled.

First Death Row Inmate Is Freed by DNA Testing

Not only has DNA evidence been useful in convicting felons, but it has also been crucial in proving the innocence of falsely convicted criminals. Kirk Bloodsworth of Maryland was the nation's first death row inmate to be exonerated based on postconviction DNA testing. Bloodsworth was convicted for the rape and murder of a nine-year-old girl in 1984. He was sentenced to death in 1985. On retrial, Bloodsworth received two life terms. DNA testing in 1992 excluded him from the crime. Finally in 1993 Bloodsworth was released from prison. In 1999 the state paid Bloodsworth $300,000 for wrongful conviction and imprisonment, including time on death row.

State and Federal Legislatures Enact Laws to Expand DNA Testing

The federal Innocence Protection Act of 2004 (P.L. 108-405) became law on October 30, 2004. The law laid down the conditions with which a federal prisoner who pleaded not guilty could receive postconviction DNA testing. If a trial defendant were to face conviction, the act called for the preservation of the defendant's biological evidence. A five-year, $25 million grant program was also established to help eligible states pay for postconviction testing.

Many state legislatures passed similar DNA testing legislation prior to the Innocence Protection Act. In 2003 Colorado, Connecticut, Georgia, Ohio, Montana, and Nevada passed legislation providing for postconviction DNA testing. As of December 31, 2004, a total of thirty-four death penalty states had statutes that provided DNA testing to felons and death row defendants.

FEDERAL DEATH PENALTY

In modern times, capital punishment generally has fallen under the purview of the states. Each year, the federal government pursues the death penalty in far fewer cases than most states with death penalty statutes. The reason for this is simple: most crimes are state crimes. Generally speaking the federal government is only involved in prosecuting a relatively small number of crimes; crimes that cross state boundaries, are committed on federal property, or that affect federal officials or the working of the federal government. The federal government, however, has been executing criminals since it was formed. In 1790 Thomas Bird became the first inmate executed under the federal death penalty. He was hanged in Maine for murder. Between 1790 and 1963 the federal government put to death 336 men and four women, according to the Death Penalty Information Center. However, most of these executions took place early in American history. Only 32 men and 2 women were executed between 1927 and 1963. On February 15, 1963, Victor Feguer was hanged in Iowa for kidnapping and murder. This was the last execution by the federal government until nearly forty years later.

Expansion of the Federal Death Penalty

In 1988 Congress enacted the first of several laws that broadened the scope of the federal death penalty. The Anti-Drug Abuse Act (P.L. 100-690) included a drug-kingpin provision allowing the death penalty for murder resulting from large-scale illegal drug dealing. The act did not provide for the method of federal execution. In 1993 President George H. W. Bush authorized the use of lethal injection under this law. As of June 30, 2005, three inmates were under sentence of death pursuant to this law.

In 1994 the Violent Crime Control and Law Enforcement Act (P.L. 103-322; also known as the Federal Death Penalty Act of 1994) added more than fifty crimes punishable by death. (See Table 1.2.) Among these federal crimes are murder of certain government officials, kid-

TABLE 1.2

Federal laws providing for the death penalty, 2003

8 U.S.C. 1342—Murder related to the smuggling of aliens.
18 U.S.C. 32-34—Destruction of aircraft, motor vehicles, or related facilities resulting in death.
18 U.S.C. 36—Murder committed during a drug-related drive-by shooting.
18 U.S.C. 37—Murder committed at an airport serving international civil aviation.
18 U.S.C. 115(b)(3) [by cross-reference to 18 U.S.C. 1111]—Retaliatory murder of a member of the immediate family of law enforcement officials.
18 U.S.C. 241, 242, 245, 247—Civil rights offenses resulting in death.
18 U.S.C. 351 [by cross-reference to 18 U.S.C. 1111]—Murder of a member of Congress, an important executive official, or a Supreme Court Justice.
18 U.S.C. 794—Espionage.
18 U.S.C. 844(d), (f), (i)—Death resulting from offenses involving transportation of explosives, destruction of government property, or destruction of property related to foreign or interstate commerce.
18 U.S.C. 924(i)—Murder committed by the use of a firearm during a crime of violence or a drug-trafficking crime.
18 U.S.C. 930—Murder committed in a federal government facility.
18 U.S.C. 1091—Genocide.
18 U.S.C. 1111—First-degree murder.
18 U.S.C. 1114—Murder of a federal judge or law enforcement official.
18 U.S.C. 1116—Murder of a foreign official.
18 U.S.C. 1118—Murder by a federal prisoner.
18 U.S.C. 1119—Murder of a U.S. national in a foreign country.
18 U.S.C. 1120—Murder by an escaped federal prisoner already sentenced to life imprisonment.
18 U.S.C. 1121—Murder of a state or local law enforcement official or other person aiding in a federal investigation; murder of a State correctional officer.
18 U.S.C. 1201—Murder during a kidnaping.
18 U.S.C. 1203—Murder during a hostage taking.
18 U.S.C. 1503—Murder of a court officer or juror.
18 U.S.C. 1512—Murder with the intent of preventing testimony by a witness, victim, or informant.
18 U.S.C. 1513—Retaliatory murder of a witness, victim, or informant.
18 U.S.C. 1716—Mailing of injurious articles with intent to kill or resulting in death.
18 U.S.C. 1751 [by cross-reference to 18 U.S.C. 1111]—Assassination or kidnaping resulting in the death of the President or Vice President.
18 U.S.C. 1958—Murder for hire.
18 U.S.C. 1959—Murder involved in a racketeering offense.
18 U.S.C. 1992—Willful wrecking of a train resulting in death.
18 U.S.C. 2113—Bank-robbery-related murder or kidnaping.
18 U.S.C. 2119—Murder related to a carjacking.
18 U.S.C. 2245—Murder related to rape or child molestation.
18 U.S.C. 2251—Murder related to sexual exploitation of children.
18 U.S.C. 2280—Murder committed during an offense against maritime navigation.
18 U.S.C. 2281—Murder committed during an offense against a maritime fixed platform.
18 U.S.C. 2332—Terrorist murder of a U.S. national in another country.
18 U.S.C. 2332a—Murder by the use of a weapon of mass destruction.
18 U.S.C. 2340—Murder involving torture.
18 U.S.C. 2381—Treason.
21 U.S.C. 848(e)—Murder related to a continuing criminal enterprise or related murder of a federal, state, or local law enforcement officer.
49 U.S.C. 1472-1473—Death resulting from aircraft hijacking.

SOURCE: Thomas P. Bonczar and Tracy L. Snell, "Appendix Table 1. Federal Laws Providing for the Death Penalty, 2003," in *Capital Punishment, 2003*, U.S. Department of Justice, Bureau of Justice Statistics, November 2004, http://www.ojp.usdoj.gov/bjs/pub/pdf/cp03.pdf (accessed June 1, 2005)

napping resulting in death, murder for hire, fatal drive-by shootings, sexual abuse crimes resulting in death, carjacking resulting in death, and other crimes not resulting in death, such as running a large-scale drug enterprise. The method of execution will be the same as that used in the state where the sentencing occurs. If the state does not allow the death penalty, the judge would choose a state with the death penalty. Under the act, more than thirty-five people had been sentenced to death as of September 2005, and three had been executed.

Antiterrorism legislation came about in the wake of the Oklahoma City bombing in 1995. In 1996 Congress passed the Antiterrorism and Effective Death Penalty Act (AEDPA; P.L. 104-132). The act, signed into law on April 24, 1996, just after the first anniversary of the Oklahoma City bombing by Timothy McVeigh, was intended "to deter terrorism, provide justice for victims, [and] provide for an effective death penalty." Another capital crime was added on June 25, 2002, as part of the Terrorist Bombings Convention Implementation Act of 2002 (P.L. 107-197). The law makes punishable by death the bombing of places of public use, government facilities, public transportation systems, and infrastructure facilities with the intent to cause death or serious physical injury or with intent to cause destruction resulting in major economic loss.

New Laws Lead to an Increase in Capital Cases

In 1992 the Administrative Office of the United States Court established the Federal Death Penalty Resource Counsel Project (FDPRCP) to serve as a clearinghouse for information helpful to defense attorneys appointed in federal death penalty cases. According to the FDPRCP, between 1988, when the Anti–Drug Abuse Act was signed into law, to June 10, 2005, the U.S. attorney general authorized the government to seek the death penalty in 356 cases. In 40% of cases, the defendants either entered a plea agreement, the government withdrew the request for the death penalty, or the government dismissed the charges. One person received clemency, and two were found innocent. Juries and judges chose the death sentence forty-four times and rejected it eighty-three times. Seventy-one inmates were on trial or awaiting trial. Thirty-six convicts were on death row in the federal penal system. Three inmates had been executed.

Federal Government Resumes Executions

Timothy McVeigh was sentenced to death for conspiracy and murder in 1997 for his bombing of the Alfred P. Murrah Federal Building in Oklahoma City, Oklahoma, on April 19, 1995, which killed 168 people. McVeigh received an execution date of May 16, 2001. U.S. Attorney General John Ashcroft, however, delayed the execution following the discovery that the Federal Bureau of Investigation (FBI) had failed to turn over more than 3,000 documents to the defense and prosecution during the trial. McVeigh appealed for a second stay of execution, but the U.S. Court of Appeals for the Tenth Circuit denied his request, affirming a U.S. District Court's ruling that there was no evidence that the federal government intentionally hid the FBI files from the defense. On June 11, 2001, the execution was carried out.

Eight days later, on June 19, 2001, Texas drug boss Juan Raul Garza became the second federal prisoner to be executed since 1963. He was the first person to be executed under the Anti-Drug Abuse Act of 1988 for murders resulting from a drug enterprise. Garza received the death sentence in 1993 for the 1990 murders of three associates.

Garza was initially scheduled to be executed in August 2000. In July 2000 President Clinton granted a four-month reprieve (a stay of execution for a short time to resolve an issue) to allow the Justice Department to establish clemency guidelines by which a death row inmate could plead for his life after exhausting all appeals. Some critics noted that the Clinton administration, which had been running the government for seven years, should have previously taken the time to put in place a clemency protocol for capital cases. Others claimed the government could have applied to capital cases the clemency guidelines that it uses for noncapital cases. It should be noted that, even with no formal guidelines in place, Garza could have pleaded for clemency.

On September 13, 2000, Garza asked President Clinton to commute his death sentence to life imprisonment without parole. Garza's lawyer argued that the Justice Department study of the federal death penalty system, released the day before, showed the federal capital punishment is "plagued by systemic bias, disparity and arbitrariness." Defense counsel claimed that it would be unfair to put Garza to death because the federal death penalty discriminates against members of minorities and is administered unevenly geographically. (Of the eighteen men on federal death row at that time, sixteen were minorities, and six had been convicted in Texas.) Again, the president delayed the execution, this time to December 12, 2000. It took another six months for the U.S. government to carry out Garza's death penalty. Newly elected President George W. Bush, formerly the governor of Texas, refused to stay the execution, and Garza was executed June 19, 2001.

Louis Jones, Jr., a retired soldier, was executed by the U.S. government on March 18, 2003. In 1995 Jones was convicted of killing a female soldier. He admitted kidnapping Tracie Joy McBride from an air force base in Texas. The federal government prosecuted Jones because his crime originally occurred at a U.S. military facility. As of November 3, 2005, Jones was the last person to have been executed by the federal government.

Federal Capital Punishment in Non–Death Penalty States

Federal prisoners in death penalty cases used to be imprisoned in the state where the trial was held, but between 1993 and 1996 the U.S. Bureau of Prisons built a fifty-cell federal death house in Terre Haute, Indiana, to accommodate the condemned. It started housing death row inmates in 1999.

According to Justice Department policy, federal criminal law can be enacted in any state. Federal law can also be enacted in any U.S. territory. In 2000 federal prosecutors in Puerto Rico sought the death penalty against two men for kidnapping and murder. Puerto Rico had its last execution in 1927 and had banned the death penalty in 1929. In August 2003 a federal jury voted to acquit the defendants.

Massachusetts outlawed capital punishment in 1975, but in 2000 the federal government sought the death penalty in the case of Kristen Gilbert in Massachusetts, a non–death penalty state. Gilbert was charged with killing four patients at the Veterans Affairs Medical Center in Northampton, a federal hospital. The jury found Gilbert guilty of first-degree murder but was deadlocked on the death sentence. As a result, Judge Michael Ponsor sentenced the defendant to life imprisonment without the possibility of parole.

On March 16, 2002, Michigan became the first non–death penalty state in which a federal jury sentenced a man to death during the modern era. Marvin Gabrion received the death penalty for killing Rachel Timmerman in 1997 on federal property in Manistee National Forest. No execution date had been set as of September 2005. Michigan has not executed an inmate under state law since it joined the Union in 1837. However, Anthony Cherboris, who killed a bystander during a bank robbery, was executed in Michigan under federal law in 1938.

In September 2003 Massachusetts was once again the scene of a federal death penalty case. The Federal Death Penalty Act of 1994 allowed federal prosecutors to seek the death penalty in the case of Gary Lee Sampson, who killed two men in separate carjacking incidents in 2001. Before the trial phase began, Sampson pleaded guilty to the crimes. The case proceeded to the penalty phase, in which a federal jury sentenced him to death. As with other death penalty cases, Sampson's case will undergo several appeals.

Prior to 2005, Vermont had not had a capital trial in nearly fifty years. On July 14, 2005, a federal court jury in Vermont recommended a death sentence for Donald Fell, who was convicted of carjacking a woman in Vermont and then murdering her in New York in 2000. Prosecutors in the case initially tried to negotiate a plea bargain for Fell in 2004, but Attorney General John Ashcroft rejected the deal.

THE U.S. MILITARY

The U.S. military has its own death penalty law—the Uniform Code of Military Justice (UCMJ) found under United States Code, Title 10, Chapter 47. Lethal injection is the method of execution. For crimes that occurred on or after November 17, 1997, the UCMJ provides the alternative sentence of life without the possibility of parole. As commander-in-chief, the president of the United States can write regulations and procedures to implement the UCMJ provisions. The military needs the president's approval to implement a death sentence.

According to the Bureau of Justice Statistics, the military executed 160 inmates between 1939 and 1961. As of April 29, 2005, eight men were on the military death row—six African-Americans, one white, and one Asian. All were convicted of premeditated murder or felony murder (murder that occurs during the commission of another serious crime, such as arson). The military's death row at the U.S. Disciplinary Barracks is located at Fort Leavenworth, Kansas.

The first American soldier to be executed since the Civil War was Army Private Edward Slovik. In 1944 he was charged with desertion while assigned to the European theater during World War II (1939–45). Although Slovik was just one of hundreds of American soldiers who were convicted of desertion and sentenced to death, he was the only one executed. It is believed that, among other reasons, the military wanted to use his case as a deterrent to future desertions. Slovik died by firing squad on January 31, 1945, in France. Since then no other soldier has been executed for desertion. The last military execution occurred on April 13, 1961, when Army Private John A. Bennett was hanged for the 1955 rape and murder of an eleven-year-old girl.

NATIVE AMERICANS

The U.S. government has let Native American nations use their own discretion regarding the death penalty. Most of the tribes have decided against using the death penalty, although according to the NAACP Legal Defense Fund & Educational Fund, Inc. (New York, NY), as of April 1, 2005, there were forty Native Americans on state death rows.

DIVERGENT VIEWS OF SUPREME COURT JUSTICES

The Supreme Court has had the final say on what crimes are eligible for the death penalty and on who can receive the death penalty. Far from being in complete agreement on the subject, justices' views have diverged dramatically.

On July 2, 2001, Supreme Court Justice Sandra Day O'Connor, a longtime supporter of the death penalty, expressed concern about capital punishment. She said in a speech before the Minnesota Women Lawyers that "if statistics are any indication, the system may well be allowing some innocent defendants to be executed." On October 18, 2001, Justice O'Connor told the Nebraska

Bar Association that, unless qualified lawyers are willing to work for indigent defendants who cannot afford counsel, innocent people may be sentenced to death. Justice O'Connor said, "More often than we want to recognize, some innocent defendants have been convicted and sentenced to death."

On April 9, 2001, Justice Ruth Bader Ginsburg expressed similar concerns at a lecture at the University of the District of Columbia. Justice Ginsburg stated:

> I have yet to see a death case among the dozens coming to the Supreme Court on eve-of-execution stay petitions, in which the defendant was well represented at trial. . . . Public funding for the legal representation of poor people in the United States is hardly generous. In capital cases, state systems for affording representation to indigent defendants vary from adequate to meager.

At a Seventh Circuit Bar Association dinner in Chicago, Illinois, on May 2004, Justice John Paul Stevens gave one of the strongest statements against the death penalty that a Supreme Court justice has ever given. In a speech to fellow judges and lawyers, he said, "I really think it's a very unfortunate part of our judicial system and I would feel much, much better if more states would really consider whether they think the benefits outweigh the very serious potential injustice, because in these cases the emotions are very, very high on both sides and to have stakes as high as you do in these cases, there is a special potential for error. We cannot ignore the fact that in recent years a disturbing number of inmates on death row have been exonerated."

Justice Antonin Scalia has voiced a different view of the death penalty. In a speech at the Pew Forum on Religion and Public Life conference, "A Call for Reckoning: Religion & the Death Penalty" (University of Chicago Divinity School, January 25, 2002), Justice Scalia explained that the Roman Catholic Church's current stand against capital punishment does not reflect historical Christian teaching. He added that the core of St. Paul's message in Romans 13 is that government

> derives its moral authority from God. It is the minister of God with powers to revenge, to execute wrath, including even wrath by the sword, which is unmistakably a reference to the death penalty.

According to Justice Scalia, judges who consider the death penalty immoral should resign rather than sabotage the death penalty. He admitted that

> [T]he Constitution that I interpret and apply is not living, but dead; or as I prefer to call it, enduring. It means today not what current society, much less the Court, thinks it ought to mean, but what it meant when it was adopted. For me, therefore, the constitutionality of the death penalty is not a difficult, soul-wrenching question. It was clearly permitted when the Eighth Amendment was adopted—not merely for murder, by the way, but for all felonies.

WORLDWIDE TREND

The *de facto* moratorium on the death penalty in the United States from 1967 to 1976 paralleled a general worldwide movement, especially among Western nations, toward the abolition of capital punishment. While the United States resumed executions in 1977, most of the Western world either formally or informally abolished capital punishment.

Today among the Western democratic nations (with which the United States traditionally compares itself), only the United States imposes the death penalty. There are technical exceptions: Israel, for example, maintains the death penalty in its statute books for "crimes against mankind" but has executed only Adolf Eichmann (1962). One of Nazi leader Adolf Hitler's SS officers, Eichmann was responsible for the murder of millions of Jews in occupied Europe during World War II. Some countries still maintain the death penalty for treason—although no Western democracy has actually imposed it. One of the first acts of the parliaments of many of the eastern European countries after the fall of communism was to abolish capital punishment.

As of May 24, 2005, seventy-six countries and territories in the world continued to maintain and use the death penalty for ordinary crimes (crimes committed during peacetime). However, some of these countries had not actually implemented a death sentence for many years. According to Amnesty International, in 2004 sixty-four countries carried out 7,395 executions.

Extradition and Capital Punishment

An increasing number of countries refuse to extradite (surrender for trial) U.S. criminals who might face the death penalty. In March 2000 French authorities arrested fugitive James Charles Kopp, who was accused of murdering Buffalo, New York, abortion provider Dr. Barnett Slepian. It took months of negotiations before the French government agreed to send Kopp back to New York for trial. The U.S. Justice Department had to guarantee in writing that the United States would not charge Kopp with capital murder. In spring 2001 the supreme courts of Canada and South Africa ruled that both nations would not extradite any criminal to the United States or any country that advocates capital punishment. In November 2001 Spain made a similar announcement, saying it will not extradite terrorist suspects to the United States unless the U.S. government agrees not to seek the death penalty.

A very controversial case also involving France concerned a fugitive convicted and sentenced to death in absentia. Ira Einhorn was accused of murdering his girlfriend, Helen Maddux, in 1977. Her body was found in 1979, eighteen months after she disappeared, in a closet in his apartment. Before his trial in 1981, Einhorn fled to

Ireland, and eventually to France. The state of Pennsylvania held a trial without him, and he was convicted of Maddux's murder in 1993. In 1997, after French authorities arrested Einhorn, the United States requested his extradition. France, following rules of the European Convention on Human Rights, does not recognize verdicts handed down in trials in absentia or verdicts that result in the death penalty. As such, France refused to extradite the fugitive. Four years later, on July 20, 2001, France finally turned Einhorn over to U.S. officials after receiving assurances that he would be retried and not face the death penalty, forcing the Pennsylvania General Assembly to create a new law allowing for a condemned man to have another trial. On October 17, 2001, Einhorn was convicted of first-degree murder and sentenced to life imprisonment without parole.

CHAPTER 2
SUPREME COURT RULINGS—CONSTITUTIONALITY OF THE DEATH PENALTY, GUIDELINES FOR JUDGES AND JURIES, JURY SELECTION, AND SENTENCING PROCEDURES

In 1967 a coalition of anti–death penalty groups sued Florida and California, the states with the most inmates on death row at that time, challenging the constitutionality of state capital punishment laws. An unofficial moratorium (temporary suspension) of executions resulted, pending Supreme Court decisions on several cases on appeal. The defendants in these cases claimed that the death penalty is "cruel and unusual punishment" in violation of the Eighth Amendment to the U.S. Constitution. Moreover, they alleged that the death penalty also violated the Fourteenth Amendment, which prevents states from denying anyone "equal protection of the laws." This moratorium lasted until January 17, 1977, when convicted murderer Gary Gilmore, virtually at his own request, was executed by the state of Utah.

IS THE DEATH PENALTY CONSTITUTIONAL?

On June 29, 1972, a split 5–4 Supreme Court reached a landmark decision in *Furman v. Georgia* (408 U.S. 238, which included *Jackson v. Georgia* and *Branch v. Texas*), holding that "as the statutes before us are now administered ... the imposition and carrying out of the death penalty constitutes cruel and unusual punishment in violation of the Eighth and Fourteenth Amendments." In other words, the justices did not address whether capital punishment as a whole is unconstitutional. Rather, they considered capital punishment in the context of its application in state statutes (laws created by state legislatures). The justices, whether they were of the majority opinion or of the dissenting opinion, could not agree on the arguments explaining why they opposed or supported the death penalty. As a result, the decision consisted of nine separate opinions, the lengthiest ruling in Court history to date.

Majority Opinions in *Furman v. Georgia*

Justice William O. Douglas, in his concurring majority opinion, quoted former Attorney General Ramsey Clark's observation in his book, *Crime in America* (1970): "It is the poor, the sick, the ignorant, the powerless, and the hated who are executed." Douglas added,

We deal with a system of law and of justice that leaves to the uncontrolled discretion of judges or juries the determination whether defendants committing these crimes should die or be imprisoned. Under these laws no standards govern the selection of the penalty. People live or die, dependent on the whim of one man or of twelve. ... Thus, these discretionary statutes are unconstitutional in their operation. They are pregnant with discrimination, and discrimination is an ingredient not compatible with the idea of equal protection of the laws that is implicit in the ban on "cruel and unusual" punishments.

Justice William J. Brennan stated,

At bottom, then, the Cruel and Unusual Punishments Clause prohibits the infliction of uncivilized and inhumane punishments. The State, even as it punishes, must treat its members with respect for their intrinsic worth as human beings. A punishment is "cruel and unusual," therefore, if it does not comport with human dignity.

Justice Potter Stewart stressed another point, saying,

These death sentences are cruel and unusual in the same way that being struck by lightning is cruel and unusual. For, of all the people convicted of rapes and murders in 1967 and 1968, many just as reprehensible as these, the petitioners are among a capriciously selected random handful upon whom the sentence of death has in fact been imposed.

This did not mean that Justice Stewart would rule out the death penalty. He believed that the death penalty was justified but would like to see a more equitable system of determining who should be executed. He explained,

I cannot agree that retribution is a constitutionally impermissible ingredient in the imposition of punishment. The instinct for retribution is part of the nature of man, and channeling that instinct in the administration of criminal justice serves an important purpose in promoting the stability of a society governed by law. When people begin to believe that organized society is unwilling or unable to impose upon criminal offenders the punishment they "deserve," then there are sown the seeds of anarchy—of self-help, vigilante justice, and lynch law.

Justice Byron White, believing that the death penalty was so seldom imposed that executions were ineffective deterrents to crime, chose instead to address the role of juries and judges in imposing the death penalty. He concluded that the cases before the courts violated the Eighth Amendment because the state legislatures, having authorized the application of the death penalty, left it to the discretion of juries and judges whether or not to impose the punishment.

Justice Thurgood Marshall thought that "the death penalty is an excessive and unnecessary punishment which violates the Eighth Amendment." He added that "even if capital punishment is not excessive, it nonetheless violates the Eighth Amendment because it is morally unacceptable to the people of the United States at this time in their history." Justice Marshall also noted that the death penalty was applied with discrimination against certain classes of people (the poor, the uneducated, and members of minority groups) and that innocent people had been executed before they could prove their innocence. He also believed that it hindered the reform of the treatment of criminals, and that it promoted sensationalism during trials.

Dissenting Opinions

Chief Justice Warren Burger, disagreeing with the majority, observed that "the constitutional prohibition against 'cruel and unusual punishments' cannot be construed to bar the imposition of the punishment of death." Justice Harry A. Blackmun was disturbed by Justices Stewart's and White's remarks that as long as capital punishment was mandated for specific crimes, it could not be considered unconstitutional. Justice Blackmun feared "that statutes struck down today will be re-enacted by state legislatures to prescribe the death penalty for specified crimes without any alternative for the imposition of a lesser punishment in the discretion of the judge or jury, as the case may be."

Justice Lewis Powell declared,

I find no support—in the language of the Constitution, in its history, or in the cases arising under it—for the view that this Court may invalidate a category of penalties because we deem less severe penalties adequate to serve the ends of penology....

This Court has long held that legislative decisions in this area, which lie within the special competency of that branch, are entitled to a presumption of validity.

In other words, the Court would not question the validity of a government entity properly doing its job unless its actions were way out of line.

Justice William H. Rehnquist agreed with Justice Powell, adding the following comment:

How can government by the elected representatives of the people co-exist with the power of the federal judiciary, whose members are constitutionally insulated from responsiveness to the popular will, to declare invalid laws duly enacted by the popular branches of government?

Summary of Court Decision

Only Justices Brennan and Marshall concluded that the Eighth Amendment prohibited the death penalty for all crimes and under all circumstances. Justice Douglas, while ruling that the death penalty statutes reviewed by the high court were unconstitutional, did not necessarily require the final abolition of the death penalty. Justices Stewart and White also did not rule on the validity of the death penalty, noting instead that, because of the capricious imposition of the sentence, the death penalty violated the Eighth Amendment. However, Justices Rehnquist, Burger, Powell, and Blackmun concluded that the U.S. Constitution allows capital punishment.

Consequently, most state legislatures went to work to revise their capital punishment laws. They strove to make these laws more equitable in order to swing the votes of Stewart and White (and later that of John Paul Stevens, who replaced the retired Justice Douglas).

PROPER IMPOSITION OF THE DEATH PENALTY

Four years later, on July 2, 1976, the Supreme Court ruled decisively on a series of cases. In *Gregg v. Georgia* (428 U.S. 153), perhaps the most significant of these cases, the justices concluded 7–2 that the death penalty was, indeed, constitutional as presented in some new state laws. With Justices Brennan and Marshall dissenting, the Court stressed (just in case *Furman* had been misunderstood) that "the death penalty is not a form of punishment that may never be imposed, regardless of the circumstances of the offense, regardless of the procedure followed in reaching the decision to impose it." Furthermore, "the infliction of death as a punishment for murder is not without justification, and thus is not unconstitutionally severe."

The Court upheld death penalty statutes in Georgia (*Gregg v. Georgia*), Florida (*Proffitt v. Florida*, 428 U.S. 242), and Texas (*Jurek v. Texas*, 428 U.S. 262), but struck down laws in North Carolina (*Woodson v. North Carolina*, 428 U.S. 280) and Louisiana (*Roberts v. Louisiana*, 428 U.S. 40). It ruled that laws in the latter two states were too rigid in imposing mandatory death sentences for certain types of murder.

Citing the new Georgia laws in *Gregg v. Georgia*, Justice Stewart supported the bifurcated (two-part) trial system, in which the accused would first be tried to determine his or her guilt. Then, in a separate trial, the jury would consider whether the convicted person deserved the death penalty or whether mitigating factors (circumstances that may lessen or increase responsibility for a crime) warranted a lesser sentence, usually life imprisonment. This system meets the requirements demanded by *Furman*. Noting how the Georgia statutes fulfilled these demands, Justice Stewart observed,

> These procedures require the jury to consider the circumstances of the crime and the criminal before it recommends sentence. No longer can a Georgia jury do as *Furman*'s jury did: reach a finding of the defendant's guilt and then, without guidance or direction, decide whether he should live or die. Instead, the jury's attention is directed to the specific "circumstances of the crime: Was it committed in the course of another capital felony? Was it committed for money? Was it committed upon a peace officer or judicial officer? Was it committed in a particularly heinous way or in a manner that endangered the lives of many persons?" In addition, the jury's attention is focused on the characteristics of the person who committed the crime: Does he have a record of prior convictions for capital offenses? Are there any special facts about this defendant that mitigate against imposing capital punishment (e.g., his youth, the extent of his cooperation with the police, his emotional state at the time of the crime)? As a result, while some jury discretion still exists, the discretion to be exercised is controlled by clear and objective standards so as to produce non-discriminatory application.

In addition, the Georgia law required that all death sentences be automatically appealed to the state supreme court, an "important additional safeguard against arbitrariness and caprice." The two-part trial system has since been adopted in the trials of all capital murder cases.

In *Proffitt v. Florida*, the high court upheld Florida's death penalty laws that had a bifurcated trial system similar to Georgia's. In Florida, however, the sentence was determined by the trial judge rather than by the jury, who assumed an advisory role during the sentencing phase. The Court found Florida's sentencing guidelines adequate in preventing unfair imposition of the death sentence.

Predictability of Future Criminal Activity

In *Jurek v. Texas*, the issue centered on whether a jury can satisfactorily determine the future actions of a convicted murderer. The Texas statute required that during the sentencing phase of a trial, after the defendant had been found guilty, the jury would determine whether it is probable the defendant would commit future criminal acts of violence that would threaten society. While agreeing with Jurek's attorneys that predicting future behavior is not easy, Justice Stewart noted,

> The fact that such a determination is difficult, however, does not mean that it cannot be made. Indeed, prediction of future criminal conduct is an essential element in many of the decisions rendered throughout our criminal justice system. The decision whether to admit a defendant to bail, for instance, must often turn on a judge's prediction of the defendant's future conduct. And any sentencing authority must predict a convicted person's probable future conduct when it engages in the process of determining what punishment to impose. For those sentenced to prison, these same predictions must be made by parole authorities. The task that a Texas jury must perform in answering the statutory question in issue is thus basically no different from the task performed countless times each day throughout the American system of criminal justice.

Flexible Guidelines for Judges and Jurors Are Required

In *Woodson v. North Carolina*, the Supreme Court addressed for the first time the question of whether the jury's handing down of a death sentence under North Carolina's mandatory death penalty for all first-degree murders constituted cruel and unusual punishment within the meaning of the Eighth and Fourteenth Amendments. If a person was convicted of first-degree murder in North Carolina, he or she was automatically sentenced to death. The justices held that as a whole the American public rejected the idea of mandatory death sentences long ago. In addition, North Carolina's new statute provided "no standards to guide the jury in its inevitable exercise of the power to determine which first-degree murderer shall live and which shall die." Furthermore, the North Carolina law did not let the jury consider the convicted defendant's character, criminal record, or the circumstances of the crime before the imposition of the death sentence.

The Louisiana mandatory death sentence for first-degree murder suffered from similar inadequacies. It did, however, permit the jury to consider lesser offenses such as second-degree murder. In *Roberts v. Louisiana*, the Supreme Court rejected the Louisiana law because it forced the jury to find the defendant guilty of a lesser crime in order to avoid imposing the death penalty. In other words, if the crime was not heinous enough to warrant the death penalty, then the jury was forced to convict the defendant of second-degree murder or a lesser charge. The jury did not have the option of first determining if the accused was indeed guilty of first-degree murder for the crime he or she had actually committed and then recommending a lesser sentence if there were mitigating circumstances to support it.

As a result of either *Furman* or *Gregg* or both, virtually every state's capital punishment statute had to be rewritten. These statutes would provide flexible guidelines for judges and juries so that they might fairly decide capital cases and consider, then impose, if necessary, the death penalty.

JURY MAY CONSIDER A LESSER CHARGE

In 1977 Gilbert Beck was convicted of robbing and murdering eighty-year-old Roy Malone. According to Beck, he and an accomplice entered Malone's home and were tying up the victim in order to rob him when Beck's accomplice unexpectedly struck and killed Malone. Beck admitted to the robbery but claimed the murder was not part of the plan. Beck was tried under an Alabama statute for "robbery or attempts thereof when the victim is intentionally killed by the defendant."

Under Alabama law, the judge was specifically prohibited from giving the jury the option of convicting the defendant of a lesser, included offense. Instead, the jury was given the choice of either convicting the defendant of the capital crime, in which case he possibly faced the death penalty, or acquitting him, thus allowing him to escape all penalties for his alleged participation in the crime. The judge could not have offered the jury the lesser alternative of felony murder, which did not deal with the accused's intentions at the time of the crime.

Beck appealed, claiming this law created a situation in which the jury was more likely to convict. The Supreme Court, in *Beck v. Alabama* (447 U.S. 625, 1980), agreed and reversed the lower court's ruling, thus vacating (annulling) his death sentence. The high court observed that, while not a matter of due process, it was virtually universally accepted in lesser offenses that a third alternative be offered. The Court noted,

> That safeguard would seem to be especially important in a case such as this. For when the evidence unquestionably establishes that the defendant is guilty of a serious, violent offense—but leaves some doubt with respect to an element that would justify conviction of a capital offense—the failure to give the jury the "third option" of convicting on a lesser included offense would seem inevitably to enhance the risk of an unwarranted conviction.

According to the ruling, such a risk could not be tolerated in a case where the defendant's life was at stake. *Beck*, however, did not require a jury to consider a lesser charge in every case, but only where the consideration would be justified.

EXCLUSION FROM JURIES OF THOSE AGAINST CAPITAL PUNISHMENT

In *Witherspoon v. Illinois* (391 U.S. 510, 1968), the Supreme Court held that a death sentence cannot be carried out if the jury that imposed or recommended such punishment was selected by excluding prospective jurors simply because they have qualms against the death penalty or reservations against its infliction. The Court found that the prosecution excluded those who opposed the death penalty without determining whether their beliefs would compel them to reject capital punishment out of hand. The defendant argued that this selective process had resulted in a jury that was not representative of the community.

The justices could not definitively conclude that the exclusion of jurors opposed to the death penalty results in an unrepresentative jury. They, however, believed that a person who opposes the death penalty can still abide by his duty as a juror and consider the facts presented at trial before making his decision about the defendant's punishment. The Court observed,

> If the State had excluded only those prospective jurors who stated in advance of trial that they would not even consider returning a verdict of death, it could argue that the resulting jury was simply "neutral" with respect to penalty. But when it swept from the jury all who expressed conscientious or religious scruples against capital punishment and all who opposed it in principle, the State crossed the line of neutrality. In its quest for a jury capable of imposing the death penalty, the State produced a jury uncommonly willing to condemn a man to die.

The Court specifically noted that their findings in *Witherspoon* did not prevent the infliction of the death sentence when the prospective jurors excluded had made it "unmistakably clear" that they would automatically vote against the death sentence without considering the evidence presented during the trial, or that their attitudes toward capital punishment would keep them from making a fair decision about the defendant's guilt. Consequently, based on *Witherspoon*, it has become the practice in most states to exclude prospective jurors who indicate that they could not possibly in good conscience return a death penalty.

This ruling was reinforced in *Lockett v. Ohio* (438 U.S. 586, 1978). The defendant in Lockett contended, among several things, that the exclusion of four prospective jurors violated her Sixth Amendment right to trial by an impartial jury and Fourteenth Amendment rights under the principles established in *Witherspoon v. Illinois*. The Supreme Court upheld *Witherspoon* in this case because the prospective jurors told the prosecutor that they were so against the death penalty they could not be impartial about the case. They had also admitted that they would not take an oath saying they would consider the evidence before making a judgment of innocence or guilt.

A Special Selection Process Is Not Required When Selecting Jurors in Capital Cases

In *Wainwright v. Witt* (469 U.S. 412, 1985), a 7–2 Supreme Court decision eased the strict requirements of

Witherspoon. Writing for the majority, Justice Rehnquist declared that the new capital punishment procedures left less discretion to jurors. Rehnquist indicated that potential jurors in capital cases should be excluded from jury duty in a manner similar to how they were excluded in noncapital cases. (In a noncapital case, the prospective jurors typically go through a selection process in which the prosecution and the defense question them about their attitudes toward the crime and the people and issues related to it to determine if they are too biased to be fair.)

No longer would a juror's "automatic" bias against imposing the death penalty have to be proved with "unmistakable clarity." A prosecutor could not be expected to ask all the questions necessary to determine if a juror would automatically rule against the death penalty or fail to convict a defendant if he or she were likely to face execution. Fundamentally, the question of exclusion from a jury should be determined by the interplay of the prosecutor and the defense lawyer and by the decision of the judge based on his or her initial observations of the prospective juror. Judges can see firsthand whether prospective jurors' beliefs would bias their ability to impose the death penalty.

In his dissent, Justice Brennan claimed that making it easier to eliminate those who opposed capital punishment from the jury created a jury not only more likely to impose the death sentence but also more likely to convict. He also attacked the majority interpretation that now treated exclusion from a capital case as being similar to exclusion from any other case.

It Does Not Matter if "Death-Qualified" Juries Are More Likely to Convict

In *Lockhart v. McCree* (476 U.S. 162, 1986), the Supreme Court firmly resolved the issue presented in *Witherspoon* regarding a fair trial with a "death-qualified" jury. (A death-qualified jury is another name for a jury that is willing to sentence a person to death after hearing the evidence of the case.)

Ardia McCree was convicted of murdering Evelyn Boughton while robbing her gift shop and service station in Camden, Arkansas, in February 1978. In accordance with Arkansas law, the trial judge removed eight prospective jurors because they indicated they could not, under any circumstances, vote for the imposition of the death sentence. The resulting jury then convicted McCree and, although the state sought the death penalty, sentenced the defendant to life imprisonment without parole.

McCree appealed, claiming that the removal of the so-called *Witherspoon*-excludables violated his right to a fair trial under the Sixth and Fourteenth Amendments. These amendments guaranteed that his guilt or innocence would be determined by an impartial jury selected from a representative cross-section of the community, which would include people strongly opposed to the death penalty. McCree cited several studies, revealing that "death-qualified" juries were more likely to convict. Both the federal district court and the federal court of appeals agreed with McCree, but in a 6–3 decision, the Supreme Court disagreed.

The high court majority did not accept the validity of the studies. Justice Rehnquist, speaking for the majority, argued that, even if the justices did accept the validity of these studies, "the Constitution does not prohibit the States from 'death qualifying' juries in capital cases." Justice Rehnquist further observed,

> The exclusion from jury service of large groups of individuals not on the basis of their inability to serve as jurors, but on the basis of some immutable characteristic such as race, gender, or ethnic background, undeniably gave rise to an "appearance of unfairness."
>
> [Nevertheless], unlike blacks, women, and Mexican-Americans, "*Witherspoon*-excludables" are singled out for exclusion in capital cases on the basis of an attribute that is within the individual's control. It is important to remember that not all who oppose the death penalty are subject to removal for cause in capital cases; those who firmly believe that the death penalty is unjust may nevertheless serve as jurors in capital cases so long as they state clearly that they are willing to temporarily set aside their own beliefs in deference to the rule of law. Because the group of "*Witherspoon*-excludables" includes only those who cannot and will not conscientiously obey the law with respect to one of the issues in a capital case, "death qualification" hardly can be said to create an "appearance of unfairness."

Writing in dissent, Justice Marshall observed that if the high court thought in *Witherspoon* that excluding those who opposed the death penalty meant that a convicted murderer would not get a fair hearing during the sentencing part of the trial, it would also logically mean that he or she would not get a fair hearing during the initial trial part. The Court minority generally accepted the studies showing "that 'death qualification' in fact produces juries somewhat more 'conviction-prone' than 'non–death-qualified' juries."

DOES THE BUCK STOP WITH THE JURY?

During the course of a robbery Bobby Caldwell shot and killed the owner of a Mississippi grocery store in October 1980. He was tried and found guilty. During the sentencing phase of the trial, Caldwell's attorney pleaded for mercy, concluding his summation by emphasizing to the jury,

> I implore you to think deeply about this matter. . . . You are the judges and you will have to decide his fate. It is an awesome responsibility, I know—an awesome responsibility.

Responding to the defense attorney's plea, the prosecutor played down the responsibility of the jury, stressing that a life sentence would be reviewed by a higher court:

> [The defense] would have you believe that you're going to kill this man and they know—they know that your decision is not the final decision.... Your job is reviewable.... [T]hey know, as I know, and as Judge Baker has told you, that the decision you render is automatically reviewable by the Supreme Court.

The jury sentenced Caldwell to death, and the case was automatically appealed. The Mississippi Supreme Court upheld the conviction, but split 4–4 on the validity of the death sentence, thereby upholding the death sentence by an equally divided court. Caldwell appealed to the U.S. Supreme Court.

In a 5–3 decision (Justice Powell took no part in the decision), the Supreme Court, in *Caldwell v. Mississippi* (472 U.S. 320, 1985), vacated the death sentence. Writing for the majority, Justice Marshall noted,

> It is constitutionally impermissible to rest a death sentence on a determination made by a sentencer who has been led to believe that the responsibility for determining the appropriateness of the defendant's death rests elsewhere.... [This Court] has taken as a given that capital sentencers would view their task as the serious one of determining whether a specific human being should die at the hands of the State.

Furthermore, the high court pointed out that the appeals court was not the place to make this life-or-death decision. Most appellate courts would presume that the sentencing was correctly done, which would leave the defendant at a distinct disadvantage. The jurors, expecting to be reversed by an appeals court, might choose to "send a message" of extreme disapproval of the defendant's acts and sentence him or her to death to show they will not tolerate such actions. Should the appeals court fail to reverse the decision, the defendant might be executed when the jury only intended to "send a message."

The three dissenting judges believed "the Court has overstated the seriousness of the prosecutor's comments" and that it was "highly unlikely that the jury's sense of responsibility was diminished."

KEEPING PAROLE INFORMATION FROM THE JURY

In 1990 Jonathan Dale Simmons beat an elderly woman to death in her home in Columbia, South Carolina. The week before his capital murder trial began, he pleaded guilty to first-degree burglary and two counts of criminal sexual conduct in connection with two prior assaults on elderly women. These guilty pleas resulted in convictions for violent offenses, which made him ineligible for parole if convicted of any other violent crime.

At the capital murder trial, over the defense counsel's objection, the court did not allow the defense to ask prospective jurors if they understood the meaning of a "life" sentence as it applied to the defendant. Under South Carolina law, a defendant who was deemed a future threat to society and receiving a life sentence was ineligible for parole. The prosecution also asked the judge not to mention parole.

During deliberation, the jurors asked the judge if the imposition of a life sentence carried with it the possibility of parole. The judge told the jury,

> You are instructed not to consider parole or parole eligibility in reaching your verdict. . . . The terms life imprisonment and death sentence are to be understood in the [plain] and ordinary meaning.

The jury convicted Simmons of murder, sentencing him to death. On appeal the South Carolina Supreme Court upheld the sentence. The case was brought before the U.S. Supreme Court. The high court, in a 6–2 decision (*Simmons v. South Carolina* [512 U.S. 154, 1994]), overruled the South Carolina Supreme Court, concluding,

> Where a defendant's future dangerousness is at issue, and state law prohibits his release on parole, due process requires that the sentencing jury be informed that the defendant is parole ineligible. An individual cannot be executed on the basis of information which he had no opportunity to deny or explain. . . . Petitioner's jury reasonably may have believed that he could be released on parole if he were not executed. To the extent that this misunderstanding pervaded its deliberations, it had the effect of creating a false choice between sentencing him to death and sentencing him to a limited period of incarceration. The trial court's refusal to apprise the jury of information so crucial to its determination, particularly when the State alluded to the defendant's future dangerousness in its argument, cannot be reconciled with this Court's well-established precedents interpreting the Due Process Clause.

JUDGE SENTENCING

Florida

Under Florida's capital trial system, the jury decides the guilt or innocence of the accused. If the jury finds the defendant guilty, it recommends an advisory sentence of either life imprisonment or death. The trial judge considers aggravating and mitigating circumstances, weighs them against the jury recommendation, and then sentences the convicted murderer to either life or death. (Mitigating circumstances may lessen responsibility for a crime, while aggravating circumstances may add to responsibility for a crime.)

In 1975 a Florida jury convicted Joseph Spaziano of torturing and murdering two women. The jury recommended that Spaziano be sentenced to life imprisonment, but the trial judge, after considering the mitigating and aggravating circumstances, sentenced the defendant to death. In his appeal, Spaziano claimed the judge's overriding of the jury's recommendation of life imprisonment violated the Eighth Amendment's prohibition against cruel and unusual punishment. The Supreme Court, in a 5–3 decision in *Spaziano v. Florida* (468 U.S. 447, 1984), did not agree.

Spaziano's lawyers claimed juries, not judges, were better equipped to make reliable capital-sentencing decisions and that a jury's decision of life imprisonment should not be superceded. They reasoned that the death penalty was unlike any other sentence and required that the jury have the ultimate word. This belief had been upheld, Spaziano claimed, because thirty out of thirty-seven states with capital punishment had the jury decide the prisoner's fate. Furthermore, the primary justification for the death penalty was retribution and an expression of community outrage. The jury served as the voice of the community and knew best whether a particular crime was so terrible that the community's response must be the death sentence.

The high court indicated that, although Spaziano's argument had some appeal, it contained two fundamental flaws. First, retribution played a role in all sentences, not just death sentences. Second, a jury was not the only source of community input. "The community's voice is heard at least as clearly in the legislature when the death penalty is authorized and the particular circumstances in which death is appropriate are defined." That trial judges imposed sentences was a normal part of the judicial system. The Supreme Court continued,

> In light of the facts that the Sixth Amendment does not require jury sentencing, that the demands of fairness and reliability in capital cases do not require it, and that neither the nature of, nor the purpose behind, the death penalty requires jury sentencing, we cannot conclude that placing responsibility on the trial judge to impose the sentence in a capital case is unconstitutional.

The Court added that just because thirty of thirty-seven states let the jury make the sentencing decision did not mean states that let a judge decide were wrong. The Court pointed out that there is no one right way for a state to establish its method of capital sentencing.

Writing for the dissenters, Justice Stevens indicated,

> Because of its severity and irrevocability, the death penalty is qualitatively different from any other punishment, and hence must be accompanied by unique safeguards to ensure that it is a justified response to a given offense.... I am convinced that the danger of an excessive response can only be avoided if the decision to impose the death penalty is made by a jury rather than by a single governmental official . . . [because a jury] is best able to "express the conscience of the community on the ultimate question of life or death."

Justice Stevens also gave weight to the fact that thirty out of thirty-seven states had the jury make the decision, attesting to the "high level of consensus" that communities strongly believe life-or-death decisions should remain with the people—as represented by the jury—rather than relegated to a single government official.

Alabama

In March 1988 Louise Harris asked a coworker, Lorenzo McCarter, with whom she was having an affair, to find someone to kill her husband. McCarter paid two accomplices one hundred dollars, with a promise of more money after they killed the husband. McCarter testified against Harris in exchange for the prosecutor's promise that he would not seek the death penalty against McCarter. McCarter testified that Harris had asked him to kill her husband so they could share in his death benefits. An Alabama jury convicted Louise Harris of capital murder. At the sentencing hearing witnesses testified to her good background and strong character. She was rearing seven children, held three jobs simultaneously, and was active in her church.

Alabama law gives capital sentencing authority to the trial judge, but requires the judge to "consider" an advisory jury verdict. The jury voted 7–5 to give Harris life imprisonment without parole. The trial judge then considered her sentence. He found one aggravating circumstance (the murder was committed for monetary gain), one statutory mitigating circumstance (Harris had no prior criminal record), and one non-statutory mitigating circumstance (Harris was a hardworking, respected member of her church).

Noting that she had planned the crime, financed it, and stood to benefit from the murder, the judge felt that the aggravating circumstance outweighed the other mitigating circumstances and sentenced her to death. On appeal, the Alabama Supreme Court affirmed the conviction and sentence. It rejected Harris's arguments that the procedure was unconstitutional because Alabama state law did "not specify the weight the judge must give to the jury's recommendation and thus permits the arbitrary imposition of the death penalty."

On appeal, the U.S. Supreme Court upheld the Alabama court's decision (*Harris v. Alabama* [513 U.S. 504], 1995). Alabama's capital-sentencing process is similar to that of Florida. Both require jury participation during sentencing but give the trial judge the ultimate sentencing authority. Nevertheless, while the Florida statute requires that a trial judge must give "great weight" to the jury recommendation, the Alabama statute requires only that the judge "consider" the jury's recommendation.

As in the *Spaziano* case, the high court ruled that the Eighth Amendment does not require the state "to define the weight the sentencing judge must give to an advisory jury verdict." The Court stated,

> Because the Constitution permits the trial judge, acting alone, to impose a capital sentence . . . it is not offended when a State further requires a judge to consider a jury recommendation and trusts the judge to give it the proper weight.

JURY SENTENCING

In 2002 the U.S. Supreme Court decided a case concerning death sentencing in Arizona involving the Sixth Amendment right to an impartial jury (as opposed to the Eighth Amendment, which bars "cruel and unusual punishment"). Timothy Stuart Ring was convicted of murder in the armed robbery of an armored-car driver in 1994. According to Arizona law, Ring's offense was punishable by life imprisonment or death. He would only be eligible for the death penalty if the trial judge held a separate hearing and found that aggravating factors warranted the death penalty.

One of Ring's accomplices, who negotiated a plea bargain in return for a second-degree murder charge, testified against him at a separate sentencing hearing without a jury present. The same judge who had presided at Ring's trial concluded that Ring committed the murder and that the crime was committed "in an especially heinous, cruel or depraved manner." Weighing the two aggravating circumstances against the mitigating evidence of Ring's minimal criminal record, the judge sentenced Ring to death.

Ring appealed to the Arizona Supreme Court, claiming that the state's capital sentencing law violated his Sixth and Fourteenth Amendment rights because it allowed a judge, rather than a jury, to make the factual findings that made him death-eligible. The court put aside Ring's argument against the Arizona's judge-sentencing system in light of the U.S. Supreme Court's ruling in *Walton v. Arizona* (497 U.S. 639, 1990). The U.S. Supreme Court held in *Walton* that Arizona's sentencing procedure was constitutional because "the additional facts found by the judge qualified as sentencing considerations, not as 'element[s] of the offense of capital murder.'" Next, the Arizona Supreme Court threw out the trial judge's finding of the heinous nature of the crime but concluded that Ring's minimal criminal record was not enough to outweigh the aggravating evidence of "planned, ruthless robbery and killing." The court affirmed the death sentence.

Timothy Ring took his case to the U.S. Supreme Court. On June 24, 2002, by a 7–2 vote (*Ring v. Arizona*, 536 U.S. 584, 2002), the Court ruled that only juries and not judges can determine the presence of aggravating circumstances that warrant the death sentence. This case differs from the *Harris* and *Spaziano* cases in which the Court ruled simply that a judge could sentence a person to death after hearing a jury's recommendation. In the *Ring* opinion the Court included a discussion of *Apprendi v. New Jersey* (530 U.S. 466, 2000), in which it held that "the Sixth Amendment does not permit a defendant to be 'expose[d] . . . to a penalty *exceeding* the maximum he would receive if punished according to the facts reflected in the jury verdict alone.'" *Apprendi* involved a defendant in a noncapital case who received a prison term beyond the maximum sentence. This occurred because New Jersey law allowed sentencing judges to increase the penalty if they found that a crime was racially motivated. In *Apprendi*, the Court held that any fact other than a prior conviction that increases the punishment for a crime beyond the maximum allowed by law must be found by a jury beyond a reasonable doubt. The Court found *Walton* and *Apprendi* irreconcilable. The Court overruled *Walton* "to the extent that it allows a sentencing judge, sitting without a jury, to find an aggravating circumstance necessary for imposition of the death penalty." Justice Ruth Bader Ginsburg, who delivered the opinion of the Court, wrote,

> The right to trial by jury guaranteed by the Sixth Amendment would be senselessly diminished if it encompassed the fact-finding necessary to increase a defendant's sentence by two years [referring to *Apprendi*], but not the fact-finding necessary to put him to death. We hold that the Sixth Amendment applies to both.

However, Justice Antonin Scalia, joined by Justice Clarence Thomas, pointed out in a separate concurring opinion that under *Ring*, states that let judges impose the death sentence may continue to do so by requiring the finding of aggravating factors necessary to the imposition of the death penalty during the trial phase.

Justice Sandra Day O'Connor, in her dissenting opinion, joined by Chief Justice Rehnquist, claimed that just as the *Apprendi* decision has overburdened the appeals courts, the *Ring* decision will cause more federal appeals. O'Connor observed that *Ring v. Arizona* also invalidates the capital sentencing procedure of four other states. These included Idaho and Montana, where a judge had the sole sentencing authority, as well as Colorado and Nebraska, where a three-judge panel made the sentencing decisions. The Court ruling also potentially affected Alabama, Delaware, Florida, and Indiana, where the jury rendered an advisory verdict, but the judge had the ultimate sentencing authority.

Impact of the *Ring* Decision

As a result of the *Ring* decision, Arizona, Colorado, Delaware, Idaho, Nebraska, Indiana, and Montana passed legislation providing for jury sentencing. As of 2005, Florida and Alabama still allowed judges to override jury sentencing recommendations.

Some researchers have suggested that states where judges previously made the life-or-death decisions would see fewer death sentences under the jury system. They noted that judges are elected public officials who may be driven by political ambitions to issue death sentences and suggested that urban juries would be less likely to impose death sentences.

However, reporting in the *Arizona Republic* in November 2003, Jim Walsh calculated that after the state sentencing laws were revised per *Ring*, juries in that state handed down death sentences at a higher rate than judges had done under the previous system. According to Walsh, within a one-year period (November 2002 to November 2003), jurors in Maricopa County sentenced seven of eight (87.5%) defendants to death. Statewide, jurors imposed a total of ten death sentences out of fifteen cases heard (66.7%). In comparison, between 1995 and 1999, Maricopa County judges imposed death sentences in eleven of seventy-five (14.7%) cases. Statewide, within that four-year period, judges sentenced twenty-nine of 143 (20.3%) defendants to death.

The Ring Decision Does Not Retroactively Apply to Those Already Sentenced to Murder

Arizona death row inmate Warren Summerlin was convicted of brutally crushing the skull of bill collector Brenna Bailey and then sexually assaulting her. Summerlin was convicted by a jury, and an Arizona trial judge sentenced him to death in 1982. After the *Ring* decision was handed down, the U.S. Court of Appeals for the Ninth Circuit ruled 8–3 in *Summerlin v. Stewart* (309 F.3d 1193 [9th Cir., 2003]) that in light of *Ring v. Arizona*, Summerlin's death sentence should be vacated. The appellate court held that the Supreme Court's ruling should apply retroactively, even to those inmates who have exhausted their appeals. The prosecution brought the case to the U.S. Supreme Court.

In *Schriro v. Summerlin* (No. 03-526, 2004), the U.S. Supreme Court reversed the appellate court's decision in a 5–4 vote. The nation's highest court concluded that the *Ring* ruling only changed the procedures involved in a sentencing trial for capital punishment cases and did not alter those fundamental legal guidelines judges and juries follow when sentencing a person to death. As such, the *Ring* ruling does not call into question the accuracy of past convictions and should not be retroactive. Speaking for the majority, Justice Scalia wrote,

[We] give retroactive effect to only a small set of "watershed rules of criminal procedure" implicating the fundamental fairness and accuracy of the criminal proceeding. That a new procedural rule is "fundamental" in some abstract sense is not enough; the rule must be one without which the likelihood of an accurate conviction is seriously diminished.

DOUBLE JEOPARDY

In 1991 David Sattazahn was convicted for the 1987 murder of a restaurant manager in Berks County, Pennsylvania. Sattazahn and an accomplice killed the manager in the process of robbing him of the day's receipts. The state sought the death sentence and included an aggravating circumstance—the commission of murder while perpetrating a felony. During the sentencing phase the jury could not reach a verdict as to life or death. The trial judge considered the jury as hung and imposed an automatic sentence of life imprisonment as mandated by state law.

On appeal to the Pennsylvania Superior Court, Sattazahn was granted a new trial. The court held that the trial judge had erred in jury instructions relating to his offenses and reversed his murder conviction. During the second trial the state again sought the death penalty, this time adding a second aggravating factor—the defendant's history of felony convictions involving using or threatening violence to the victim. The jury convicted Sattazahn of first-degree murder and sentenced him to death.

Next, the Pennsylvania Supreme Court heard Sattazahn's case. The death row inmate claimed, among other things, that the Pennsylvania Constitution prohibits the imposition of the death penalty in his case because it guarantees protection from double jeopardy. The Double Jeopardy Clause of the Fifth Amendment states that "[n]o person shall...be subject for the same offence to be twice put in jeopardy of life or limb." In other words, no person can be tried or punished twice for the same crime.

Relying on its ruling in *Commonwealth v. Martorano* (634 A.2d 1063,1071 [Pa. 1993]), the Pennsylvania Supreme Court affirmed both Sattazahn's conviction and death sentence. In *Martorano*, the Court noted that the jury, as in Sattazahn's first trial, was deadlocked. The hung jury did not "acquit" the defendant of the death sentence. Therefore, there was no double jeopardy prohibition against the death penalty during the second trial.

On January 14, 2003, the U.S. Supreme Court, by a 5–4 vote, agreed with the ruling of the Pennsylvania Supreme Court (*Sattazahn v. Pennsylvania*, 537 U.S. 101). Justice Scalia, writing the majority opinion, concluded that double jeopardy did not exist in this case. According to the Court,

[T]he touchstone for double-jeopardy protection in capital-sentencing proceedings is whether there has been an "acquittal." Petitioner here cannot establish that the jury or the court "acquitted" him during his first capital-sentencing proceeding. As to the jury: The verdict form returned by the foreman stated that the jury deadlocked 9-to-3 on whether to impose the death penalty; it made no findings with respect to the alleged aggravating circumstance. That result—or more appropriately, that non-result—cannot fairly be called an acquittal. . . .

The Court added that the imposition of a life sentence by the judge did not "acquit" the defendant of the death penalty either because the judge was just following the state law. "A default judgment does not trigger a double jeopardy bar to the death penalty upon retrial."

Justice Ginsburg, writing for the dissent, was joined by Justices Stevens, Souter, and Breyer. The dissenters argued that jeopardy terminated after the judge imposed a final judgment of life imprisonment when the jury was deadlocked. Therefore, he was "acquitted" of the death penalty the first time, which means that the state could not seek the death penalty the second time. Justice Ginsburg also pointed out,

> [T]he Court's holding confronts defendants with a perilous choice. . . . Under the Court's decision, if a defendant sentenced to life after a jury deadlock chooses to appeal her underlying conviction, she faces the possibility of death if she is successful on appeal but convicted on retrial. If, on the other hand, the defendant loses her appeal, or chooses to forgo an appeal, the final judgment for life stands. In other words, a defendant in Sattazahn's position must relinquish either her right to file a potentially meritorious appeal, or her state-granted entitlement to avoid the death penalty.

SENTENCING PROCEDURES

"Comparative Proportionality Review"—Comparing Similar Crimes and Sentences

On July 5, 1978, in Mira Mesa, California, Robert Harris and his brother decided to steal a car they would need for a getaway in a planned bank robbery. Robert Harris approached two teenage boys eating hamburgers in a car. He forced them at gunpoint to drive to a nearby wooded area. The teenagers offered to delay telling the police of the car robbery and even to give the authorities misleading descriptions of the two robbers. When one of the boys appeared to be fleeing, Harris shot both of them. Harris and his brother later committed the robbery, were soon caught, and confessed to the robbery and murders.

Harris was found guilty. In California, a convicted murderer could be sentenced to death or life imprisonment without parole only if "special circumstances" existed and the murder had been "willful, deliberate, premeditated, and committed during the commission of kidnapping and robbery." This had to be proven during a separate sentencing hearing.

The state showed that Harris was convicted of manslaughter in 1975; he was found in possession of a makeshift knife and garrote (an instrument used for strangulation) while in prison; he and other inmates sodomized another inmate; and he threatened that inmate's

life. Harris testified that he had a very unhappy childhood, had little education, and his father had sexually molested his sisters. The jury sentenced Harris to death, and the judge concurred.

Harris claimed the U.S. Constitution, as interpreted in previous capital punishment rulings, required the state of California to give his case "comparative proportionality review" to determine if his death sentence was not out of line with that of others convicted of similar crimes. In "comparative proportionality review," a court considers the seriousness of the offense, the severity of the penalty, the sentences imposed for other crimes, and the sentencing in other jurisdictions for the same crime. Courts have occasionally struck down punishments inherently disproportionate and, therefore, cruel and unusual. Georgia, by law, and Florida, by practice, had incorporated such reviews in their procedures. Other states, such as Texas and California, had not.

When the case reached the U.S. Ninth Circuit Court of Appeals, the court agreed with Harris and ordered California to establish proportionality or lift the death sentence. The U.S. Supreme Court (*Pulley v. Harris*, 465 U.S. 37, 1984), in a 7–2 decision, did not agree. The Court noted that the California procedure contained enough safeguards to guarantee a defendant a fair trial and those convicted, a fair sentence. The high court added,

> That some [state statutes] providing proportionality review are constitutional does not mean that such review is indispensable. . . . To endorse the statute as a whole is not to say that anything different is unacceptable. . . . Examination of our 1976 cases makes clear that they do not establish proportionality review as a constitutional requirement.

Justice Brennan, joined by Justice Marshall, dissented. He noted that the Supreme Court had thrown out the existing death penalty procedures during the 1970s because they were deemed arbitrary and capricious. He believed they still were, but the introduction of "proportionality" might "eliminate some, if only a small part, of the irrationality that currently surrounds the imposition of the death penalty."

Due Process and Advance Notice of Imposing the Death Penalty

Robert and Cheryl Bravence were beaten to death at their campsite near Santiam Creek, Idaho, in 1983. Two brothers, Bryan and Mark Lankford, were charged with two counts of first-degree murder. At the arraignment (a summoning before a court to hear and answer charges), the trial judge advised Bryan Lankford that, if convicted of either of the two charges (he was charged with both murders), the maximum punishment he might receive was either life imprisonment or death.

After the arraignment Bryan Lankford's attorney made a deal with the prosecutor. Bryan Lankford entered a plea bargain in which he agreed to take two lie-detector tests in exchange for a lesser sentence. Although the results were somewhat unclear, they convinced the prosecutor that Lankford's older brother, Mark, was primarily responsible for the crimes and was the actual killer of both victims. Bryan Lankford's attorney and the prosecutor agreed on an indeterminate sentence with a ten-year minimum in exchange for a guilty plea, subject to commitment from the trial judge that he would impose that sentence. The judge refused to make such a commitment, and the case went to trial.

The judge also refused to instruct the jury that a specific intent to kill was required to support a conviction of first-degree murder. The jury found Bryan Lankford guilty on both counts. The sentencing hearing was postponed until after Mark's trial. He was also charged with both murders.

Before the sentencing trial, at Bryan Lankford's request, the trial judge ordered the prosecutor to notify the court and Lankford whether it would seek the death penalty and, if so, to file a statement of the aggravating circumstance on which the death penalty would be based. The prosecutor notified the judge that the state would not recommend the death penalty. Several proceedings followed, including Lankford's request for a new attorney, a motion for a new trial, and a motion for continuance of the sentencing hearing. At none of the proceedings was there any mention that Lankford might receive the death penalty.

At the sentencing hearing the prosecutor recommended a life sentence, with a minimum ranging between ten and twenty years. The trial judge indicated that he considered Lankford's testimony unbelievable and that the seriousness of the crime warranted more severe punishment than recommended by the state. He sentenced Lankford to death.

Lankford appealed, asserting that the trial judge violated the Constitution by failing to give notice that he intended to impose the death penalty in spite of the state's earlier notice that it would not seek the death penalty. The judge maintained that the Idaho Code provided Lankford with sufficient notice. The judge added that the fact the prosecutor said he would not seek the death penalty had "no bearing on the adequacy of notice to petitioner [Lankford] that the death penalty might be sought." The Idaho Supreme Court agreed with the judge's decision.

In *Lankford v. Idaho* (500 U.S. 110, 1991), the U.S. Supreme Court reversed the state supreme court ruling and remanded the case for a new trial. Writing for the majority, Justice Stevens stated that the due process clause of the Fourteenth Amendment was violated. Stevens noted,

> If the defense counsel had been notified that the trial judge was contemplating a death sentence based on five specific aggravating circumstances, presumably she would have advanced arguments that addressed these circumstances; however, she did not make these arguments because they were entirely inappropriate in a discussion about the length of the petitioner's possible incarceration.

Stevens further indicated that the trial judge's silence, in effect, hid from Lankford and his attorney, as well as from the prosecutor, the principal issues to be decided.

In a dissenting opinion, Justice Scalia wrote that Lankford's due process rights were not violated because he knew that he had been convicted of first-degree murder, and the Idaho Code clearly states that "every person guilty of murder of the first degree shall be punished by death or by imprisonment for life." At the arraignment the trial judge told Lankford that he could receive either punishment. Scalia further noted that, in Idaho, the death penalty statute places full responsibility for determining the sentence on the judge.

CHAPTER 3

SUPREME COURT RULINGS—CIRCUMSTANCES THAT DO AND DO NOT WARRANT THE DEATH PENALTY, RIGHT TO EFFECTIVE COUNSEL, APPEALS BASED ON NEW EVIDENCE, AND CONSTITUTIONALITY OF EXECUTION METHODS

CIRCUMSTANCES FOUND NOT TO WARRANT THE DEATH PENALTY

Rape and Kidnapping

On June 29, 1977, a 5–4 divided Supreme Court ruled, in *Coker v. Georgia* (433 U.S. 584) and in *Eberheart v. Georgia* (433 U.S. 917), that the death penalty may not be imposed for the crime of raping an adult woman that does not result in death. The Court stated,

Rape is without doubt deserving of serious punishment, but in terms of moral depravity and of the injury to the person and to the public, it does not compare with murder which does involve the unjustified taking of human life.... The murderer kills; the rapist, if no more than that, does not. Life is over for the victim of the murderers; for the rape victim, life may not be nearly so happy as it was, but it is not over and normally is not beyond repair. We have the abiding conviction that the death penalty, which is unique in its severity and irrevocability...is an excessive penalty for the rapist who, as such, does not take human life.

Chief Justice Warren Earl Burger, joined by Justice William Rehnquist, dissented. The justices stated,

A rapist not only violates a victim's privacy and personal integrity, but inevitably causes serious psychological as well as physical harm in the process. . . . Rape is not a mere physical attack—it is destructive of the human personality. The remainder of the victim's life may be gravely affected, and this in turn may have a serious detrimental effect upon her husband and any children she may have. . . . Victims may recover from the physical damage of knife or bullet wounds, or a beating with fists or a club, but recovery from such a gross assault on the human personality is not healed by medicine or surgery. To speak blandly, as the plurality does, of rape victims who are "unharmed," or to classify the human outrage of rape, as does Mr. Justice Powell, in terms of "excessively brutal," versus "moderately brutal," takes too little account of the profound suffering the crime imposes upon the victims and their loved ones.

The Court also held that kidnapping did not warrant the death penalty. While the victims usually suffered tremendously, they had not lost their lives. (If the kidnapped victim were killed, then the kidnapper would be tried for murder.) These high court decisions left only murder and treason as justifiable grounds for the imposition of the death penalty. So far, no cases involving the death penalty for treason have been brought to the Supreme Court.

An "Unconstitutionally Vague" Statute

During a heated dispute with his wife of twenty-eight years, Robert Godfrey threatened her with a knife. Mrs. Godfrey, saying she was leaving her husband, went to stay with relatives. That same day she went to court to file for aggravated assault. Several days later she initiated divorce proceedings and moved in with her mother. During subsequent telephone conversations, the couple argued over the wife's determination to leave Godfrey permanently.

About two weeks later Robert Godfrey killed his wife and mother-in-law. Godfrey told police that his wife phoned him, telling him she expected all the money from the planned sale of their home. She also told Godfrey she was never reconciling with him. Godfrey confessed that he went to his mother-in-law's nearby trailer and shot his wife through a window, killing her instantly. He then entered the trailer, struck his fleeing eleven-year-old daughter on the head with the gun, and shot his mother-in-law in the head, killing her. Godfrey believed his mother-in-law was responsible for his wife's reluctance to reconcile with him.

Godfrey was convicted of killing his wife and mother-in-law and of the aggravated assault of his daughter. The Georgia Code permits the imposition of the death penalty in the case of a murder that "was outrageously or wantonly vile, horrible, or inhuman in that it involved torture, depravity of mind, or an aggravated brutality to the victim." Aware of this law, the jury sentenced Godfrey to die. He appealed, claiming that the statute was unconstitutionally vague. After the Georgia Supreme Court upheld the lower court decision, the case was appealed to the U.S. Supreme Court.

The U.S. Supreme Court, in *Godfrey v. Georgia* (446 U.S. 420, 1980), noted that the victims were killed instantly (i.e., there was no torture), the victims had been "causing [Godfrey] extreme emotional trauma," and he acknowledged his responsibility. The high court concluded that, in this case, the Georgia law was unconstitutionally vague. Moreover, the Georgia Supreme Court did not attempt to narrow the definition of "outrageously and wantonly vile." In a concurring opinion, Justice Thurgood Marshall, whom Justice William Brennan joined, found this an example of the inherently "arbitrary" (subject to individual judgment) and "capricious" (unpredictable) nature of capital punishment, since even the prosecutor in Godfrey's case observed numerous times that there was no torture or abuse involved.

CRIMINAL INTENT

On April 1, 1975, Sampson and Jeanette Armstrong, on the pretext of requesting water for their overheated car, tried to rob Thomas Kersey at home. Earl Enmund waited in the getaway car. Kersey called for his wife, who tried to shoot Jeanette Armstrong. The Armstrongs killed the Kerseys. Enmund was tried for aiding and abetting in the robbery-murder and sentenced to death.

In *Enmund v. Florida* (458 U.S. 782, 1982), a 5–4 split Supreme Court ruled that, in this case, the death penalty violated the Eighth and Fourteenth Amendments to the U.S. Constitution. The majority noted that only nine of the thirty-six states with capital punishment permitted its use on a criminal who was not actually present at the scene of the crime. The exception was the case where someone paid a hit man to murder the victim.

Furthermore, over the years juries had tended not to sentence to death criminals who had not actually been at the scene of the crime. Certainly Enmund was guilty of planning and participating in a robbery, but murder had not been part of the plan. Statistically, since someone is killed in one out of two hundred robberies, Enmund could not have expected the Kerseys' murders during the robbery attempt. The Court concluded that, because Enmund did not kill or plan to kill, he should be tried only for his participation in the robbery. The Court observed,

> We have no doubt that robbery is a serious crime deserving serious punishment. It is not, however, a crime "so grievous an affront to humanity that the only adequate response may be the penalty of death" [from *Gregg v. Georgia*, 428 U.S. 153, 1976]. It does not compare with murder, which does involve the unjustified taking of human life. . . . The murderer kills; the robber, if no more than that, does not. Life is over for the victim of the murderer; for the [robbery] victim, life . . . is not over and normally is not beyond repair.

Writing for the minority, Justice Sandra Day O'Connor concluded that intent is a complex issue. It should be left to the judge and jury trying the accused to decide intent, not a federal court far removed from the actual trial.

Enmund Revisited

Just because a person had no intent to kill, however, does not mean that he or she cannot be sentenced to death. In the early morning of September 22, 1978, Crawford Bullock and his friend Ricky Tucker had been drinking at a bar in Jackson, Mississippi, and were offered a ride home by Mark Dickson, an acquaintance.

During the drive an argument ensued over money that Dickson owed Tucker, and Dickson stopped the car. The argument escalated into a fistfight, and, outside the car, Bullock held Dickson while Tucker punched Dickson and hit him in the face with a whiskey bottle. When Dickson fell, Tucker smashed his head with a concrete block, killing him. Tucker and Bullock disposed of the body. The next day police spotted Bullock driving the victim's car. After his arrest Bullock confessed.

Under Mississippi law a person involved in a robbery that results in murder may be convicted of capital murder regardless of "the defendant's own lack of intent that any killing take place." The jury never was asked to consider whether Bullock in fact killed, attempted to kill, or intended to kill. He was convicted and sentenced to death as an accomplice to the crime. During the appeals process, the Mississippi Supreme Court confirmed that Bullock was indeed a participant in the murder.

In January 1986 a divided U.S. Supreme Court modified the *Enmund* decision with a 5–4 ruling in *Cabana v. Bullock* (474 U.S. 376). The Court indicated that while *Enmund* had to be considered at some point during the judicial process, the initial jury trying the accused did not necessarily have to consider the *Enmund* ruling. The high court ruled that, while the jury had not been made aware of the issue of intent, the Mississippi Supreme Court had considered this question. Since *Enmund* did not require that intent be presented at the initial jury trial, only that it be considered at some time during the judicial process, the state of Mississippi had met that requirement.

The four dissenting justices claimed that it was difficult for any appeals court to determine intent from reading a typed transcript of a trial. Seeing the accused and others involved was important in helping determine who was telling the truth and who was not. This was why *Enmund* must be raised to the jury so it could consider the question of intent in light of what it had seen and heard directly.

"Reckless Indifference to the Value of Human Life"

Gary Tison was a convicted criminal who had been sentenced to life imprisonment for murdering a prison guard during an escape from the Arizona State Prison in Florence, Arizona. Tison's three sons, his wife, his brother, and other relatives planned a prison escape involving Tison and a fellow prisoner, Randy Greenawalt, also a convicted murderer.

On the day of the planned escape in July 1978, Tison's sons smuggled guns into the prison's visitation area. After locking up the guards and visitors, the five men fled in a car. They later transferred to another car and waited in an abandoned house for a plane to take them to Mexico. When the plane did not come, the men got back on the road. The car soon had flat tires. One son flagged down a passing car. The motorist who stopped to help was driving with his wife, their two-year-old son, and a fifteen-year-old niece.

Gary Tison then told his sons to go get some water from the motorists' car, presumably to be left with the family they planned to abandon in the desert. While the sons were gone, Gary Tison and Randy Greenawalt shot and killed the family. Several days later two of Tison's sons and Greenawalt were captured. The third son was killed, and Tison escaped into the desert, where he later died of exposure.

The surviving Tisons and Greenawalt were found guilty and sentenced to death. The sons, citing *Enmund*, appealed, claiming that they had neither pulled the triggers nor intended the deaths of the family who had stopped to help them. The 5–4 Supreme Court decision (*Tison v. Arizona*, 481 U.S. 137, 1987) upheld the death sentence, indicating that the Tison sons had shown a "reckless indifference to the value of human life [which] may be every bit as shocking to the moral sense as an 'intent to kill.'"

The Tisons may not have pulled the triggers (and the Court fully accepted the premise that they did not do the shootings or directly intend them to happen), but they released and then assisted two convicted murderers. They should have realized that freeing two killers and giving them guns could very well put innocent people in great danger. Moreover, they continued to help the escapees even after the family was killed.

"These facts," concluded Justice O'Connor for the majority, "not only indicate that the Tison brothers' participation in the crime was anything but minor, they also would clearly support a finding that they both subjectively appreciated that their acts were likely to result in the taking of innocent life." Unlike the situation in the *Enmund* case, they were not sitting in a car far from the murder scene. They were direct participants in the whole event. The death sentence would stand.

Writing for the minority, Justice William J. Brennan observed that had a prison guard been murdered (Gary Tison had murdered a prison guard in a previous escape attempt), then the Court's argument would have made sense. The murder of the family, however, made no sense and was not even necessary for the escape. The Tison sons were away from the murder scene getting water for the victims and could have done nothing to save them. While they were guilty of planning and carrying out an escape, the murder of the family who stopped to help them was an unexpected outcome of the escape.

Furthermore, the father had promised his sons that he would not kill during the escape, a promise he had kept despite several opportunities to kill during the actual prison escape. It was, therefore, not unreasonable for the sons to believe that their father would not kill in a situation that did not appear to warrant it. Justice Brennan concluded that "like Enmund, the Tisons neither killed nor attempted or intended to kill anyone. Like Enmund, the Tisons have been sentenced to death for the intentional acts of others, which the Tisons did not expect, which were not essential to the felony, and over which they had no control."

RIGHT TO EFFECTIVE COUNSEL

In 1989 Kevin Eugene Wiggins received a death sentence for the 1988 drowning of an elderly Maryland woman in her home. The Maryland Court of Appeals affirmed his sentence in 1991. With the help of new counsel, Wiggins sought postconviction relief, challenging the quality of his initial lawyers. Wiggins claimed his lawyers failed to investigate and present mitigating evidence of his horrendous physical and sexual abuse as a child. The sentencing jury never heard that he was starved, that his mother punished him by burning his hand on the stove, and that after the state put him in foster care at age six, he suffered more physical and sexual abuse.

In 2001 a federal district court concluded that Wiggins's first lawyers should have conducted a more thorough investigation into his childhood abuse, which would have kept the jury from imposing a death sentence. However, the U.S. Court of Appeals for the Fourth Circuit reversed the district court decision, ruling that the original attorneys had made a "reasonable strategic decision" to concentrate their defense on raising doubts about Wiggins's guilt instead.

On June 26, 2003, the U.S. Supreme Court threw out the death sentence. In *Wiggins v. Smith* (No. 02-311,

2003), the Court ruled 7–2 that Wiggins's lawyers violated his Sixth Amendment right to effective assistance of counsel. The Court noted,

> Counsel's investigation into Wiggins' background did not reflect reasonable professional judgment. . . . Given the nature and extent of the abuse, there is a reasonable probability that a competent attorney, aware of this history, would have introduced it at sentencing, and that a jury confronted with such mitigating evidence would have returned with a different sentence.

When Does the Right to Counsel End?

Joseph Giarratano was a Virginia prisoner under sentence of death. He received full counsel for his trial and for his initial appeal. Afterwards, Virginia would no longer provide him with his own lawyer. He went to court, complaining that, because he was poor, the state of Virginia should provide him with counsel to help prepare postconviction appeals. Virginia permitted the condemned prisoner the right to use the prison libraries to prepare an appeal, but it did not provide the condemned with his own personal attorney.

Virginia had "unit attorneys" who were assigned to help prisoners with prison-related legal matters. A unit attorney could give guidance to death row inmates but could not act as the personal attorney for any one particular inmate. This case became a class action in which the federal district court certified a class comprising "all current and future Virginia inmates awaiting execution who do not have and cannot afford counsel to pursue postconviction proceedings."

The federal district court and the federal court of appeals agreed with Giarratano, but the U.S. Supreme Court, in *Murray v. Giarratano* (492 U.S. 1, 1989), disagreed. Writing for the majority (Justices Byron White, O'Connor, and Scalia, with Justice Anthony Kennedy filing a concurring opinion), Chief Justice Rehnquist concluded that, while the Sixth and Fourteenth Amendments to the U.S. Constitution assured an impoverished defendant the right to counsel at the trial stage of a criminal proceeding, they do not provide for counsel for postconviction proceedings, as the Court ruled in *Pennsylvania v. Finley* (481 U.S. 551, 1987). Since *Finley* had not specifically considered prisoners on death row, but all prisoners in general, the majority did not believe the decision needed to be reconsidered just because death row prisoners had more at stake.

Chief Justice Rehnquist agreed that those facing the death penalty have a right to counsel for the trial and during the initial appeal. During these periods, the defendant needs a heightened measure of protection because the death penalty is involved. Later appeals, however, involve more procedural matters that "serve a different and more limited purpose than either the trial or appeal."

In dissent, Justice John Paul Stevens (joined by Justices Brennan, Marshall, and Harry A. Blackmun) indicated that he thought condemned prisoners in Virginia faced three critical differences from those considered in *Finley*. First, the Virginia prisoners had been sentenced to death, which made their condition different from a sentence of life imprisonment. Second, Virginia's particular judicial decision forbids certain issues to be raised during the direct review or appeal process and forces them to be considered only during later postconviction appeals. This means that very important issues may be considered without the benefit of counsel. Finally,

> Unlike the ordinary inmate, who presumably has ample time to use and reuse the prison library and to seek guidance from other prisoners experienced in preparing . . . petitions. . . , a grim deadline imposes a finite limit on the condemned person's capacity for useful research.

He continued, quoting from the District Court, decision in the matter,

> [An] inmate preparing himself and his family for impending death is incapable of performing the mental functions necessary to adequately pursue his claims.

Federal Judges Can Delay Executions to Allow *Habeus Corpus* Reviews

In 1988 Congress passed the Anti-Drug Abuse Act, which guaranteed qualified legal representation for poor death row defendants wanting to file for *habeas corpus* (a prisoner's petition to be heard in federal court) so that the counsel could assist in the preparation of the appeal. In 1994 this law was brought to question before the U.S. Supreme Court by death row inmate Frank McFarland.

In November 1989 a Texas jury found McFarland guilty of stabbing to death a woman he had met in a bar. The state appellate court upheld his conviction, and two lower federal courts refused his request for a stay (postponement) of execution. The federal courts ruled that they did not have jurisdiction to stop the execution until McFarland filed a *habeas corpus*. The inmate argued that without the stay, he would be executed before he could obtain a lawyer to prepare the petition.

The Supreme Court granted a stay of execution. In a 5–4 decision (*McFarland v. Scott*, 512 U.S. 849, 1994), the Court upheld the 1988 federal law. Once a defendant requested counsel, the federal court could postpone execution so the lawyer would have time to prepare an appeal. Justice Blackmun stated that "by providing indigent capital defendants with a mandatory right to qualified legal counsel in these proceedings, Congress has recognized that Federal *habeas corpus* has a particularly important role to play in promoting fundamental fairness in the imposition of the death penalty."

This case illustrated a problem in many states. For example, in 1994 there were 386 inmates on death row and only 118 lawyers with the Texas Resource Center, a federally financed legal office that handled capital cases. In 1993 judges in Texas set one hundred execution dates. (State policy dictated that an execution must be scheduled about forty-five days after the death sentence had been upheld on direct review.) If McFarland had drafted his own *habeas* petition, it would probably have been rejected as inadequate.

Does the Right to Counsel Extend to Crimes That Have Not Been Charged?

In 1994 Raymond Levi Cobb confessed to burglarizing the home of Lindsey Owings the previous year. He claimed no knowledge, however, of the disappearances of Owings's wife and infant at the time of the burglary. The court subsequently assigned Cobb a lawyer to represent him in the burglary offense. With the permission of Cobb's lawyer, investigators twice questioned Cobb regarding the disappearance of the Owings family. Both times Cobb denied any knowledge of the missing pair.

In 1995, while free on bond for the burglary and living with his father, Cobb told his father he killed Margaret Owing and buried her baby, while still alive, with her. The father reported his son's confession to the police. When brought in, Cobb confessed to the police and waived his Miranda rights, which include the right to counsel. Cobb was convicted of the murders and sentenced to death. On appeal, Cobb claimed that his confession, obtained in violation of his Sixth Amendment right to counsel, should have been suppressed. He argued that his right to counsel attached (went into full effect) when he was reported for the burglary case, and despite his open confession to the police, he never officially gave up this right to counsel.

The Texas Court of Criminal Appeals reversed Cobb's conviction, ordering a new trial. The court considered Cobb's confession to the murders inadmissible, holding that "once the right to counsel attaches to the offense charged [burglary], it also attaches to any other offense [in this case, murder] that is very closely related factually to the offense charged."

The state appealed to the U.S. Supreme Court. On April 2, 2001, in *Texas v. Cobb* (532 U.S. 162), the Court, in a 5–4 decision, stated,

> The Sixth Amendment right to counsel is . . . "offense specific." It cannot be invoked once for all future prosecutions, for it does not attach until a prosecution is commenced, that is, at or after the initiation of adversary judicial proceedings—whether by way of formal charge, preliminary hearing, indictment, information, or arraignment [citing *McNeil v. Wisconsin*, 501 U.S. 171, 1991].

This means that Cobb's right to counsel did not extend to crimes with which he had not been charged. Since this right did not prohibit investigators from questioning him about the murders without first notifying his lawyer, Cobb's confession was admissible.

CASES INVOLVING ERROR BY THE PROSECUTION
Coerced Confessions

Oreste C. Fulminante called the Mesa, Arizona, police to report the disappearance of his eleven-year-old stepdaughter, Jeneane Michelle Hunt. Fulminante was caring for the child while his wife, Jeneane's mother, was in the hospital. Several days later Jeneane's body was found in the desert east of Mesa with two shots to the head, fired at close range by a large-caliber weapon. There was a ligature (a cord used in tying or binding) around her neck. Because of the decomposed state of her body, it was not possible to determine whether she had been sexually assaulted.

Fulminante's statements about the child's disappearance and his relationship to her included inconsistencies that made him a suspect in her death. He was not, however, charged with the murder. Fulminante left Arizona for New Jersey, where he was eventually convicted on federal charges of unlawful possession of a firearm by a felon.

While incarcerated, he became friendly with Anthony Sarivola, a former police officer. Sarivola had been involved in loan-sharking for organized crime, but then became a paid informant for the Federal Bureau of Investigation. In prison he masqueraded as an organized crime figure. When Fulminante was getting some tough treatment from the other inmates, Sarivola offered him protection, but only on the condition that Fulminante tell him everything.

Fulminante was later indicted in Arizona for the first-degree murder of Jeneane. In a hearing prior to the trial, Fulminante moved to suppress the statement he had made to Sarivola in prison and then later to Sarivola's wife, Donna, following his release from prison. He maintained that the confession to Sarivola was coerced, and that the second confession was the "fruit" of the first one.

The trial court denied the motion to remove the statements from the record, finding that, based on the specified facts, the confessions were voluntary. Fulminante was convicted of Jeneane's murder and subsequently sentenced to death.

In his appeal Fulminante argued, among other things, that his confession to Sarivola was coerced and that its use at the trial violated his rights of due process under the Fifth and Fourteenth Amendments to the U.S. Constitution. The Arizona Supreme Court ruled that the confession was coerced, but initially determined that the admission of the confession at the trial was a harmless error because of the overpowering evidence against Fulminante. In legal terms, "harmless error" refers to an error committed during the trial that had no bearing on the outcome of the trial, and as such, is not harmful enough to reverse the outcome of the trial on appeal.

After Fulminante motioned for reconsideration, however, the Arizona Supreme Court ruled that the U.S. Supreme Court had set a precedent that prevented the use of harmless error in the case of a coerced confession. The harmless-error standard, as stated in *Chapman v. California* (386 U.S. 18, 1967), held that an error is harmless if it appears "beyond a reasonable doubt that the error complained of did not contribute to the verdict obtained." The Arizona Supreme Court reversed the conviction and ordered that Fulminante be retried without the use of his confession to Sarivola. Because of differences in the state and federal courts over the admission of a coerced confession with regard to harmless-error analysis, the U.S. Supreme Court agreed to hear the case.

In *Arizona v. Fulminante* (499 U.S. 279, 1991), Justice White, writing for the majority, stated that although the question was a close one, the Arizona Supreme Court was right in concluding that Fulminante's confession had been coerced. He further noted,

> The Arizona Supreme Court found a credible threat of physical violence unless Fulminante confessed. Our cases have made clear that a finding of coercion need not depend upon actual violence by a government agent; a credible threat is sufficient. As we have said, "coercion can be mental as well as physical, and . . . the blood of the accused is not the only hallmark of an unconstitutional inquisition."

Justice White further argued that the state of Arizona had failed to meet its burden of establishing, beyond a reasonable doubt, that the admission of Fulminante's confession to Sarivola was harmless. He added,

> A confession is like no other evidence. Indeed, "the defendant's own confession is probably the most probative [providing evidence] that can be admitted against him. . . . [T]he admissions of a defendant come from the actor himself, the most knowledgeable and unimpeachable source of information about his past conduct. Certainly confessions have profound impact on the jury, so much so that we may justifiably doubt its ability to put them out of mind even if told to do so." [From *Bruton v. United States*, 391 U.S. 123, 1968]

Presumption of Malice

Dale Robert Yates and Henry Davis planned to rob a country store in Greenville County, South Carolina, in February 1981. When they entered the store, only the owner, Willie Wood, was present. Yates and Davis showed their weapons and ordered Wood to give them money from the cash register. Davis handed Yates the $3,000 and ordered Wood to lie across the counter. Wood, who had a pistol beneath his jacket, refused.

Meanwhile, Yates was backing out of the store with his gun pointed at the owner. After being told to do so by Davis, Yates fired two shots. The first bullet caused flesh wounds in Wood; the second shot missed. Yates then jumped into the car and waited for Davis. When Davis did not appear, Yates drove off. Inside the store, although wounded, Wood pursued Davis. As the two struggled, Wood's mother came in and ran to help her son. During the struggle, Mrs. Wood was stabbed once in the chest and died at the scene. Wood then shot Davis five times, killing him.

After Yates was arrested and charged with murder, his primary defense was that Mrs. Wood's death was not the probable natural consequence of the robbery he had planned with Davis. He claimed that he had brought the weapon only to induce the owner to give him the cash and that neither he nor Davis intended to kill anyone during the robbery.

The prosecutor's case for murder hinged on the agreement between Yates and Davis to commit an armed robbery. He argued that they planned to kill any witness, thereby making homicide a probable or natural result of the robbery. The prosecutor concluded, "It makes no difference who actually struck the fatal blow, the hand of one is the hand of all."

The judge told the jury that under South Carolina law murder is defined as "the unlawful killing of any human being with malice aforethought either express or implied." In his instructions to the jury, the judge said,

> Malice is implied or presumed by the law from the willful, deliberate and intentional doing of an unlawful act without any just cause or excuse. In its general signification, malice means the doing of a wrongful act, intentionally, without justification or excuse.... I tell you, also, that malice is implied or presumed from the use of a deadly weapon.

The judge continued to instruct the jury on the theory of accomplice liability. The jury returned guilty verdicts on the murder charge and on all other counts in the indictment. Yates was sentenced to death.

Yates petitioned the South Carolina Supreme Court, asserting that the jury charge that "malice is implied or presumed from the use of a deadly weapon" was an unconstitutional burden-shifting instruction. The case was twice reviewed by the South Carolina Supreme Court, which agreed that the jury instructions were unconstitutional, but that allowing the jury to presume malice was a harmless error, one that had no bearing on the outcome of the trial. The South Carolina court found that the jury did not have to rely on presumptions of malice because Davis's "lunging" at Mrs. Wood and stabbing her were acts of malice.

The U.S. Supreme Court, in *Yates v. Evatt* (500 U.S. 391, 1991), reversed the decisions of the South Carolina Supreme Court and remanded the case (sent it back to the lower court for further proceedings). Justice David Souter, writing for the high court, ruled that the state supreme court failed to apply the proper harmless-error standard as stated in *Chapman*. "The issue under *Chapman* is whether the jury actually rested its verdict on evidence establishing the presumed fact beyond a reasonable doubt, independently of the presumption."

Justice Souter concluded by stating that there was clear evidence of Davis's attempt to kill Wood because he could have left the store with Yates but stayed to pursue Wood with a deadly weapon. The evidence that Davis intended to kill Mrs. Wood was not as clear. The record also showed that Yates heard a woman scream as he left the store but did not attempt to return and kill her.

The jury could have interpreted Yates's behavior to confirm his claim that he and Davis had not originally intended to kill anyone. Even the prosecutor, in summation, conceded that Mrs. Wood could have been killed inadvertently by Davis.

APPEALS BASED ON NEW EVIDENCE
Newly Discovered Evidence Does Not Stop Execution

On an evening in late September 1981 the body of Texas Department of Public Safety Officer David Rucker was found lying beside his patrol car. He had been shot in the head. At about the same time, police officer Enrique Carrisalez saw a vehicle speeding away from the area where Rucker's body had been found. Carrisalez and his partner chased the vehicle and pulled it over. Carrisalez walked to the car. The driver opened his door and exchanged a few words with the police officer before firing at least one shot into Carrisalez's chest. The officer died nine days later.

Leonel Torres Herrera was arrested a few days after the shootings and charged with capital murder. In January 1982 he was tried and found guilty of murdering Carrisalez. In July 1982 he pleaded guilty to Rucker's murder.

At the trial Officer Carrisalez's partner identified Herrera as the person who fired the gun. He also testified that there was only one person in the car. In a statement by Carrisalez before he died, he also identified Herrera. The speeding car belonged to Herrera's girlfriend, and Herrera had the car keys in his pocket when he was arrested. Splatters of blood on the car and on Herrera's clothes were the same type as Rucker's. Strands of hair found in the car also belonged to Rucker. Finally, a handwritten letter,

which strongly implied that he had killed Rucker, was found on Herrera when he was arrested.

In 1992, ten years after the initial trial, Herrera appealed to the federal courts, alleging that he was innocent of the murders of Rucker and Carrisalez and that his execution would violate the Eighth and Fourteenth Amendments. He presented affidavits (sworn statements) claiming that he had not killed the officers, but that his now dead brother had. The brother's attorney, one of Herrera's cellmates, and a school friend all swore that the brother had killed the police officers. The dead brother's son also said that he had witnessed his father killing the men.

The U.S. Supreme Court, in *Herrera v. Collins* (506 U.S. 390, 1993), ruled in a 6–3 decision that executing Herrera would not violate the Eighth and Fourteenth Amendments. The high court said that the trial—not the appeals process —judges a defendant's guilt or innocence. Appeals courts determine only the fairness of the proceedings.

Writing for the majority, Chief Justice Rehnquist stated,

> A person when first charged with a crime is entitled to a presumption of innocence and may insist that his guilt be established beyond a reasonable doubt. . . . Once a defendant has been afforded a fair trial and convicted of the offense for which he was charged, the presumption of innocence disappears. . . . Here, it is not disputed that the State met its burden of proving at trial that petitioner was guilty of the capital murder of Officer Carrisalez beyond a reasonable doubt. Thus, in the eyes of the law, petitioner does not come before the Court as one who is "innocent," but on the contrary as one who has been convicted by due process of two brutal murders.
>
> Based on affidavits here filed, petitioner claims that evidence never presented to the trial court proves him innocent. . . .
>
> Claims of actual innocence based on newly discovered evidence have never been held to state a ground for [court] relief, absent an independent constitutional violation occurring in the underlying state criminal proceeding. . . .
>
> This rule is grounded in the principle that . . . [appeals] courts sit to ensure that individuals are not imprisoned in violation of the Constitution—not to correct errors of fact.

Rehnquist continued that states all allow the introduction of new evidence. Texas was one of seventeen states that require a new trial motion based on new evidence within sixty days. Herrera's appeal came ten years later. The chief justice, however, emphasized that Herrera still had options, saying,

> For under Texas law, petitioner may file a request for executive clemency. . . . Executive clemency has

provided the "fail safe" in our criminal justice system.... It is an unalterable fact that our judicial system, like the human beings who administer it, is fallible. But history is replete with examples of wrongfully convicted persons who have been pardoned in the wake of after-discovered evidence establishing their innocence.

The majority opinion found the information presented in the affidavits inconsistent with the other evidence. The justices questioned why the affidavits were produced at the very last minute. The justices also wondered why Herrera had pleaded guilty to Rucker's murder if he had been innocent. They did note that some of the information in the affidavits might have been important to the jury, "but coming ten years after the... trial, this showing of innocence falls far short of that which would have to be made in order to trigger the sort of constitutional claim [to decide for a retrial]."

Speaking for the minority, Justice Blackmun wrote,

We really are being asked to decide whether the Constitution forbids the execution of a person who has been validly convicted and sentenced but who, nonetheless, can prove his innocence with newly discovered evidence. Despite the State of Texas' astonishing protestation to the contrary . . . I do not see how the answer can be anything but "yes."

The Eighth Amendment prohibits "cruel and unusual punishments." This proscription is not static but rather reflects evolving standards of decency. I think it is crystal clear that the execution of an innocent person is "at odds with contemporary standards of fairness and decency...." The protection of the Eighth Amendment does not end once a defendant has been validly convicted and sentenced.

Claim of Miscarriage of Justice

Lloyd Schlup, a Missouri prisoner, was convicted of participating in the murder of a fellow inmate in 1984 and sentenced to death. He had filed one petition for *habeas corpus*, arguing that he had inadequate counsel. He claimed the counsel did not call fellow inmates and other witnesses to testify that could prove his innocence. He filed a second petition, alleging that constitutional error at his trial deprived the jury of crucial evidence that would again have established his innocence.

Using a previous U.S. Supreme Court ruling (*Sawyer v. Whitley*, 505 U.S. 333, 1992), the district court claimed that Schlup had not shown "by clear and convincing evidence that, but for a constitutional error, no reasonable juror would have found him guilty." Schlup's lawyers argued that the district court should have used another ruling (*Murray v. Carrier*, 477 U.S. 478, 1986), in which a petitioner need only to show that "a constitutional violation has probably resulted in the conviction of one who is actually innocent." The appellate court affirmed the district court's ruling, noting that Schlup's guilt,

which had been proven at the trial, barred any consideration of his constitutional claim.

The U.S. Supreme Court, upon appeal, reviewed the case to determine whether the *Sawyer* standard provides enough protection from a miscarriage of justice that would result from the execution of an innocent person. In *Schlup v. Delo* (513 U.S. 298, 1995), the Court observed,

If a petitioner such as Schlup presents evidence of innocence so strong that a court cannot have confidence in the outcome of the trial... the petitioner should be allowed to... argue the merits of his underlying claims.

The justices concluded that the less stringent *Carrier* standard, as opposed to the rigid *Sawyer* standard, focuses the investigation on the actual innocence, allowing the Court to review relevant evidence that might have been excluded or unavailable during the trial.

Suppressed Evidence Means a New Trial

Curtis Lee Kyles was convicted by a Louisiana jury of the first-degree murder of a woman in a grocery store parking lot in 1984. He was sentenced to death. It was revealed on review that the prosecutor had never disclosed certain evidence favorable to the defendant. Among the evidence were conflicting statements by an informant who, the defense believed, wanted to get rid of Kyles in order to get his girlfriend. The state supreme court, the federal district court, and the Fifth Circuit Court denied Kyles's appeals. The U.S. Supreme Court, in *Kyles v. Whitley* (514 U.S. 419, 1995), reversed the lower courts' decisions. The high court ruled,

[F]avorable evidence is material, and constitutional error results from its suppression by the government, if there is a "reasonable probability" that, had the evidence been disclosed to the defense, the result of the proceeding would have been different.... [The] net effect of the state-suppressed evidence favoring Kyles raises a reasonable probability that disclosure would have produced a different result at trial.

The conviction was overturned. Four mistrials followed. On February 18, 1998, after his fifth and final trial ended with a hung jury, Curtis Lee Kyles was released from prison. He had spent fourteen years on death row.

CHALLENGING THE ANTITERRORISM AND EFFECTIVE DEATH PENALTY ACT OF 1996

The Antiterrorism and Effective Death Penalty Act (AEDPA; P. L. 104-132) became law on April 24, 1996, shortly after the first anniversary of the Oklahoma City bombing. AEDPA aims in part to "provide for an effective death penalty." After passage of the law the lower courts differed in their interpretations of certain core provisions. For the first time, on October 18, 2000, the

U.S. Supreme Court addressed these problems. Note that the defendants in the two cases share the same last name.

Federal *Habeas Corpus* Relief and the AEDPA

The AEDPA restricts the power of federal courts to grant *habeas corpus* relief to state inmates who have exhausted their state appeals. Through the writ of *habeas corpus*, an inmate could have a court review his or her conviction or sentencing. The AEDPA bars a federal court from granting an application for a writ of *habeas corpus* unless the state court's decision "was contrary to, or involved an unreasonable application of, clearly established federal law, as determined by the Supreme Court of the United States." The idea was to curtail the amount of *habeas* reviews filed by convicts and thus save the overbooked federal courts time and money.

In 1986 Terry Williams, while incarcerated in a Danville, Virginia, city jail, wrote to police that he had killed two people and that he was sorry for his acts. He also confessed to stealing money from one of the victims. He was subsequently convicted of robbery and capital murder.

During the sentencing hearing, the prosecutor presented numerous crimes Williams had committed in addition to the murder for which he was convicted. Two state witnesses also testified to the defendant's future dangerousness.

Williams's lawyer, however, called on his mother to testify to his being a nonviolent person. The defense also played a taped portion of a psychiatrist's statement, saying that Williams told the psychiatrist he had removed bullets from a gun used during a robbery so as not to harm anyone. During his closing statement, however, the lawyer noted that the jury would probably find it hard to give his client mercy because he did not show mercy to his victims. The jury sentenced Williams to death, and the trial judge imposed the sentence.

In 1988 Williams filed a state *habeas corpus* petition. The Danville Circuit Court found Williams's conviction valid. The court found, however, that the defense lawyer's failure to present several mitigating factors at the sentencing phase violated Williams's right to effective assistance of counsel as prescribed by *Strickland v. Washington* (466 U.S. 668, 1984). The mitigating circumstances included early childhood abuse and borderline mental retardation. The *habeas corpus* hearing further revealed that the state expert witnesses had testified that if Williams were kept in a "structured environment," he would not be a threat to society. The circuit court recommended a new sentencing hearing.

In 1997 the Virginia Supreme Court rejected the district court's recommendation for a new sentencing hearing, concluding that the omitted evidence would not have affected the sentence. In making their ruling, the state supreme court relied on what they considered to be an established U.S. Supreme Court precedent.

Next, Williams filed a federal *habeas corpus* petition. The federal trial judge ruled not only that the death sentence was "constitutionally infirm" but that defense counsel was ineffective. The Fourth Circuit Court of Appeals, however, reversed the federal trial judge's decision, holding that the AEDPA prohibits a federal court from granting *habeas corpus* relief unless the state court's decision "was contrary to, or involved an unreasonable application of, clearly established federal law, as determined by the Supreme Court of the United States."

On April 18, 2000, the U.S. Supreme Court, in *(Terry) Williams v. Taylor* (529 U.S. 362, 2000), reversed the Fourth Circuit Court's ruling by a 6–3 decision. The Court concluded that the Virginia Supreme Court's decision rejecting Williams's claim of ineffective assistance was contrary to a Supreme Court established precedent (*Strickland v. Washington*), as well as an unreasonable application of that precedent. This was the first time the Supreme Court had granted relief on such a claim.

On November 14, 2000, during a court hearing Terry Williams accepted a plea agreement of a life sentence without parole after prosecutors agreed not to seek the death penalty again.

Federal Evidentiary Hearings for Constitutional Claims

Under an AEDPA provision, if the petitioner has failed to develop the facts of his or her challenges of a constitutional claim in state court proceedings, the federal court shall not hold a hearing on the claim unless the facts involve an exception listed by the AEDPA.

In 1993, after robbing the home of Morris Keller Jr. and his wife, Mary Elizabeth, Michael Wayne Williams and his friend Jeffrey Alan Cruse raped the woman and then killed the couple. In exchange for the state's promise not to seek capital punishment, Cruse described details of the crimes. Williams received the death sentence for the capital murders. The prosecution told the jury about the plea agreement with Cruse. The state later revoked the plea agreement after discovering that Cruse had also raped the wife and failed to disclose it. After Cruse's court testimony against Williams, however, the state gave Cruse a life sentence, which Williams alleged amounted to a second, informal plea agreement.

Williams filed a *habeas* petition in state court, claiming he was not told of the second plea agreement between the state and his codefendant. The Virginia Supreme Court dismissed the petition (1994), and the U.S. Supreme Court refused to review the case (1995).

In 1996, upon appeal, a federal district court agreed to an evidentiary hearing of Williams's claims of the undisclosed second plea agreement. The defendant had also claimed that a psychiatric report about Cruse, which was not revealed by prosecution, could have shown that Cruse was not credible. Moreover, a certain juror might have had possible bias, which the prosecution failed to disclose. Before the hearing could be held, the state concluded that the AEDPA prohibited such a hearing. Consequently, the federal district court dismissed Williams's petition.

When the case was brought before the U.S. Court of Appeals for the Fourth Circuit, the court, interpreting the AEDPA, concluded that the defendant had failed to develop the facts of his claims. On April 18, 2000, in *(Michael) Williams v. Taylor* (529 U.S. 420), a unanimous U.S. Supreme Court did not address Williams's claim of the undisclosed plea agreement between Cruse and the state. Instead, the high court held that the defendant was entitled to a federal district court evidentiary hearing regarding his other claims. According to the Court,

> Under the [AEDPA], a failure to develop the factual basis of a claim is not established unless there is lack of diligence, or some greater fault, attributable to the prisoner or the prisoner's counsel. We conclude petitioner has met the burden of showing he was diligent in efforts to develop the facts supporting his juror bias and prosecutorial misconduct claims in collateral proceedings before the Virginia Supreme Court.

High Court Upholds Restriction on Federal Appeals

Although the Supreme Court ruled in favor of new resentencing hearings for Terry Williams and Michael Williams, it stressed that the AEDPA places a new restriction on federal courts with respect to granting *habeas* relief to state inmates. The Court noted that under the AEDPA,

> the writ may issue only if one of the following two conditions is satisfied—the state-court adjudication resulted in a decision that (1) "was contrary to...clearly established Federal law, as determined by the Supreme Court of the United States," or (2) "involved an unreasonable application of...clearly established Federal law, as determined by the Supreme Court of the United States." Under the "contrary to" clause, a federal *habeas* court may grant the writ if the state court arrives at a conclusion opposite to that reached by this Court on a question of law or if the state court decides a case differently than this Court has on a set of materially indistinguishable facts. Under the "unreasonable application" clause, a federal *habeas* court may grant the writ if the state court identifies the correct governing legal principle from this Court's decisions but unreasonably applies that principle to the facts of the prisoner's case.

METHODS OF EXECUTION
Lethal Injection May Be Used for Executions

The injection of a deadly combination of drugs has become the method of execution in most states permitting capital punishment. Condemned prisoners from Texas and Oklahoma, two of the first states to introduce this method, brought suit claiming that, while the drugs used had been approved by the U.S. Food and Drug Administration (FDA) for medical purposes, they had never been approved for use in nor tested for human executions.

The petitioners further claimed that, since the drugs would likely be administered by untrained personnel, they might not cause the quick and painless death intended. They alleged these drugs had been "misbranded," a violation of 21 U.S.C. para. 352 (f), which states, "A drug or device shall be deemed to be misbranded . . . unless its labeling bears (1) adequate directions for use." In addition, since the drugs were being put to a new use, they had to be reapproved by the FDA to determine if they were "safe and effective" for human execution.

The FDA commissioner refused to act, claiming serious questions as to whether the agency had jurisdiction in the area. He further noted,

> Generally, enforcement proceedings in this area are initiated only when there is a serious danger to the public health or a blatant scheme to defraud. We cannot conclude that those dangers are present under State lethal injections laws, which are duly authorized statutory enactments in furtherance of proper State [goals].

The U.S. District Court for the District of Columbia disagreed with the condemned prisoners that the FDA had a responsibility to determine if the lethal mixture used during execution was safe and effective. The court noted that decisions by a federal agency not to take action were not reviewable in court.

A divided Court of Appeals for the District of Columbia reversed the lower court ruling, noting that the FDA's own policy required the FDA to investigate the unapproved use of an approved drug when such use became "widespread" or "endanger[ed] the public health." Therefore, the prisoners who risked a "cruel and protracted" death were entitled to a more thorough investigation of the drugs used in their execution.

A generally irritated U.S. Supreme Court agreed to hear the case "to review the implausible result that the FDA is required to exercise its enforcement power to ensure that States use only drugs that are 'safe and effective' for human execution."

In *Heckler v. Chaney* (470 U.S. 821, 1985), the unanimous Court agreed that, in this case, the FDA did not have jurisdiction, although Justices Brennan and Marshall indicated that the limitation on court jurisdiction should not apply to all agency decisions not to intervene. The remaining justices, however, thought the courts had no right to question an agency's decision not to take action.

Writing for all but Justices Marshall and Brennan, Justice Rehnquist explained why the majority of justices concluded that the FDA decision not to investigate the prisoners' request was simply not the high court's business:

> First, an agency decision not to enforce often involves a complicated balancing of a number of factors which are peculiarly within its expertise. Thus, the agency must not only assess where a violation has occurred, but whether agency resources are best spent on this violation or another, whether the agency is likely to succeed if it acts, whether the particular enforcement action requested best fits the agency's overall policies, and indeed, whether the agency has enough resources to undertake the action at all. An agency generally cannot act against each technical violation of the statute it is charged with enforcing. The agency is better equipped than the courts to deal with the many variables involved in the proper ordering of its priorities.

Is Execution by Hanging Constitutional?

Washington state law imposes capital punishment either by "hanging by the neck" or, if the condemned chooses, by lethal injection. Charles Rodham Campbell was convicted of three counts of murder in 1982 and sentenced to death. Campbell, in challenging the constitutionality of hanging under the Washington statute, claimed that execution by hanging violated his Eighth Amendment right because it was cruel and unusual punishment. Furthermore, the direction that he be hanged unless he chose lethal injection was cruel and unusual punishment. He claimed that such instruction further violated his First Amendment right by forcing him to participate in his own execution to avoid hanging.

In *Campbell v. Wood* (18 F.3d. 662, 9th Cir. 1994), the U.S. Court of Appeals for the Ninth Circuit noted,

> We do not consider hanging to be cruel and unusual simply because it causes death, or because there may be some pain associated with death. . . . As used in the Constitution, "cruel" implies "something inhuman and barbarous, something more than the mere extinguishment of life." . . . Campbell is entitled to an execution free only of "the unnecessary and wanton infliction of pain."

According to the Court, just because the defendant was given a choice of a method of execution did not mean that he was being subjected to cruel and unusual punishment:

> We believe that benefits to prisoners who may choose to exercise the option and who may feel relieved that they can elect lethal injection outweigh the emotional

costs to those who find the mere existence of an option objectionable.

Campbell argued that the state was infringing on his First Amendment right of free exercise of his religion. He claimed that it was against his religion to participate in his own execution by being allowed to elect lethal injection over hanging.

The Court contended that Campbell did not have to choose an execution method or participate in his own execution. "He may remain absolutely silent and refuse to participate in any election." The death penalty statute does not require him to choose the method of execution; it simply offers a choice. Upon appeal (*Campbell v. Wood*, 511 U.S. 1119, 1994), the U.S. Supreme Court decided not to hear the case.

Is Execution by Lethal Gas Constitutional?

On April 17, 1992, three California death row inmates (David Fierro, Alejandro Gilbert Ruiz, and Robert Alton Harris) filed a suit on behalf of themselves and all others under sentence of execution by lethal gas. In *Fierro v. Gomez* (790 F. Supp. 966 [N.D. Cal. 1992], also referred to as *Fierro I*), the inmates alleged that California's method of execution by lethal gas violated the Eighth and Fourteenth Amendments. Harris was scheduled to be executed four days later, on April 21, 1992.

The district court prohibited James Gomez, director of the California Department of Corrections, and Arthur Calderon, warden of San Quentin Prison, from executing any inmate until a hearing was held. On appeal from Gomez and Calderon, the U.S. Court of Appeals for the Ninth Circuit vacated the district court's ruling. On his execution day Harris had filed a *habeas corpus* petition with the California Supreme Court, challenging the constitutionality of the gas chamber. The court declined to review the case, and Harris was put to death that day. In the aftermath of Harris's execution, the California legislature, in 1993, amended its death penalty statute, providing that, if lethal gas "is held invalid, the punishment of death shall be imposed by the alternative means," lethal injection.

In October 1994 a federal district judge, Marilyn Hall Patel, ruled that execution by lethal gas "is inhumane and has no place in civilized society" (865 F. Supp. at 1415; also referred to as *Fierro II*). She then ordered California's gas chamber closed and that lethal injection be used instead. This was the first time a federal judge had ruled that any method of execution violated the Eighth and Fourteenth Amendments. While the state of California maintained that cyanide gas caused almost instant unconsciousness, the judge referred to doctors' reports and witnesses' accounts of gas chamber executions, which indicated that the dying inmates stayed conscious for fifteen seconds to a minute or longer and suffered "intense physical pain."

Gomez and Calderon appealed Judge Patel's ruling on the unconstitutionality of the gas chamber before the U.S. Court of Appeals for the Ninth Circuit. They also appealed the permanent injunction against the use of lethal gas as a method of execution. In February 1996, in *Fierro v. Gomez* (77 F.3d. 301, 9th Cir.), the appellate court affirmed Judge Patel's ruling.

Gomez and Calderon appealed the case to the U.S. Supreme Court. In October 1996 a 7–2 Supreme Court, in *Gomez v. Fierro* (519 U.S. 918), vacated the appellate court's ruling and returned the case to the appellate court for additional proceedings, citing the death penalty statute amended in 1993 (lethal injection as an alternative to lethal gas).

Does Electrocution Constitute a Cruel and Unusual Punishment?

In the 1990s, although Florida had three botched executions using the electric chair, the state supreme court ruled each time that electrocution does not constitute cruel or unusual punishment. In 1990 and 1997 flames shot out from the headpiece worn by the condemned man. On July 8, 1999, Allen Lee Davis developed a nosebleed during his execution in the electric chair.

Thomas Provenzano, scheduled to be electrocuted after Davis, challenged the use of the electric chair as Florida's sole method of execution. In *Provenzano v. Moore* (No. 95,973, September 24, 1999), the Florida Supreme Court, in a 4–3 decision, ruled that the electric chair was not cruel and unusual punishment. The court further reported that Davis's nosebleed occurred prior to the execution and did not result from the electrocution.

Subsequently, the court, as it routinely does with all its rulings, posted the *Provenzano* decision on the Internet. Three photographs of Davis, covered with blood, were posted as part of Justice Leander Shaw's dissenting opinion. The photographs brought public outcry worldwide. Justice Shaw claimed that Davis was "brutally tortured to death."

In October 1999, for the first time, the U.S. Supreme Court agreed to consider the constitutionality of electrocution. Death row inmate Anthony Braden Bryan asked the U.S. Supreme Court to review his case, based on the unreliability of the electric chair. Before the high court could hear the case, however, the Florida legislature, in a special session, voted to replace electrocution with lethal injection as the primary method of execution, but allowing a condemned person to choose the electric chair as an alternative.

On January 24, 2000, the Supreme Court dismissed *Bryan v. Moore* (No. 99-6723) as moot, or irrelevant,

based on Florida's new legislation. Governor Jeb Bush agreed to sign the bill in conjunction with a second bill that limits, in most cases, death row inmates to two appeals in state courts, with the second appeal to be filed within six months of the first. This provision cut in half the time limit for the second appeal.

In 2001 the Georgia Supreme Court became the first appellate court to rule a method of execution unconstitutional. On October 5 the court held that electrocution was cruel and unusual punishment in violation of the state constitution. Voting 4–3 in two consolidated cases (*Dawson v. State*, S01A1041, and *Moore v. State*, S01A1210), the majority stated,

> The United States Supreme Court has recognized that punishment is cruel and unusual when it unnecessarily involves "something more than the mere extinguishment of life." *In re Kemmler*, 136 U.S. 436, 446 (1890). . . . [W]e conclude that death by electrocution . . . "inflicts purpose-less physical violence and needless mutilation that makes no measurable contribution to accepted goals of punishment." *Fleming v. Zant*, supra, 259 Ga. at 689 (3).

Justice Hugh P. Thompson, joined by Justices George H. Carley and P. Harris Hines, dissented. The justices observed that courts are supposed to interpret the laws, not make them, which was what the majority did when it decided that lethal injection will be the method of execution for the state of Georgia. The justices added,

> However tempted, however much they may dislike a law, courts should not use judicial powers to transform their preferences into constitutional mandates. Because today's decision reflects not the evolving standards of decency of the people of Georgia, but the evolving opinions of the majority members of this Court, I dissent.

In 2000 the Georgia legislature had passed a law making lethal injection the sole method of execution. Prior to the state supreme court ruling in October 2001, that law applied only to those sentenced after May 1, 2000.

As of 2005 ten states authorized the use of electrocution, although Nebraska was the only state that required it as its sole means of execution. Other states had laws that allowed electrocution under certain circumstances. For example, in Alabama lethal injection is used unless an inmate requests electrocution. In Oklahoma and Illinois, electrocution may be used if lethal injection is ever held to be unconstitutional.

DOES EXTENDED STAY ON DEATH ROW CONSTITUTE CRUEL AND UNUSUAL PUNISHMENT?

In 2002 Charles Kenneth Foster, a Florida inmate, asked the U.S. Supreme Court to consider whether his long wait for execution constitutes cruel and unusual punishment prohibited by the Eighth Amendment. Foster has been on death row since 1975 for a murder conviction. In 1981 and again in 1984 the defendant was granted a stay of execution to allow his federal *habeas corpus* petition.

Justice Breyer dissented from the Court's refusal to hear the case (*Foster v. Florida*, No. 01-10868, October 21, 2002). Justice Breyer pointed out that the defendant's long wait on death row resulted partly from Florida's repeated errors in proceedings. The justice added,

> Death row's inevitable anxieties and uncertainties have been sharpened by the issuance of two death warrants

and three judicial reprieves. If executed, Foster, now fifty-five, will have been punished both by death and also by more than a generation spent in death row's twilight. It is fairly asked whether such punishment is both unusual and cruel.

Concurring with the Court opinion not to hear Foster's case, Justice Thomas observed that the defendant could have ended the "anxieties and uncertainties" of death row had he submitted to execution, which the people of Florida believe he deserves. Foster remained in Florida prison under sentence of death as of September 2005.

CHAPTER 4

SUPREME COURT RULINGS— MITIGATING CIRCUMSTANCES, YOUTH, INSANITY, MENTAL RETARDATION, THE ADMISSIBILITY OF VICTIM IMPACT STATEMENTS, AND THE INFLUENCE OF RACE IN CAPITAL CASES

MITIGATING CIRCUMSTANCES

Mitigating circumstances may lessen responsibility for a crime, while aggravating circumstances may add to responsibility for a crime. In 1978 an Ohio case highlighted the issue of mitigating circumstances before the Supreme Court after Sandra Lockett was convicted of capital murder for her role in a pawnshop robbery that resulted in the shooting death of the shop owner. Lockett helped to plan the robbery, drove the getaway car, and hid her accomplices in her home, but was not present in the store at the time the storeowner was shot. According to the Ohio death penalty statute, capital punishment had to be imposed on Lockett unless "(1) the victim induced or facilitated the offense; (2) it is unlikely that the offense would have been committed but for the fact that the offender was under duress, coercion, or strong provocation; or (3) the offense was primarily the product of the offender's psychosis or mental deficiency." Lockett was found guilty and sentenced to die.

Lockett appealed, claiming that the Ohio law did not give the sentencing judge the chance to consider the circumstances of the crime, the defendant's criminal record, and the defendant's character as mitigating factors, lessening her responsibility for the crime. In July 1978 the Supreme Court, in *Lockett v. Ohio* (438 U.S. 586), upheld Lockett's contention. Chief Justice Burger observed,

> A statute that prevents the sentencer in capital cases from giving independent mitigating weights to aspects of the defendant's character and record and to the circumstances of the offense . . . creates the risk that the death penalty will be imposed in spite of factors that may call for a less severe penalty, and when the choice is between life and death, such risk is unacceptable and incompatible with the commands of the Eighth and Fourteenth Amendments.

Mitigating Circumstances Must Always Be Considered

In *Hitchcock v. Dugger* (481 U.S. 393, 1987), a unanimous Supreme Court further emphasized that all mitigating circumstances had to be considered before the convicted murderer could be sentenced. A Florida judge had instructed the jury not to consider evidence of mitigating factors that were not specifically indicated in the Florida death penalty law. Writing for the Court, Justice Antonin Scalia stressed that a convicted person had the right "to present any and all relevant mitigating evidence that is available."

CAN A MINOR BE SENTENCED TO DEATH?

On April 4, 1977, sixteen-year-old Monty Lee Eddings and several friends were pulled over by a police officer as they traveled in a car in Oklahoma. Eddings had several guns in the car, which he had taken from his father. When the police officer approached the car, Eddings shot and killed him. Eddings was tried as an adult even though he was sixteen at the time of the murder. He was convicted of first-degree murder for killing a police officer and was sentenced to death.

At the sentencing hearing following the conviction, Eddings's lawyer presented substantial evidence of a turbulent family history, beatings by a harsh father, and serious emotional disturbance. The judge refused, as a matter of law, to consider the mitigating circumstances of Eddings's unhappy upbringing and emotional problems. He ruled that the only mitigating circumstance was the petitioner's youth, which was insufficient to outweigh the aggravating circumstances.

In *Eddings v. Oklahoma* (455 U.S. 104, 1982), the Supreme Court, in a 5–4 opinion, ordered the case remanded (sent back to the lower courts for further proceedings). The justices based their ruling on *Lockett v. Ohio*, which required the trial court to consider and weigh all of the mitigating evidence concerning the petitioner's family background and personal history.

By implication, since the majority did not reverse the case on the issue of age, the decision let stand Oklahoma's decision to try Eddings as an adult. Meanwhile, Chief Justice Warren Burger, who filed the dissenting opinion in which Justices Byron White, Harry A. Blackmun, and William H. Rehnquist joined, observed,

> The Constitution does not authorize us to determine whether sentences imposed by state courts are sentences we consider "appropriate"; our only authority is to decide whether they are constitutional under the Eighth Amendment. The Court stops far short of suggesting that there is any constitutional proscription against imposition of the death penalty on a person who was under age eighteen when the murder was committed.

Hence, while the high court did not directly rule on the question of minors being sentenced to death, the sense of the Court would appear to be that it would uphold such a sentencing.

Not at Fifteen Years Old

With three adults, William Thompson brutally murdered a former brother-in-law in Oklahoma. Thompson was fifteen at the time of the murder, but the state determined that Thompson, who had a long history of violent assault, had "virtually no reasonable prospects for rehabilitation . . . within the juvenile system and . . . should be held accountable for his acts as if he were an adult and should be certified to stand trial as an adult." Thompson was tried as an adult and found guilty. As in *Eddings*, Thompson's age was considered a mitigating circumstance, but the jury still sentenced him to death.

Thompson appealed, and while the Court of Criminal Appeals of Oklahoma upheld the decision, the U.S. Supreme Court, in *Thompson v. Oklahoma* (487 U.S. 815, 1988), did not. In a 5–3 majority vote, with Justice Sandra Day O'Connor agreeing to vacate (annul) the sentence but not agreeing with the majority reasoning, the case was reversed. (Justice Anthony Kennedy took no part in the decision.)

Writing for the majority (Justices John Paul Stevens, William J. Brennan, Thurgood Marshall, and Blackmun), Justice Stevens observed,

> [I]nexperience, less education, and less intelligence make the teenager less able to evaluate the consequences of his or her conduct, while at the same time he or she is much more apt to be motivated by mere emotion or peer pressure than is an adult. The reasons why juveniles are not trusted with the privileges and responsibilities of an adult also explain why their irresponsible conduct is not as morally reprehensible as that of an adult.

Justice Stevens noted that eighteen states required the age of at least sixteen years before the death penalty could be considered. Counting the fourteen states prohibiting capital punishment, a total of thirty-two states did not execute people under sixteen.

Justice O'Connor agreed with the judgment of the Court that the appellate court's ruling should be reversed. O'Connor pointed out, however, that, although most fifteen-year-old criminals are generally less blameworthy than adults who commit the same crimes, some may fully understand the horrible deeds they have done. Individuals, after all, have different characteristics, including their capability to distinguish right from wrong.

Writing for the minority (Justices Antonin Scalia, Rehnquist, and White), Justice Scalia found no national consensus forbidding the execution of a person who was sixteen at the commission of the murder. The justice could not understand the majority's calculations establishing a "contemporary standard" that forbade the execution of young minors. He reasoned that abolitionist states (states with no death penalty) should not be considered in the issue of executing minors since they did not have executions in the first place. Rather, the eighteen states that prohibited the execution of offenders who were younger than age sixteen when they murdered should be compared to the nineteen states that applied the death penalty to young offenders.

For a Number of Years Minors Could Be Sentenced to Death at Sixteen or Seventeen

In 1989 a majority of the Court, with Justice O'Connor straddling the fence, found the death penalty unacceptable for an offender who was less than sixteen when he or she committed murder. A majority of the Court, however, found the death sentence acceptable for a minor who was sixteen or seventeen during the commission of murder. The Supreme Court, in two jointly considered cases, *Stanford v. Kentucky* and *Wilkins v. Missouri* (492 U.S. 361, 1989), ruled that inmates who committed their crimes at ages sixteen or seventeen could be executed for murder.

In January 1981, when he was seventeen years old, Kevin Stanford and an accomplice raped Barbel Poore, an attendant at a Kentucky gas station they were robbing. They then took the woman to a secluded area near the station, where Stanford shot her in the face and in the back of her head. Stressing the seriousness of the offense and Stanford's long history of criminal behavior, the court certified him as an adult. He was tried, found guilty, and sentenced to death.

In July 1985, when he was sixteen years old, Heath Wilkins stabbed Nancy Allen to death while he was robbing the convenience store where she worked. Wilkins indicated he murdered Allen because "a dead person can't talk." Based on his long history of juvenile delinquency, the court ordered Wilkins tried as an adult. He was found guilty and sentenced to die.

Writing for the majority (Justices Scalia, Rehnquist, White, and Kennedy), Justice Scalia could find no national consensus that executing minors ages sixteen and seventeen constituted cruel and unusual punishment. Scalia observed that of the thirty-seven states whose statutes allowed the death penalty, just twelve refused to impose it on seventeen-year-old offenders, and in addition to those twelve, only three more states refused to impose it on sixteen-year-old offenders.

Further, Justice Scalia saw no connection between the defendant's argument that those under eighteen were denied the right to drive, drink, or vote because they were not considered mature enough to do so responsibly and whether this standard of maturity should be applied to a minor's understanding that murder is terribly wrong. Scalia added,

> Even if the requisite degrees of maturity were comparable, the age statutes in question would still not be relevant. . . . These laws set the appropriate ages for the operation of a system that makes its determinations in gross, and that does not conduct individualized maturity tests for each driver, drinker, or voter. . . . In the realm of capital punishment in particular, "individualized consideration [is] a constitutional requirement," and one of the individualized mitigating factors that sentencers must be permitted to consider is the defendant's age.

Writing for the minority (Justices Brennan, Marshall, Blackmun, and Stevens), Justice Brennan found a national consensus among thirty states when he added the twelve states forbidding the execution of a person who was sixteen years during the commission of the crime to those with no capital punishment, and the states that, in practice if not in law, did not execute minors. Justice Brennan, taking serious exception to the majority's observation that they had to find a national consensus in the laws passed by the state legislatures, stated,

> Our judgment about the constitutionality of a punishment under the Eighth Amendment is informed, though not determined . . . by an examination of contemporary attitudes toward the punishment, as evidenced in the actions of legislatures and of juries. The views of organizations with expertise in relevant fields and the choices of governments elsewhere in the world also merit our attention as indicators whether a punishment is acceptable in a civilized society.

The Court Reverses Its Decision Regarding Minors

For fifteen years the nation's highest court held fast on its decision to allow for the execution of minors who committed capital crimes. The Court even rejected another appeal by Stanford in 2002. In *Roper v. Simmons* (543 U.S. 633, 2005), however, the Supreme Court reversed its earlier opinion when it ruled that executing Christopher Simmons was "cruel and unusual" based on the fact that Simmons was a minor when he committed murder.

In 1993, seventeen-year-old Simmons and two friends, Charles Benjamin and John Tessmer, planned the elaborate burglary and murder of Shirley Cook, who lived in Fenton, Missouri. The three teenagers wanted to experience the thrill of the crime, reasoning that they would not be held accountable as they were under the age of eighteen. On the night of the murder, Tessmer and Simmons broke into Cook's house. (Benjamin backed out.) When Cook identified who the boys were, they covered her eyes and mouth with duct tape and bound her hands. The teenagers drove Cook to a state park, wrapped more duct tape over her entire face, tied her hands and feet together with electrical wire, and threw her off a railroad trestle into a river.

The next day Simmons began bragging about the murder at school and was picked up by the police along with the two other teenagers. Simmons confessed on videotape and was tried and sentenced to death. He made a number of unsuccessful appeals and pleas for *habeas corpus*. Just weeks before he was scheduled to die, the Missouri Supreme Court called off the execution and reopened the debate in light of the Supreme Court's Atkins decision. (In *Atkins v. Virginia* [536 U.S. 304; see below], the U.S. Supreme Court ruled that executing mentally retarded criminals was a violation of the Eighth Amendment because the mentally retarded do not have as strong a sense of lasting consequences or of right and wrong as normal adults.) The state court overturned Simmons's death sentence 6–3, stating that a national consensus had developed against executing minors since *Stanford* and *Wilkins* were decided.

The U.S. Supreme Court upheld the Missouri court's decision in a 5–4 vote, reversing *Stanford*. The majority reasoned that adolescents do not have the emotional maturity and understanding of lasting consequences that adults have. As such, they cannot be held to as high of a standard and should not be sentenced to death. The majority also agreed with the Missouri court in that a national and international consensus had changed over the past fifteen years. The court noted, "To implement this framework we have established the propriety and affirmed the necessity of referring to the evolving standards of decency that mark the progress of a maturing society."

Justices O'Connor, Scalia, Thomas, and Rehnquist dissented, claiming the guidelines for executing minors should not be inflexible and that a great many citizens of the United States still favor the death penalty for teenagers who commit especially heinous crimes. Scalia stated that the majority was bowing to international pressures. In his dissent, he wrote, "Though the views of our own citizens are essentially irrelevant to the Court's decision today, the views of other countries and the so-called international community take center stage.

Youth—A Mitigating Circumstance Even for Those over Eighteen

On March 23, 1986, Dorsie Lee Johnson Jr. and an accomplice staked out a convenience store in Snyder, Texas, with the intention of robbing it. They found out that only one employee worked during the predawn hours. Agreeing to leave no witnesses to the crime, nineteen-year-old Johnson shot and killed the clerk, Jack Huddleston. They then emptied the cash register and stole some cigarettes.

The following month Johnson was arrested and subsequently confessed to the murder and the robbery. During jury selection the defense attorneys asked potential jurors whether they believed that people were capable of change and whether they, the potential jurors, had ever done things in their youth that they would not now do.

The only witness the defense called was Johnson's father, who told of his son's drug use, grief over the death of his mother two years before the crime, and the murder of his sister the following year. He spoke of his son's youth and the fact that, at age nineteen, he did not evaluate things the way a person of thirty or thirty-five would.

Johnson was tried and convicted of capital murder. Under Texas law, the homicide qualified as a capital offense because Johnson intentionally or knowingly caused Huddleston's death. Moreover, the murder was carried out in the course of committing a robbery.

In the sentencing phase of the trial, the judge instructed the jury to answer two questions: (1) whether Johnson's actions were deliberate and intended to kill, and (2) whether there was a possibility that he would continue to commit violent crimes and be a threat to society. If the jury answered "yes" to both questions, Johnson would be sentenced to death. If the jury returned a "no" answer to either question, the defendant would be sentenced to life in prison. The jury was not to consider or discuss the possibility of parole.

Of equal importance was the instruction that the jury could consider all the evidence, both aggravating and mitigating, in either phase of the trial. The jury unanimously answered yes to both questions, and Johnson was sentenced to death.

Five days after the state appellate court denied Johnson's motions for a rehearing, the U.S. Supreme Court issued its opinion in another case, *Penry v. Lynaugh* (492 U.S. 302, 1989) (holding that the jury should have been instructed that it could consider men-

tal retardation as a mitigating factor during the penalty phase). Based on the *Penry* ruling, Dorsie Lee Johnson Jr. appealed once more, claiming that a separate instruction should have been given to the jurors that would have allowed them to consider his youth. Again, the appellate court rejected Johnson's petition.

Affirming the Texas appellate court decision, Justice Kennedy delivered the opinion of the Supreme Court in *Johnson v. Texas* (509 U.S. 350, 1993). He was joined by Justices Rehnquist, White, Scalia, and Clarence Thomas. Kennedy noted that the Texas special-issues system (two questions asked of the jury and instruction to consider all evidence) allowed for adequate consideration of Johnson's youth. Justice Kennedy stated,

> Even on a cold record, one cannot be unmoved by the testimony of petitioner's father urging that his son's actions were due in large part to his youth. It strains credulity to suppose that the jury would have viewed the evidence of petitioner's youth as outside its effective reach in answering the second special issue. The relevance of youth as a mitigating factor derives from the fact that the signature qualities of youth are transient; as individuals mature, the impetuousness and recklessness that may dominate in younger years can subside. . . . As long as the mitigating evidence is within "the effective reach of the sentencer," the requirements of the Eighth Amendment are satisfied.

Justice O'Connor, in a dissenting opinion joined by Justices Blackmun, Stevens, and David Souter, stated that the jurors were not allowed to give full effect to his strongest mitigating circumstance: his youth. Hearing of his less than exemplary youth, a jury might easily conclude, as Johnson's did, that he would continue to be a threat to society.

ROLE OF PSYCHIATRISTS

Validity of a Psychiatrist's Testimony

In 1978 Thomas Barefoot was convicted of murdering a police officer in Bell County, Texas. During the sentencing phase of his trial, the prosecution put two psychiatrists on the stand. Neither psychiatrist had actually interviewed Barefoot, nor did either ask to do so. Both psychiatrists agreed that an individual with Barefoot's background and who had acted as Barefoot had in murdering the policeman represented a future threat to society. Partially based on their testimony, the jury sentenced Barefoot to death.

Barefoot's conviction and sentence were appealed numerous times, and in 1983 his case was argued before the U.S. Supreme Court. Among the issues debated was the validity of the testimony of psychiatrists. Barefoot's lawyers questioned whether it was necessary for the psychiatrists to have interviewed Barefoot or if it was enough for them to answer hypothetical questions that pertained to a hypothetical individual who acted like Barefoot.

Barefoot's attorneys claimed that psychiatrists could not reliably predict that a particular offender would commit other crimes in the future and be a threat to society. They further argued that psychiatrists should also not be allowed to testify about an offender's future dangerousness in response to hypothetical situations presented by the prosecutor and without having first examined the offender.

In *Barefoot v. Estelle* (463 U.S. 880, 1983), the Supreme Court ruled 6–3 that local juries were in the best position to decide guilt and impose a sentence. The Court referred to *Jurek v. Texas* (428 U.S. 262, 1976), an earlier case that, among other things, upheld the testimony of laypersons concerning a defendant's possible future actions. The Court, therefore, looked upon psychiatrists as just another group of people presenting testimony to the jury for consideration. The Court claimed that like all evidence presented to the jury, a psychiatric observation

> should be admitted and its weight left to the fact finder, who would have the benefit of cross examination and contrary evidence by the opposing party. Psychiatric testimony predicting dangerousness may be countered not only as erroneous in a particular case but as generally so unreliable that it should be ignored. If the jury may make up its mind about future dangerousness unaided by psychiatric testimony, jurors should not be barred from hearing the views of the State's psychiatrists along with opposing views of the defendant's doctors.

The high court dismissed the *amicus curiae* brief (a friend-of-the-court brief prepared to enlighten the court) presented by the American Psychiatric Association (APA), indicating that psychiatric testimony was "almost entirely unreliable" in determining future actions. The Court countered that such testimony had been traditionally accepted. The high court also observed that arguments, such as the APA brief, were founded "on the premise that a jury will not be able to separate the wheat from the chaff," a sentiment with which the Court did not agree.

The high court also dismissed Barefoot's contention that the psychiatrists should have personally interviewed him. Such methods of observation and conclusion were quite normal in courtroom procedures, and the psychiatric observations had been based on established facts. Barefoot's appeal was denied.

Justice Blackmun strongly dissented from the majority decision. He declared,

> In the present state of psychiatric knowledge, this is too much for me. One may accept this in a routine lawsuit for money damages, but when a person's life is at stake—no matter how heinous his offense—a requirement of greater reliability should prevail. In a capital case, the specious testimony of a psychiatrist, colored in the eyes of an impressionable jury by the inevitable untouchability of a medical specialist's words, equates with death itself.

A Prisoner Maintains Rights during Psychiatric Examination

During the commission of a robbery in 1973, Ernest Smith's accomplice fatally shot a grocery clerk (Smith had tried to shoot the clerk, but his weapon had jammed). The state of Texas sought the death penalty against Smith based on the Texas law governing premeditated murder.

Thereafter, the judge ordered a psychiatric examination of Smith by Dr. James P. Grigson to determine if Smith was competent to stand trial. Without permission from Smith's lawyer, Dr. Grigson interviewed Smith in jail for about ninety minutes and found him competent. Dr. Grigson then discussed his conclusions and diagnosis with the state attorney. Smith was found guilty. During the sentencing phase of the trial, over the protests of the defendant's lawyers, Dr. Grigson testified that Smith was a "very severe sociopath," who would continue his previous behavior, which would get worse. The jury sentenced Smith to death.

Smith appealed his sentence, claiming he was not informed of his rights. Both the federal district court and the appeals court agreed. So did a unanimous Supreme Court. In *Estelle v. Smith* (451 U.S. 454, 1981), the Court ruled that the trial court had the right to determine if Smith was capable of standing trial. It had no right, however, to use the information gathered without first advising him of his Fifth Amendment right against self-incrimination. According to the Court, the psychiatrist was "an agent of the state" about whom the defendant had not been warned, but who was reporting about the defendant. Noting *Miranda v. Arizona* (384 U.S. 436, 1966), the Court continued,

> The Fifth Amendment privilege is available outside of criminal court proceedings and serves to protect persons in all settings in which their freedom of action is curtailed in any significant way from being compelled to incriminate themselves.

The Court reiterated that the prosecution may not use any statements made by a suspect under arrest "unless it demonstrates the use of procedural safeguards effective to secure the privilege against self-incrimination."

Needing a Psychiatrist to Prove Insanity

In 1979 Glen Burton Ake and Steven Hatch shot and killed the Reverend Richard and Marilyn Douglass and wounded their children, Brooks and Leslie, in Canadian County, Oklahoma. Before the trial, due to Ake's bizarre behavior, the trial judge ordered him examined by a psychiatrist to determine if he should be put under observation. The psychiatrist diagnosed Ake as a probable paranoid schizophrenic and reported that his client claimed "to be the 'sword of vengeance' of the Lord." The physician recommended a long-term psychiatric examination to determine Ake's competency to stand trial.

Ake's psychiatric evaluation confirmed his paranoid schizophrenia. Consequently, the court pronounced him incompetent to stand trial and ordered him committed to the state mental hospital.

Six weeks later the hospital psychiatrist informed the court that Ake had become competent to stand trial. Under daily treatment with an antipsychotic drug, he could stand trial. The state of Oklahoma resumed proceedings against the accused murderer.

Prior to the trial Ake's lawyer told the court of his client's insanity defense. He also informed the court that in order for him to defend Ake adequately, he needed to have Ake examined by a psychiatrist to determine his mental condition at the time he committed murder. During his stay at the mental hospital, Ake was evaluated as to his "present sanity" to stand trial but not his mental state during the murder. Since Ake could not afford a psychiatrist, his counsel asked the court to provide a psychiatrist or the money to hire one. The trial judge refused his request, claiming the state is not obligated to provide a psychiatrist, even to poor defendants in capital cases.

Ake was tried for two counts of first-degree murder and for two counts of shooting with intent to kill. During the trial Ake's only defense was insanity; none of the psychiatrists at the state mental hospital, however, could testify to his mental state at the time of the crime.

The judge instructed the jurors that Ake could be found not guilty by reason of insanity if he could not distinguish right from wrong when he committed murder. The jurors were told they could presume Ake sane at the time of the crime unless he presented sufficient evidence to raise a reasonable doubt about his sanity during the crime. The jury found him guilty on all counts. The jury sentenced Ake to death based on the earlier testimony of the psychiatrist who concluded he was a threat to society. Upon appeal, the Oklahoma Court of Appeals agreed with the trial court that the state did not have the responsibility to provide an impoverished defendant with a psychiatrist to help with his defense.

The U.S. Supreme Court disagreed. In an 8–1 ruling, the Court, in *Ake v. Oklahoma* (470 U.S. 68, 1985), reversed the lower court's ruling, finding that "there was no expert testimony for either side on Ake's sanity at the time of the offense." The high court further observed:

This Court has long recognized that when a State brings its judicial power to bear on an indigent defendant in a criminal proceeding, it must take steps to assure that the defendant has a fair opportunity to present his defense. This elementary principle, grounded in significant part on the Fourteenth Amendment's due process guarantee of fundamental fairness, derives from the belief that justice cannot be equal where, simply as a result of his poverty, a defendant is denied the opportunity to participate meaningfully in a judicial proceeding in which his liberty is at stake.

INSANITY AND EXECUTION

Can an Insane Person Be Executed?

In 1974 Alvin Ford was convicted of murder and sentenced to death in Florida. There was no question that he was completely sane at the time of his crime, at the trial, and at the sentencing. Eight years later, Ford began to show signs of delusion—from thinking that people were conspiring to force him to commit suicide to believing that family members were being held hostage in prison.

Ford's lawyers had a psychiatrist examine their client. After fourteen months of evaluation and investigation, the doctor concluded that Ford suffered from a severe mental disorder that would preclude him from assisting in the defense of his life. A second psychiatrist concluded that Ford did not understand why he was on death row.

Florida law required the governor to appoint a panel of three psychiatrists to determine whether Ford was mentally capable of understanding the death penalty and the reasons he was being sentenced to death. The three state-appointed doctors met with Ford once for about thirty minutes and then filed separate reports. Ford's lawyers were present but were ordered by the judge not to participate in the examination "in any adversarial manner."

The three psychiatrists submitted different diagnoses, but all agreed that Ford was sane enough to be executed. Ford's lawyers attempted to submit the reports of the first two psychiatrists along with other materials. The governor, refusing to inform the lawyers whether he would consider these reports, proceeded to sign Ford's death warrant.

Ford's appeals were denied in state and federal courts, but a 7–2 Supreme Court, in *Ford v. Wainwright* (477 U.S. 399, 1986), reversed the earlier judgments. In light of the fact that there had been no precedent formed for such a case in U.S. history, the justices turned to English law. Writing for the majority, Justice Marshall observed that, while the reasons appear unclear, English common law forbade the execution of the insane. The English jurist Sir William Blackstone (1723–80) had labeled such a practice "savage and inhuman." Likewise, the other noted English judicial resource, Sir Edward Coke (1552–1634), observed that, while the execution of a criminal was to serve as an example, the execution of a madman was considered "of extreme inhumanity and cruelty, and can be no example to others." Consequently, since the Eighth Amendment forbidding cruel and unusual punishment was prepared by men who accepted English common law, there could be no question that the Eighth Amendment prohibited the execution of the insane.

The issue then became the method the state used to determine Ford's insanity. The high court noted that Florida did not allow the submission of materials that might be relevant to the decision whether or not to execute the condemned man. In addition, Ford's lawyers were not given the chance to question the state-appointed psychiatrists about the basis for finding their client competent. Questions the defense could have asked included the possibility of personal bias on the doctors' part toward the death penalty, any history of error in their judgment, and their degree of certainty in reaching their conclusions. Finally, the justices pointed out that the greatest defect in Florida's practice is its entrusting the ultimate decision about the execution entirely to the executive branch. The high court observed,

> Under this procedure, the person who appoints the experts and ultimately decides whether the State will be able to carry out the sentence that it has long sought is the Governor, whose subordinates have been responsible for initiating every stage of the prosecution of the condemned from arrest through sentencing. The commander of the State's corps of prosecutors cannot be said to have the neutrality that is necessary for reliability in the fact-finding proceeding.

The high court further observed that, even though a prisoner has been sentenced to death, he is still protected by the Constitution. Therefore, ascertaining his sanity as a basis for a legal execution is as important as other proceedings in a capital case.

In dissent, Justice Rehnquist, joined by Chief Justice Burger, thought the Florida procedure consistent with English common law, which had left the decision to the executive branch. Rehnquist warned,

> A claim of insanity may be made at any time before sentence and, once rejected, may be raised again; a prisoner found sane two days before execution might claim to have lost his sanity the next day, thus necessitating another judicial determination of his sanity and presumably another stay of his execution.

Can an Insane Person Stabilized by Drugs Be Executed?

In 1979 Charles Singleton stabbed Mary Lou York twice in the neck after robbing her grocery store in Hamburg, Arkansas. The police arrested Singleton. He was tried, convicted, and sentenced to death. Singleton was sane during the murder and through the trial.

While in prison, Singleton developed schizophrenia. At one point during his incarceration, Singleton claimed his prison cell was possessed by demons. When given antipsychotic medication, however, Singleton regained his sanity. Fearing a psychotic outburst from Singleton, the prison forced medication on him when he refused to take it. Singleton filed several *habeas corpus* petitions in state and federal courts, claiming that in light of *Ford*, he was not competent enough to be executed. He also argued that the forcible administration of antipsychotic medication was a violation of the Eighth Amendment, which forbids "cruel and unusual punishment."

The case was taken up by the U.S. Court of Appeals for the Eighth Circuit. In *Singleton v. Norris* (319 F.3d 1018 [8th Cir., 2003]), the appellate court upheld the death penalty for Singleton in a 5–4 decision. The majority felt that as long as Singleton was on medication and in full control of his faculties, his execution was not a violation of the Eighth Amendment. Singleton appealed to the U.S. Supreme Court, but the high court turned the case down, effectively endorsing the decision of the appellate court. Singleton was executed by the state of Arkansas on January 6, 2004.

CAN A MENTALLY RETARDED PERSON BE EXECUTED?
Penry I

In 1979 Pamela Carpenter was brutally raped, beaten, and stabbed with a pair of scissors in Livingston, Texas. Before she died, she was able to describe her attacker, and as a result, Johnny Paul Penry was arrested for, and later confessed to, the crime. At the time of the crime, Penry was out on parole for another rape. He was found guilty for the murder of Carpenter and sentenced to die.

Among the issues considered in his appeal was whether the state of Texas could execute a mentally retarded person. At Penry's competency hearing a psychiatrist testified that the defendant had an intelligence quotient (IQ) of fifty-four. Penry had been tested in the past as having an IQ between fifty and sixty-three, indicating mild to moderate retardation. According to the psychiatrist, during the commission of the crime, twenty-two-year-old Penry had the mental age of a child six-and-a-half years old and the social maturity of someone who was nine to ten years old. Penry's attorneys argued,

> Because of their mental disabilities, mentally retarded people do not possess the level of moral culpability to justify imposing the death sentence.... [T]here is an emerging national consensus against executing the retarded.

Writing for the five-person majority (Justices O'Connor, Rehnquist, White, Scalia, and Kennedy) regarding the execution of mentally retarded persons, Justice O'Connor, in *Penry v. Lynaugh* (492 U.S. 302, 1989), found no emerging national consensus against such executions. Furthermore, while profoundly retarded persons had not been executed for murder historically, Penry did not fall into this group.

Justice O'Connor noted that Penry was found competent to stand trial. He was able to consult rationally with his lawyer and understood the proceedings against him. Justice O'Connor thought that the defense was guilty of lumping all mentally retarded persons together, ascribing, among other things, a lack of moral capacity to be culpable for actions that call for the death punishment. Justice O'Connor wrote,

> Mentally retarded persons are individuals whose abilities and experiences can vary greatly. . . . [If the mentally retarded were not treated as individuals, but as an undifferentiated group,] a mildly mentally retarded person could be denied the opportunity to enter into contracts or to marry by virtue of the fact that he had a "mental age" of a young child. . . . In light of the diverse capacities and life experiences of mentally retarded persons, it cannot be said on the record before us today that all mentally retarded people, by definition, can never act with the level of culpability associated with the death penalty.

Further, the majority could find no national movement toward any type of consensus on this issue. While *Penry* produced several public opinion polls that indicated strong public opposition to executing the retarded, almost none of this public opinion was reflected in death penalty legislation. Only the federal Anti-Drug Abuse Act of 1988 (P.L. 100-690) and the states of Georgia and Maryland at the time banned the execution of retarded persons found guilty of a capital crime.

Justice Brennan disagreed. While he agreed that lumping mentally retarded people together might result in stereotyping and discrimination, he believed there are characteristics that fall under the clinical definition of mental retardation. Citing the *amicus curiae* brief prepared by the American Association on Mental Retardation, Justice Brennan noted,

> Every individual who has mental retardation—irrespective of his or her precise capacities or experiences—has a substantial disability in cognitive ability and adaptive behavior. . . . Though individuals, particularly those who are mildly retarded, may be quite capable of overcoming these limitations to the extent of being able to "maintain themselves independently or semi-independently in the community," nevertheless, the mentally retarded, by definition, "have a reduced ability to cope with and function in the everyday world."

Justice Brennan did not believe that executing a person not fully responsible for his or her actions would serve the "penal goals of retribution or deterrence." What is the point of executing someone who did not fully recognize the terrible evil that he or she had done? Furthermore, he argued, executing a mentally retarded person would not deter nonretarded people, those who would be aware of the possibility of an execution.

Although the Supreme Court held that executing persons with mental retardation was not a violation of the Eighth Amendment, it ruled that Penry's Eighth Amendment right was violated because the jury was not instructed that it could consider mental retardation as a mitigating factor during sentencing. The case was sent back to the lower court. In 1990 Texas retried Penry, and he was again found guilty of capital murder. During the sentencing phase the prosecution used a specific portion of a psychiatric report to point out the doctor's opinion that, if released from custody, Penry would be a threat to society. Penry appealed his case all the way to the Supreme Court. Ten years later, in November 2000, with Penry less than three hours from being put to death, the Supreme Court granted a stay of execution in order to hear Penry's claims.

Penry II

Penry once again appealed to the Supreme Court after his case was retried. In his appeal to the Supreme Court, Penry argued that the use of a portion of an old psychiatric report at his 1990 retrial violated his Fifth Amendment right against self-incrimination. In 1977 Penry was arrested in connection with another rape. During this rape case, the state of Texas provided Penry with a psychiatrist at the request of his lawyer. The psychiatrist was to determine the defendant's competency to stand trial. In 2000 Penry argued that the psychiatrist was an "agent of the state," and the prosecution's use of his report in the 1990 retrial for murder violated Penry's right against self-incrimination. Penry also claimed jury instructions were inadequate.

On June 4, 2001, the Supreme Court, in *Penry v. Johnson* (532 U.S. 782), ruled 6–3 that the admission of the psychiatrist's report did not violate Penry's Fifth Amendment right. The Court held that this case was different from *Estelle v. Smith*, discussed earlier, in which the justices found that the psychiatrist's testimony about the defendant's future dangerousness based on the defendant's statements without his lawyer present violated his Fifth Amendment right. The justices emphasized that *Estelle* was restricted to that particular case.

The justices, however, sent the case back to the trial court for resentencing because, as in the original *Penry*, the state did not give the sentencing jury adequate instructions about how to weigh mental retardation as a mitigating factor.

The Court Revisits Mental Retardation

Daryl Renard Atkins was convicted and sentenced to death for a 1996 abduction, armed robbery, and capital murder. On appeal to the Virginia Supreme Court, Atkins argued that he could not be executed because he was mentally retarded. Relying on *Penry v. Lynaugh*, the court affirmed the conviction. The court ordered a sentencing retrial because the trial court had used the wrong verdict form. As with the first penalty trial, a psychologist testified that Atkins was "mildly mentally retarded," having an IQ of fifty-nine. The jury sentenced Atkins to death for a second time. Atkins again appealed to the Virginia Supreme Court, which upheld the trial court ruling.

The U.S. Supreme Court unanimously agreed to hear Atkins's case. Thirteen years after ruling that executing the mentally retarded does not violate the Constitution, the Supreme Court, in a 6–3 decision, reversed its 1989 *Penry* decision. On June 20, 2002, in *Atkins v. Virginia* (536 U.S. 304), the majority of the Court held that "executions of mentally retarded criminals are 'cruel and unusual punishments' prohibited by the Eighth Amendment."

Justice Stevens delivered the opinion of the Court. Justices O'Connor, Kennedy, Souter, Ginsburg, and Breyer joined the opinion. According to the Court, since *Penry*, many states had concluded that death is not a suitable punishment for mentally retarded offenders, reflecting society's sentiments that these individuals are less culpable than average offenders. The Court observed,

> Mentally retarded persons . . . have diminished capacities to understand and process information, to communicate, to abstract from mistakes and learn from experience, to engage in logical reasoning, to control impulses, and to understand the reactions of others. . . . Their deficiencies do not warrant an exemption from criminal sanctions, but they do diminish their personal culpability.

The Justices also noted that, while the theory is that capital punishment would serve as deterrence to those contemplating murder, this theory does not apply to the mentally retarded because their diminished mental capacities prevent them from appreciating the possibility of execution as punishment. Moreover, the lesser culpability of mentally retarded criminals does not warrant the severe punishment of death.

Justice Scalia disagreed with the ruling that a person who is slightly mentally retarded does not possess the culpability to be sentenced to death. He claimed that the ruling finds "no support in the text or history of the Eighth Amendment." The justice also noted that current social attitudes do not support the majority decision. He pointed out that the state laws that the majority claimed reflect society's attitudes against executing the mentally retarded are still in their infancy and have not undergone the test of time.

On the relationship between a criminal's culpability and the deserved punishment, Justice Scalia stated,

> Surely culpability, and deservedness of the most severe retribution, depends not merely (if at all) upon the mental capacity of the criminal (above the level where he is able to distinguish right from wrong) but also upon the depravity of the crime—which is precisely why this sort of question has traditionally been thought answerable not by a categorical rule of the sort the Court today imposes upon all trials, but rather by the sentencer's weighing of the circumstances (both degree of retardation and depravity of crime) in the particular case. The fact that juries continue to sentence mentally retarded offenders to death for extreme crimes shows that society's moral outrage sometimes demands execution of retarded offenders. By what principle of law, science, or logic can the Court pronounce that this is wrong? There is none. Once the Court admits (as it does) that mental retardation does not render the offender morally *blameless* . . . there is no basis for saying that the death penalty is *never* appropriate retribution, no matter *how* heinous the crime.

Penry Is Sentenced a Third Time

On July 3, 2002, about two weeks after the U.S. Supreme Court ruled that it is unconstitutional to execute a mentally retarded person, a Texas jury concluded that Penry is not mentally retarded. For the third time, Penry received the death penalty, and his case continued under appeal. As of September 2005 Penry remained on death row in Texas.

COMPETENCY STANDARD

In Las Vegas, Nevada, on August 2, 1984, Richard Allen Moran fatally shot a bartender and a patron four times each. Several days later he went to the home of his former wife and fatally shot her, then turned the gun on himself. However, his suicide attempt failed, and Moran confessed to his crimes. Later the defendant pleaded not guilty to three counts of first-degree murder. Two psychiatrists examined Moran and concluded that he was competent to stand trial. Approximately ten weeks after the evaluations, the defendant decided to dismiss his attorneys and change his plea to guilty. After review of the psychiatric reports, the trial court accepted the waiver for counsel and the guilty plea. The defendant was later sentenced to death.

Seven months later Moran appealed his case, claiming that he had been "mentally incompetent to represent himself." The appellate court reversed the conviction, ruling that "competency to waive constitutional rights requires a higher level of mental functioning than that required to stand trial." A defendant is considered competent to stand trial if he can understand the proceedings and help in his defense. Yet, for a defendant to be considered competent to waive counsel or to plead guilty, he has to be capable of "'reasoned choice' among the alternatives available to him." The appellate court found Moran mentally incapable of the reasoned choice needed to be in a position to waive his constitutional rights.

In a 7–2 decision, the Supreme Court, in *Godinez v. Moran* (509 U.S. 389, 1993), reversed the judgment of the court of appeals, holding that the standard for measuring a criminal defendant's competency to plead guilty or to waive his right to counsel is not higher than the standard for standing trial. The high court then sent the case back to the lower courts for further proceedings. Moran was executed in March 1996.

VICTIM IMPACT STATEMENTS
First, They Are Not Constitutional

John Booth and Willie Reid stole money from elderly neighbors to buy heroin in 1983. Booth, knowing his neighbors could identify him, tied up the elderly couple and then repeatedly stabbed them in the chest with a kitchen knife. The couple's son found their bodies two days later. Booth and Reid were found guilty.

The state of Maryland permitted a victim impact statement (VIS) to be read to the jury during the sentencing phase of the trial. The VIS prepared in this case explained the tremendous pain caused by the murder of the parents and grandparents to the family. A 5–4 Supreme Court, in *Booth v. Maryland* (482 U.S. 496, 1987), while recognizing the agony caused to the victim's family, ruled that victim impact statements, as required by Maryland's statute, were unconstitutional and could not be used during the sentencing phase of a capital murder trial.

Writing for the majority, Justice Lewis Powell indicated that a jury must determine whether the defendant should be executed, based on the circumstances of the crime and the character of the offender. These factors had nothing to do with the victim. The high court noted that it is the crime and the criminal that are at issue. Had Booth and Reid viciously murdered a drunken bum, the crime would have been just as horrible. Furthermore, some families could express the pain and disruption they suffered as a result of the murder better than other families, and a sentencing should not depend on how well a family could express its grief.

. . . And Then They Are

Pervis Tyrone Payne spent the morning and early afternoon of June 27, 1987, injecting cocaine and drinking beer. Later, he drove around town with a friend, each of them taking turns reading a pornographic magazine. In mid-afternoon, Payne went to his girlfriend's apartment, who was away visiting her mother in Arkansas. Charisse Christopher lived across the hall from the apartment. Payne entered Christopher's apartment and made sexual advances toward Christopher, who resisted. Payne became violent.

When the police arrived, they found Christopher on the floor with forty-two direct knife wounds and forty-two defensive wounds on her arms and hands. Her two-year-old daughter had suffered stab wounds to the chest, abdomen, back, and head. The murder weapon, a butcher knife, was found at her feet. Christopher's three-year-old son, despite several stab wounds that went completely through his body, was still alive. Payne was arrested, and a Tennessee jury convicted him of the first-degree murders of Christopher and her daughter and of the first-degree assault, with intent to murder, of Christopher's son, Nicholas.

During the sentencing phase of the trial, Payne called his parents, his girlfriend, and a clinical psychologist to testify about the mitigating aspects of his background and character. The prosecutor, however, called Nicholas's grandmother, who testified how much the child missed his mother and baby sister. In arguing for the death penalty, the prosecutor commented on the continuing effects the crime was having on Nicholas and his family. The jury sentenced Payne to death on each of the murder counts. The state supreme court agreed, rejecting Payne's claim that the admission of the grandmother's testimony and the state's closing argument violated his Eighth Amendment rights under *Booth v. Maryland*.

On hearing the appeal (*Payne v. Tennessee*, 501 U.S. 808, 1991), a 6–3 U.S. Supreme Court upheld the death penalty and overturned *Booth v. Maryland*. In *Payne*, the Court ruled that the Eighth Amendment does not prohibit a jury from considering, at the sentencing phase of a capital trial, victim impact evidence relating to a victim's personal characteristics and the emotional impact of the murder on the victim's family. The Eighth Amendment also does not bar a prosecutor from arguing such evidence at the sentencing phase.

The Court reasoned that the assessment of harm caused by a defendant as a result of a crime has long been an important concern of criminal law in determining both the elements of the offense and the appropriate punishment. Victim impact evidence is simply another form or method of informing the sentencing jury or judge about the specific harm caused by the crime in question.

The *Booth* case unfairly weighted the scales in a capital trial. No limits were placed on the mitigating evidence the defendant introduced relating to his own circumstances. The state, however, was potentially barred from offering a glimpse of the life of the victim or from showing the loss to the victim's family or to society. *Booth* was decided by narrow margins, the Court continued, and had been questioned by members of the Supreme Court as well as by the lower courts.

Justice Stevens, dissenting, stated that a victim impact statement

> sheds no light on the defendant's guilt or moral culpability and thus serves no purpose other than to encourage jurors to decide in favor of death rather than life on the basis of their emotions rather than their reason.

THE ISSUE OF RACE IN CAPITAL CASES

In 1978 Willie Lloyd Turner, a black man, robbed a jewelry store in Franklin, Virginia. Angered because the owner had set off a silent alarm, Turner first shot the owner in the head, wounding him, and then shot him twice in the chest, killing him for "snitching." Turner's lawyer submitted to the judge the following question for the jurors:

> The defendant, Willie Lloyd Turner, is a member of the Negro race. The victim, W. Jack Smith, Jr., was a white Caucasian. Will these facts prejudice you against Willie Lloyd Turner or affect your ability to render a fair and impartial verdict based solely on the evidence?

The judge refused to allow this question to be asked. A jury of eight whites and four blacks convicted Turner and then, in a separate sentencing hearing, recommended the death sentence, which the judge imposed.

Turner appealed his conviction, claiming that the judge's refusal to ask prospective jurors about their racial attitudes deprived him of his right to a fair trial. Although his argument failed to convince state and federal appeals courts, the U.S. Supreme Court heard his case. In *Turner v. Murray* (476 U.S. 28, 1986), the high court, in a 7–2 decision, overturned Turner's death sentence, but not his conviction.

Writing for the majority, Justice White noted that, in considering a death sentence, the jury makes a subjective decision that is uniquely his or her own regarding what punishment should be meted out to the offender. Justice White further stated,

> Because of the range of discretion entrusted to a jury in a capital sentencing hearing, there is a unique opportunity for racial prejudice to operate but remain undetected. On the facts of this case, a juror who believes that blacks are violence-prone or morally inferior might well be influenced by that belief in deciding whether petitioner's crime involved the aggravating factors specified under Virginia law. Such a juror might also be less favorably inclined toward petitioner's evidence of mental disturbance as a mitigating circumstance. More subtle, less consciously held racial attitudes could also influence a juror's decision in this case. Fear of blacks, which could easily be stirred up by the violent facts of petitioner's crime, might incline a juror to favor the death penalty.

The high court recognized that the death sentence differs from all other punishments and, therefore, requires a more comprehensive examination of how it is imposed. The lower court judge, by not asking prospective jurors about their racial attitudes, had not exercised this thorough examination. Consequently, the Supreme Court reversed Turner's death sentence. Justice Lewis Powell, in his dissent, observed that the Court ruling seemed to be

> based on what amounts to a constitutional presumption that jurors in capital cases are racially biased. Such presumption unjustifiably suggests that criminal justice in our courts of law is meted out on racial grounds.

Limits to Consideration of Racial Attitudes

On May 13, 1978, Warren McCleskey and three armed men robbed a furniture store in Fulton County, Georgia. A police officer, responding to a silent alarm, entered the store, was shot twice, and died. McCleskey was black; the officer was white. McCleskey admitted taking part in the robbery but denied shooting the policeman. The state proved that at least one shot came from the weapon McCleskey was carrying and produced two witnesses who had heard McCleskey admit to the shooting. A jury found him guilty, and McCleskey, offering no mitigating circumstances during the sentencing phase, received the death penalty.

McCleskey eventually appealed his case all the way to the U.S. Supreme Court. Part of his appeal was based on two major statistical studies of more than two thousand Georgia murder cases that occurred during the 1970s. Prepared by David C. Baldus, George Woodworth, and Charles Pulanski, the statistical analyses were referred to as the Baldus study. (The two studies were "Comparative Review of Death Sentences: An Empirical Study of the Georgia Experience," *Journal of Criminal Law and Criminology* 74, 1983, and "Monitoring and Evaluating Contemporary Death Sentencing Systems: Lessons from Georgia," *University of California Davis Law Review* 18, 1985.)

The Baldus study found that defendants charged with killing white persons received the death penalty in 11% of cases, but defendants charged with killing blacks received the death penalty in only 1% of the cases. The study also found a reverse racial difference, based on the defendant's race—4% of the black defendants received the death penalty, as opposed to 7% of the white defendants.

Furthermore, the Baldus study reported on the cases based on the combination of the defendant's race and that of the victim. The death penalty was imposed in 22% of the cases involving black defendants and white victims, in 8% of the cases involving white defendants and white victims, in 3% of the cases involving white defendants and black victims, and in 1% of the cases involving black defendants and black victims.

The Baldus study also found that prosecutors sought the death penalty in 70% of the cases involving black defendants and white victims, in 32% of the cases involving white defendants and white victims, in 19% of the cases involving white defendants and black victims, and in 15% of the cases involving black defendants and black victims.

Finally, after taking account of variables that could have explained the differences on nonracial grounds, the study concluded that defendants charged with killing white victims were 4.3 times as likely to receive the death penalty as defendants charged with killing blacks. In addition, black defendants were 1.1 times as likely to get a death sentence as other defendants were. Therefore, McCleskey, who was black and killed a white victim, had the greatest likelihood of being sentenced to death.

In court testimony Dr. Baldus testified that, in really brutal cases where there is no question the death penalty should be imposed, racial discrimination on the part of the jurors tends to disappear. The racial factors usually come into play in midrange cases, such as McCleskey's, where the jurors were faced with choices.

While the federal district court did not accept the Baldus study, both the court of appeals and the U.S. Supreme Court accepted the study as valid. A 5–4 Supreme Court, however, in *McCleskey v. Kemp* (481 U.S. 279, 1987), rejected McCleskey's appeal. McCleskey had to show that the state of Georgia had acted in a discriminatory manner in his case, and the Baldus study was not enough to support the defendant's claim that any of the jurors had acted with discrimination.

Justice Powell noted that statistics, at most, may show that a certain factor might likely enter some decision-making processes. The Court recognized that a jury's decision could be influenced by racial prejudice, but the majority believed previous rulings had built in enough safeguards to guarantee equal protection for every defendant. The Court declared,

> At most, the Baldus study indicates a discrepancy that appears to correlate with race. Apparent disparities in sentencing are an inevitable part of our criminal justice system. . . . We hold that the Baldus study does not demonstrate a constitutionally significant risk of racial bias affecting the Georgia capital-sentencing process.

The Court expressed concern that if it ruled that Baldus's findings did represent a risk, the findings might well be applied to lesser cases. It further noted that it is the job of the legislative branch to consider these findings and incorporate them into the laws to guarantee equal protection in courts of law.

Justice Brennan, who, along with Justice Marshall, believed capital punishment constitutes cruel and unusual punishment and, therefore, is unconstitutional, thought the Baldus study powerfully demonstrated that it is impossible to eliminate arbitrariness in the imposition of the death penalty. Therefore, he argued, the death penalty must be abolished altogether because the Court cannot rely on legal safeguards to guarantee a black defendant a fair sentencing. While the Baldus study did not show that racism necessarily led to McCleskey's death sentence, it had surely shown that McCleskey faced a considerably greater likelihood of being sentenced to death because he was a black man convicted of killing a white man.

Also writing in dissent, Justice Blackmun thought the Court majority had concentrated too much on the potential racial attitudes of the jury. As important, he thought, were the racial attitudes of the prosecutor's office, which the Baldus study found to be much more likely to seek the death penalty for a black person who had killed a white person than for other categories.

The district attorney for Fulton County had testified that no county policy existed on how to prosecute capital cases. Decisions to seek the death penalty were left to the judgment of the assistant district attorneys who handled the cases. Blackmun thought that such a system was certainly open to abuse. Without guidelines, the prosecutors could let their racial prejudices influence their decisions.

Blackmun also noted that the Court majority had totally dismissed Georgia's history of racial prejudice as past history. While it should not be the overriding factor, this bias should be considered in any case presented to the high court, he thought. Justice Blackmun found most disturbing the Court's concern that, if the Baldus findings were upheld, they might be applied to other cases, leading to constitutional challenges. Blackmun thought that a closer scrutiny of the effects of racial discrimination would benefit the criminal justice system and, ultimately, society.

Prosecutor's Racially Based Use of Peremptory Challenges in Jury Selection

James Ford, a black man, was charged with the kidnapping, rape, and murder of a white woman on February 29, 1984. The state of Georgia informed Ford that it planned to seek the death penalty. Before the trial, Ford filed a "Motion to Restrict Racial Use of Peremptory Challenges," claiming that the prosecutor had consistently excluded black persons from juries where the victims were white.

At a hearing on the defendant's motion, Ford's lawyer noted that it had been his experience that the district attorney and his assistants had used their peremptory challenges (the right to reject a juror without giving a reason) to excuse potential black jurors. Ford's lawyer asked the trial judge to prevent this from happening by ordering the district attorney to justify on the record his reasons for excusing potential black jurors.

The prosecutor denied any discrimination on his part. He referred to the U.S. Supreme Court decision in *Swain v. Alabama* (380 U.S. 202, 1965), which said, in part, "It would be an unreasonable burden to require an attorney for either side to justify his use of peremptory challenges." The judge denied Ford's attorney's motion because he had previously seen the district attorney passing over prospective white jurors in favor of potential black jurors.

During jury selection the prosecutor used nine of his ten peremptory challenges to dismiss prospective black jurors, leaving only one black member seated on the jury. In closed sessions, the judge allowed Ford's attorney's observation, for the record, that nine of the ten black prospective members had been dismissed on peremptory challenges by the prosecutor. The judge, however, told the prosecutor that he did not have to offer any reasons for his peremptory actions.

Ford was convicted on all counts and was sentenced to death. His attorney, believing that the jury did not represent a fair cross-section of the community, called for a new trial and claimed that Ford's "right to an impartial jury as guaranteed by the Sixth Amendment of the United States Constitution was violated by the prosecutor's exercise of his peremptory challenges on a racial basis." On appeal, the Supreme Court of Georgia affirmed the conviction.

Ford appealed to the U.S. Supreme Court. In *Ford v. Georgia* (498 U.S. 411, 1991), the high court reversed the decision of the Georgia Supreme Court. The Court vacated (annulled) Ford's conviction and ruled that its decision on *Batson v. Kentucky* (476 U.S. 79, 1986) could be applied retroactively to Ford's case, which had been tried in 1984. In 1986 the high court had superceded *Swain* when it ruled in *Batson* that a defendant could make a case claiming the denial of equal protection of the laws solely on evidence that the prosecutor had used peremptory challenges to exclude members of the defendant's race from the jury.

Delivering the opinion for a unanimous Court, Justice Souter held that the Georgia Supreme Court had erred when it ruled that Ford had failed to present a proper equal protection claim. Although Ford's pretrial motion did not mention the Equal Protection Clause (of the Fourteenth Amendment), and his new trial motion had cited the Sixth Amendment rather than the Fourteenth, the motion referring to a pattern of excluding black members "over a long period of time asserts an equal protection claim." As of September 2005 Ford was in the Georgia State Prison serving a sentence of life with the possibility of parole.

Using Race/Ethnicity to Obtain a Death Sentence

On June 5, 2000, the Supreme Court, in a summary disposition, ordered the Texas Court of Criminal Appeals to hold a new sentencing hearing for Victor Saldano, an Argentine national on death row. In a summary disposition, the Court decides a case in a simple proceeding without a jury. Generally, a summary disposition is rare in criminal cases. In this instance, the crime was committed by a foreign national and thus fell outside of a trial jury's mandate. In *Saldano v. Texas* (99-8119), the Court cited the confession of error by Texas Attorney General John Cornyn regarding the use of race as a factor in sentencing the defendant.

Texas death penalty statutes require that the jury consider a defendant's future dangerousness to determine whether or not to impose the death penalty. At the sentencing hearing court-appointed psychologist Dr. Walter Quijano testified that Saldano was "a continuing threat to society" because he is Hispanic. Dr. Quijano told the jury that because Hispanics are "overrepresented" in prisons they are more likely to be dangerous. Following this decision, other death row inmates whose cases reflected similar circumstances were granted new sentencing hearings. Saldano's own case continued in the courts; in March 2004 the 5th U.S. Circuit Court of Appeals refused to reinstate Saldano's death sentence.

CHAPTER 5

DEATH PENALTY STATUTES AND METHODS: CHANGES AND CHALLENGES

CAPITAL OFFENSES

Prior to the late 1960s, death penalty laws in the United States varied considerably from state to state and from region to region. Few national standards existed on how a murder trial should be conducted or which types of crimes deserved the death penalty. In South Carolina, for instance, a person could be executed for rape or robbery. In Georgia and a number of other states, juries were given complete discretion in delivering a sentence along with the conviction. Though verdicts were swift, the punishments such juries meted out were frequently arbitrary and at times discriminatory.

In the late 1960s and early 1970s, the U.S. Supreme Court undertook a series of cases that questioned the constitutionality of state capital punishment laws. In *Furman v. Georgia* (408 U.S. 238, 1972), the U.S. Supreme Court ruled that the death penalty, as it was then being administered, constituted cruel and unusual punishment in violation of the Eighth and Fourteenth Amendments to the U.S. Constitution. According to the court, the state laws that were then in effect led to arbitrary sentencing of the death penalty. As a result, many states changed their laws to conform to standards set by the *Furman* decision. Since *Furman*, review of individual state statutes has continued as appeals of capital sentences reach state courts or the U.S. Supreme Court.

Under revised laws, most states now use a bifurcated (two-part) trial system where the first trial is used to determine a defendant's guilt, and the second trial determines the sentence of a guilty defendant. In most trials, jurors are usually only given the option of either sentencing a convicted felon to life in prison or to death. During a sentencing hearing, juries must consider all the aggravating circumstances presented by the prosecution and the mitigating circumstances presented by the defense. Mitigating circumstances may lessen responsibility for a crime, while aggravating circumstances may add to responsibility for a crime.

Different types of capital murder have been specifically defined as well. Although varying somewhat from one jurisdiction to another, the types of homicide most commonly specified are murder carried out during the commission of a felony (serious offense such as rape, robbery, or arson); murder of a peace officer, corrections employee, or firefighter engaged in the performance of official duties; murder by an inmate serving a life sentence; and murder for hire (contract murder). Different statutory terminology may be used in different states to designate essentially similar crimes. Such terms as "capital murder," "first-degree murder," "capital felony," or "murder Class 1 felony" may indicate the same offense in different states. Table 1.1 and Table 1.2 in Chapter 1 show capital offenses by state and federal laws providing for the death penalty as of year-end 2003. As of August 30, 2005, the death penalty remained authorized for certain cases of homicide by the statutes of thirty-eight states and by the federal government. However, the death penalty statutes of Kansas and New York were declared unconstitutional by the U.S. Supreme Court in 2004, and five states that authorized the death penalty—New Hampshire, New Jersey, Kansas, New York, and South Dakota—had not executed anyone since 1976.

While other offenses (most notably, treason and air piracy, or hijacking) also carry the death penalty, most have not yet had their constitutionality tested. The U.S. Supreme Court has held, in *Coker v. Georgia* (433 U.S. 584, 1977) and *Eberheart v. Georgia* (433 U.S. 917, 1977), that rape and kidnapping, as horrible as they are, do not result in death and, therefore, do not warrant the death penalty. Nonetheless, in 1995 the Louisiana legislature amended statute La. R. S. 14:42(C) to allow for the death penalty when the victim of rape is less than twelve years old.

STATE STATUTES AND STATUTORY CHANGES SINCE 2001

Terrorism

As in the past, states with the death penalty have continued to revise their statutory provisions relating to the death penalty. In the aftermath of the September 11, 2001, attacks on the World Trade Center and the Pentagon, several states expanded their laws, including both death penalty and non–death penalty states. According to Donna Lyons in "States Enact New Terrorism Crimes and Penalties" in the *National Conference of State Legislatures' State Legislative Report* (November 2002), New York, Florida, and North Carolina amended their death penalty statutes in 2001, making murder committed in furtherance of a terrorist act a capital crime. In 2002, ten more states—Georgia, Idaho, New Jersey, Ohio, Oklahoma, South Carolina, South Dakota, Tennessee, Utah, and Virginia—added murder committed in the perpetration of terrorism punishable by death.

Arkansas and Texas expanded their definitions of criminal homicide to include terrorism in 2003, the same year in which Colorado authorized the death penalty for anyone who used chemical, biological, or radiological weapons to kill more than one person.

Aggravating Circumstances

As noted, aggravating circumstances are factors surrounding a capital crime that tend to increase the culpability of the defendant. During the sentencing trial, the jury must consider the aggravating and mitigating circumstances and base their sentencing decision on these factors. In their statutory laws, many states list the specific aggravating factors a sentencing jury must consider in their deliberation as well as the number of factors a jury is required to agree on before convicting a person to death. Aggravating factors include the murder of a policeman, the murder of multiple people, and the murder of a child.

Many of the statutory changes occurring after 2001 involved the addition of aggravating circumstances that made an offender death-eligible. Arkansas added to its aggravating circumstances the murder of a child age twelve or under. Connecticut added murder committed to avoid arrest or prosecution as an aggravating factor. Wyoming added as an aggravating circumstance the murder of an on-duty officer of the law or an officer or member of the court, including "a judicial officer, former judicial officer, district attorney, former district attorney, defending attorney, peace officer, juror or witness."

In 2002 South Carolina added to its aggravating circumstances for death penalty eligibility the murder of a current or former law enforcement officer, peace officer, corrections officer, or fireman during or because of the performance of his official duties. Colorado made the killing of a pregnant woman by a defendant who had knowledge of the pregnancy an aggravating factor in 2003.

Jury Determination

The U.S. Supreme Court ruled in 2002 (*Ring v. Arizona*, 536 U.S. 584) that juries and not judges should weigh the aggravating circumstances in a sentencing trial where the death penalty is involved. Juries, in other words, were required to decide if the particular circumstances of a murder warranted the death penalty. At the time the Supreme Court ruling was handed down, judges were responsible for sentencing defendants in capital murder trials in nine states. In Idaho and Montana, one judge had the sentencing authority, whereas in Colorado and Nebraska, a three-judge panel sentenced a guilty defendant. Juries in Alabama, Delaware, Florida, and Indiana deliberated on the aggravating circumstances and then gave an advisory verdict to a judge who had the ultimate sentencing authority.

In light of *Ring v. Arizona*, Arizona, Colorado, Delaware, Indiana, and Nebraska all revised their capital statutes in 2002 to allow for jury determination of a death sentence. Idaho and Nevada followed suit in 2003. With the exception of Delaware, all of these states did away with judge sentencing. Under the new Delaware statute, the judge still had the discretion to sentence the defendant. If the judge's sentencing decision differed from the jury's advisory verdict, however, the judge was required to write an opinion stating why.

Minimum Age for Execution

Under state laws, the term *juvenile* refers to people below the age of eighteen. Literature on the death penalty typically considers "juvenile offenders" as persons younger than eighteen at the time of their crimes. According to Victor L. Streib in *The Juvenile Death Penalty Today: Death Sentences and Executions for Juvenile Crimes, January 1, 1973–December 31, 2004* (Ada, OH: Ohio Northern University, Claude W. Pettit College of Law, 2005), the first execution of a juvenile in the United States took place in Plymouth Colony, Massachusetts, in 1642. Since that time, Streib reported, an estimated 366 inmates who were juveniles during the commission of their crimes have been executed in the United States. Inmates spent from six years to more than twenty years on death row prior to execution.

Prior to 1999, the last execution of a person who was sixteen at the time of his crime occurred on April 10, 1959, when Maryland executed Leonard Shockley. After a forty-year respite in the United States, in February 1999 Oklahoma executed Sean Sellers, who was sixteen when he committed his crime and twenty-nine years old at the time of execution. He had been convicted for the murders

TABLE 5.1

TABLE 5.2

Juveniles executed since January 1, 1973

Name	Date of execution	Place of execution	Race	Age at crime	Age at execution
Charles Rumbaugh	9/11/85	Texas	White	17	28
J. Terry Roach	1/10/86	South Carolina	White	17	25
Jay Pinkerton	5/15/86	Texas	White	17	24
Dalton Prejean	5/18/90	Louisiana	Black	17	30
Johnny Garrett	2/11/92	Texas	White	17	28
Curtis Harris	7/1/93	Texas	Black	17	31
Frederick Lashley	7/28/93	Missouri	Black	17	29
Ruben Cantu	8/24/93	Texas	Latino	17	26
Chris Burger	12/7/93	Georgia	White	17	33
Joseph Cannon	4/22/98	Texas	White	17	38
Robert Carter	5/18/98	Texas	Black	17	34
Dwayne Allen Wright	10/14/98	Virginia	Black	17	24
Sean Sellers	2/4/99	Oklahoma	White	16	29
Douglas Christopher Thomas	1/10/00	Virginia	White	17	26
Steven Roach	1/13/00	Virginia	White	17	23
Glen McGinnis	1/25/00	Texas	Black	17	27
Shaka Sankofa (Gary Graham)	6/22/00	Texas	Black	17	36
Gerald Mitchell	10/22/01	Texas	Black	17	33
Napoleon Beazley	5/28/02	Texas	Black	17	25
T.J. Jones	8/8/02	Texas	Black	17	25
Toronto Patterson	8/28/02	Texas	Black	17	24
Scott Allen Hain	4/3/03	Oklahoma	White	17	32

Note: No juveniles were executed between January 1, 1973 and September 10, 1985.

SOURCE: "Juveniles Executed in the United States in the Modern Era (Since January 1, 1973)," in *Age Requirements of the Death Penalty and the Execution of Juveniles*, Death Penalty Information Center, 2005, http://www.deathpenaltyinfo.org/article.php?scid=27&did=203 (accessed June 1, 2005)

Minimum death penalty ages, by jurisdiction, prior to March 1, 2005

Minimum age	States
Age sixteen (14 states)	Alabama, Arizona[a], Arkansas[a], Delaware[a], Idaho[a], Kentucky, Louisiana[a], Mississippi[a], Nevada, Oklahoma[a], Pennsylvania[a], South Carolina[a], Utah[a], Virginia
Age seventeen (5 states)	Florida[b], Georgia, New Hampshire, North Carolina, Texas
Age eighteen (19 states and 2 federal jurisdictions)	California, Colorado, Connecticut, Illinois, Indiana, Kansas, Maryland, Missouri, Montana, Nebraska, New Jersey, New Mexico, New York , Ohio, Oregon, South Dakota, Tennessee, Washington, Wyoming, federal civilian government, federal military

Express minimum age in statute, unless otherwise indicated:
[a]Minimum age required by U.S. Constitution per U.S. Supreme Court in *Thompson v. Oklahoma* (1988)
[b]Minimum age required by Florida Constitution per Florida Supreme Court in *Brennan v. State* (1999). Florida's minimum age may have been lowered to 16 by a 2002 referendum.
[c]New York's death penalty statute was ruled unconstitutional on June 24, 2004.

SOURCE: "Minimum Age Requirements for the Death Penalty by State," in *Age Requirements of the Death Penalty and the Execution of Juveniles*, Death Penalty Information Center, 2005, http://www.deathpenaltyinfo.org/article.php?scid=27&did=203 (accessed June 1, 2005)

of his mother, stepfather, and a convenience-store clerk. His supporters claimed Sellers suffered from multiple personality disorder, which was diagnosed after his conviction.

According to the Death Penalty Information Center, in the modern death penalty era (1973–2005), twenty-two inmates who were juveniles at the time of their crimes had been executed. (See Table 5.1.) Texas implemented the death penalty of thirteen juvenile offenders, followed by Virginia (three) and Oklahoma (two). Florida, Georgia, Missouri, and South Carolina each executed one juvenile offender.

On March 1, 2005, the Supreme Court ruled in *Roper v. Simmons* (543 U.S. 633) that the execution of a person who committed a crime as a minor was unconstitutional. The Court reversed an opinion issued fifteen years earlier in *Stanford v. Kentucky* (492 U.S. 361, 1989), where it held that juvenile murderers below the age of eighteen could be executed. In light of *Roper*, states are required to amend their statutes regarding juvenile executions.

As of spring 2005, nineteen states and the federal government (including the military courts) required that a person had to be at least eighteen years old to receive the death sentence. Five states had statutes that continued to specify seventeen as the minimum age for the death

penalty, and fourteen states still designated a minimum age of sixteen. Of these fourteen states, four states had the minimum age requirement in their statutes, and the remaining ten states followed court decisions. (See Table 5.2.) However, all are required by *Roper* to amend their laws. Prior to 2005, the number of states that executed juvenile offenders had been dwindling. In September 2003 sixteen states designated a minimum age of sixteen for the death penalty. South Dakota and Wyoming had changed their statutes to forbid the execution of minors in 2004.

Executing Mentally Retarded Persons

In 1989 the U.S. Supreme Court held, in *Penry v. Lynaugh* (492 U.S. 302), that it was not unconstitutional to execute a mentally retarded person found guilty of a capital crime. According to the Court, there was no emerging national consensus against such execution. Just two death-penalty states—Georgia and Maryland—banned putting mentally retarded persons to death. In 1988 Georgia became the first state to prohibit the execution of murderers found "guilty but mentally retarded." The legislation resulted from the 1986 execution of Jerome Bowden, who had an IQ (intelligence quotient) of sixty-five. It is generally accepted that an IQ below seventy is evidence of mental retardation. (Normal IQ is considered ninety and above). In 1988 Maryland passed similar legislation, which took effect in July 1989.

Between 1989 and 2001, eighteen states outlawed the execution of offenders with mental retardation. The federal government also forbids the execution of mentally retarded inmates. In the Anti-Drug Abuse Act of 1988 (P.L. 100-690), the government permits the death penalty for any person working "in furtherance of a continuing criminal enterprise or any person engaging in a drug-related felony offense, who intentionally kills or counsels, commands, or causes the intentional killing of an individual," but forbids the imposition of the death penalty against anyone who is mentally retarded who commits such a crime. In 1994, when Congress enacted the Federal Death Penalty Act (P.L. 103-322), adding more than fifty crimes punishable by death, it also exempted persons with mental retardation from the death sentence.

Although the U.S. Supreme Court had agreed to review the case of North Carolina death row inmate Ernest McCarver in 2001 to consider whether it is unconstitutional to execute inmates with mental retardation, the case was rendered moot when a state bill was passed that banned such executions. On June 20, 2002, the U.S. Supreme Court finally ruled on a case involving the execution of mentally retarded convicts. In *Atkins v. Virginia* (536 U.S. 304), the Court ruled 6–3 that executing the mentally retarded violates the Eighth Amendment ban against cruel and unusual punishment. The Supreme Court did not say what mental retardation consists of and left it to the states to set their own definitions. Since the *Atkins* ruling, eight states—California, Delaware, Idaho, Illinois, Louisiana, Nevada, Utah, and Virginia—passed legislation banning such executions, according to the Death Penalty Information Center (as of June 1, 2005). Table 5.3 lists the definitions each state uses to classify mental retardation.

DEATH PENALTY METHODS

The Eighth Amendment of the U.S. Bill of Rights, using the language of the English Bill of Rights of 1689, prohibits the use of "cruel and unusual punishment" in carrying out an execution. For the most part, neither the colonies nor the United States ever used excessively brutal methods of execution, such as drawing and quartering, burying alive, boiling in oil, sawing in half, or crucifixion. Throughout most of the nineteenth century civilians sentenced to death were hanged, while the military usually shot spies, traitors, and deserters.

The federal government currently authorizes the method of execution under two different laws. Crimes prosecuted under 28 Code of Federal Regulations (CFR), Part 26, call for execution by lethal injection, while offenses covered by the Violent Crime Control and Law Enforcement Act of 1994 (P.L. 103-322, also known as the Federal Death Penalty Act of 1994) are referred to the state where the conviction occurred.

The Bureau of Justice Statistics in *Capital Punishment, 2003* reported that thirty-seven states used lethal injection as the primary method of execution in 2003. Of these states, twenty used lethal injection as the sole means of execution. Seventeen states authorized more than one method of execution—lethal injection and an alternative method—generally letting the condemned prisoner choose the method. Of these seventeen states, Arizona, Arkansas, Delaware, Kentucky, and Tennessee specified which method must be used, depending on the date of sentencing. (See Table 5.4.)

Idaho, Oklahoma, and Utah authorized the firing squad method in 2003. On May 3, 2005, Utah dropped the firing squad as a means of execution. Idaho, which still had a firing squad in 2005, authorized the firing squad only if lethal injection is "impractical." For example, an inmate might have collapsed veins from using drugs and, therefore, could not be given lethal injection. Like Idaho, Oklahoma kept the firing squad method only as a backup. It authorized electrocution if lethal injection is ever held to be unconstitutional and the firing squad if both lethal injection and electrocution are held unconstitutional. So far, Utah has been the only state that has used the firing squad. In 1977 Gary Gilmore asked the state of Utah to carry out his execution using the firing squad. Nineteen years later, in January 1996, John Albert Taylor was executed by firing squad. Both inmates chose that method of execution.

Lethal Injection

In 1977 Oklahoma became the first state to authorize lethal injection. It was not until 1982, however, that lethal injection was first used, when Texas executed Charles Brooks. Following several legal challenges, the Supreme Court, in *Heckler v. Chaney* (470 U.S. 821, 1985), upheld the use of lethal injection as a method of execution. By 1993 twenty-five of thirty-six states with capital punishment used lethal injection as the primary method of execution, according to the Bureau of Justice Statistics. Since then, most states with the death penalty have adopted lethal injection as a more humane alternative to other methods of execution—from twenty-seven states in 1994 to thirty-seven states in 2003. On February 18, 1993, the federal government adopted lethal injection as its sole means of execution.

Electrocution

At the end of the nineteenth century, alternating current (AC) electricity became one of the dominant symbols of progress. Many people thought this modern convenience would provide a more humane method of execution. In 1888 New York built the first electric chair and in 1890 executed William Kemmler with the crude mechanism.

By 2001 just two states—Alabama and Nebraska—authorized electrocution as the sole method of execution. In 2002 Alabama amended its capital statute, authorizing lethal injection as the primary means of execution,

TABLE 5.3

Death penalty states that enacted laws banning execution of mentally retarded offenders before *Atkins* decision in 2001

State	Statute citation	Definition of mental retardation	Qualified examiners
Arizona	Ariz. Rev. Stat. Sect. 13-3982	A condition based on a mental deficit that has resulted in significantly subaverage general intellectual functioning existing concurrently with significant limitations in adaptive functioning, where the onset of the forgoing conditions occurred before the defendant reached the age of eighteen.	Requires the trial court in a capital case to appoint a licensed psychologist to conduct a prescreening evaluation to determine the defendant's IQ.
Arkansas	Ark. Code Ann. Sect. 5-4-618 (1993)	Significantly subaverage general intellectual functioning accompanied by significant deficits or impairments in adaptive functioning, and manifested in the developmental period. The age of onset is 18. There is a rebuttable presumption of mental retardation when the defendant has an IQ of 65 or below.	There is no information on this aspect of the statute.
Colorado	Colo. Rev. Stat. Sect. 16-9-401-403	Any defendant with significantly subaverage general intellectual functioning existing concurrently with substantial deficits in adaptive behavior and manifested and documented during the developmental period. The requirements for documentation may be excused by the court upon a finding that extraordinary circumstances exist. The court does not define extraordinary circumstances. The law does not give a numerical IQ level.	There is no information on this aspect of the statute.
Connecticut	Public Act No, 01-151	Significantly subaverage general intellectual functioning existing concurrently with deficits in adaptive behavior and manifested during the developmental period. (as defined in Conn. Gen. Stat. § 1-1g (2001))	There is no information on this aspect of the statute.
Florida	Florida Statutes, Sect. 921.137	Significantly subaverage general intellectual functioning existing concurrently with deficits in adaptive behavior and manifested during the period from conception to age 18	Court-appointed experts in the field of mental retardation shall evaluate the defendant and report their findings to the court and all interested parties prior to the final sentencing hearing.
Georgia	Ga. Code. Ann. Sect. 17-7-131(i)	"...Significantly subaverage intellectual functioning resulting in or associated with impairments in adaptive behavior which manifests during the developmental period."	Court-appointed licensed psychologists or psychiatrists; or physicians or licensed clinical rsychologists chosen and paid for by the defendant.
Indiana	Ind. Code Sect. 35-36-9-1 et. seq.	An individual before becoming 22 years of age manifests: (1) significantly subaverage intellectual functioning; and (2) substantial impairment of adaptive behavior that is documented in a court-ordered evaluative report.	State does not specify if the court can appoint psychologists or psychiatrists. Attorneys should probably obtain this information from trial court at pre-trial.
Kansas	Kan. Stat. Ann. Sect. 21-4623	An individual having significantly subaverage general intellectual functioning to an extent that substantially impairs one's capacity to appreciate the criminality of one's conduct or conform one's conduct to the requirements of law. The statute does not define adaptive behavior or the age of onset. However, Kan. Stat. Ann Sect. 76-12b01 defines these terms. Adaptive behavior refers to the effectiveness of personal independence and social responsibility expected of that person's age, cultural group and community. The age of onset must be prior to 18 years old.	There is no information on this aspect of the statute.
Kentucky	Ky. Rev. Stat. Sect. 532.130-140	A significant subaverage intellectual functioning existing concurrently with substantial deficits in adaptive behavior and manifested during the developmental period. The age of onset is 18 years old. Significantly subaverage general intellectual functioning is defined as an IQ of 70 or below.	There is no information on this aspect of the statute.
Maryland	Md. Code. Ann. art. 27 Sect. 412	An individual who has significantly subaverage intellectual functioning as evidenced by an IQ of 70 or below on an individually administered IQ test, and impairment in adaptive behavior. The age of onset is before the age of 22.	There is no information on this aspect of the statute.
Missouri	RSMo 565.030	Significantly subaverage general intellectual functioning which originates before age eighteen; and is associated with a significant impairment in adaptive behavior.	There is no information on this aspect of the statute.
New Mexico	N.M. Stat. Ann. Sect. 31-20A-2.1 (1978)	Mental retardation refers to significantly subaverage general intellectual functioning existing concurrently with deficits in adaptive behavior. An IQ of 70 or below on a reliably administered IQ test shall be presumptive evidence of mental retardation.	There is no information on this aspect of the statute.
Nebraska	R.R.S. Neb. Sect. 28-105.01 (2000)	Mental retardation means significantly subaverage general intellectual functioning existing concurrently with deficits in adaptive behavior. An IQ of 70 or below on a reliably administered IQ test shall be presumptive evidence of mental retardation.	There is no information on this aspect of the statute.
New York (except for murder by a prisoner)	N.Y. Crim. Proc. Sect. 400.27(12)	The statute uses the most recent American Association on Mental Retardation definition (1992).* The N.Y Statute does not list specific levels of intelligence, nor does it go into detail regarding adaptive skills.	No specifics noted—"psychiatrist, psychologist or other trained individual."

TABLE 5.3

Death penalty states that enacted laws banning execution of mentally retarded offenders before *Atkins* decision in 2001 [CONTINUED]

State	Statute citation	Definition of mental retardation	Qualified examiners
North Carolina	2001 N.C. Sess. Laws 346	Significantly subaverage general intellectual functioning (defined as having an IQ of 70 or below), existing concurrently with significant limitations in adaptive functioning (defined as having significant limitations in two or more of the following adaptive skill areas: communication, self-care, home living, social skills, community use, self-direction, health and safety, functional academics, leisure skills and work skills) both of which were manifested before the age of 18.	A licensed psychiatrist or psychologist
South Dakota	S.D. Codified Laws Sect. 23A-27A-26.1 (2000)	Mental retardation means significant subaverage general intellectual functioning existing concurrently with substantial related deficits in applicable adaptive skill areas. An IQ exceeding 70 on a reliable standardized measure of intelligence is presumptive evidence that the defendant does not have significant subaverage general intellectual functioning. Mental retardation must have been manifested and documented before the age of 18 years.	A psychiatrist, licensed psychologist, or licensed psychiatric social worker designated by the state's attorney, for the purpose of rebutting evidence offered by the defendant.
Tennessee	Tenn. Code. Ann. tit.39. Ch. 13 pt. 2 sect. 39-13-203	(1) Significantly subaverage general intellectual functioning as evidenced by a functional IQ of 70 or below; (2) deficits in adaptive behavior; (3) the mental retardation must have been manifested during the developmental period or by age 18. The state does not define "deficits in adaptive behavior." The statute clearly provides that adaptive behavior and intellectual functioning are independent criteria.	There is no information on this aspect of the statute.
Washington	Was. Rev. Code Ann. Sect. 10.95.030 (West)	The individual has (1) significantly subaverage general intellectual functioning; (2) existing concurrently with deficits in adaptive behavior; and (3) both significantly subaverage general intellectual functioning and deficits in adaptive behavior were manifested during the developmental period. The age of onset is 18 years of age. The required IQ level is 70 or below.	A court-appointed licensed psychiatrist or psychologist experienced in the diagnosis and evaluation of metal retardation. This leaves open the issue of whether or not the defendant may hire his own expert.
Federal government	18 U.S.C.A. Sect. 3596(c) (Federal Crime Bill of 1994)	In 1994, Congress adopted legislation to ban the execution of individuals with mental retardation. The statute states that a sentence of death shall not be carried out upon a person who has mental retardation. The statute does not define mental retardation, or discuss at what stage in the criminal proceedings the determination of mental retardation must be made. Earlier, Congress had also provided a form of an exemption for this issue in the Anti-Drug Abuse Act of 1988 (pub. L. No. 100-690).	

Note: The statutes listed in this chart were all passed prior to the United States Supreme Court Ruling in Atkins v. Virginia.
*Mental retardation refers to substantial limitations in present functioning. It is characterized by significantly subaverage intellectual functioning, existing concurrently with related limitations in two or more of the following applicable adaptive skill areas: communication, self-care, home living, social skills, community use, self-direction, health and safety, functional academics, leisure, and work. Mental retardation manifests before age 18.

SOURCE: "State Statutes Prohibiting the Death Penalty for People with Mental Retardation," in *Mental Retardation and the Death Penalty*, Death Penalty Information Center, 2005, http://www.deathpenaltyinfo.org/article.php?scid=28&did=138 (accessed June 1, 2005)

TABLE 5.4

Methods of execution, by state, 2003

Lethal injection	Electrocution	Lethal gas	Hanging	Firing squad
Alabama[a]	Alabama[a]	Arizona[a,b]	Delaware[a,g]	Idaho[a]
Arizona[a,b]	Arkansas[a,c]	California[a]	New Hampshire[a,i]	Oklahoma[f]
Arkansas[a,c]	Florida[a]	Missouri[a]	Washington[a]	Utah[a]
California[a]	Kentucky[a,d]	Wyoming[a,e]		
Colorado	Nebraska			
Connecticut	Oklahoma[f]			
Delaware[a,g]	South Carolina[a]			
Florida[a]	Tennessee[a,h]			
Georgia	Virginia[a]			
Idaho[a]				
Illinois				
Indiana				
Kansas				
Kentucky[a,d]				
Louisiana				
Maryland				
Mississippi				
Missouri[a]				
Montana				
Nevada				
New Hampshire[a]				
New Jersey				
New Mexico				
New York				
North Carolina				
Ohio				
Oklahoma[a]				
Oregon				
Pennsylvania				
South Carolina[a]				
South Dakota				
Tennessee[a,h]				
Texas				
Utah[a]				
Virginia[a]				
Washington[a]				
Wyoming[a]				

[a]Authorizes 2 methods of execution.
[b]Authorizes lethal injection for persons sentenced after 11/15/92; the condemned sentenced before that date may select lethal injection or gas.
[c]Authorizes lethal injection for those whose capital offense occurred on or after 7/4/83; the condemned whose offense occurred before that date may select lethal injection or electrocution.
[d]Authorizes lethal injection for persons sentenced on or after 3/31/98; the condemned sentenced before that date may select lethal injection or electrocution.
[e]Authorizes lethal gas if lethal injection is held to be unconstitutional.
[f]Authorizes electrocution if lethal injection is held to be unconstitutional, and firing squad if both lethal injection and electrocution are held to be unconstitutional.
[g]Authorizes lethal injection for those whose capital offense occurred on or after 6/13/86; those who committed the offense before that date may select lethal injection or hanging.
[h]Authorizes lethal injection for those whose capital offense occurred after 12/31/98; those who committed the offense before that date may select electrocution.
[i]Authorizes hanging only if lethal injection cannot be given.

SOURCE: Thomas P. Bonczar and Tracy L. Snell, "Table 2. Method of Execution, by State, 2003," in *Capital Punishment, 2003*, U.S. Department of Justice, Bureau of Justice Statistics, November 2004, http://www.ojp.usdoj.gov/bjs/pub/pdf/cp03.pdf (accessed June 1, 2005)

although an inmate may request electrocution. According to *Capital Punishment, 2003*, nine states continued to authorize electrocution as a method of execution in 2003. Except for Nebraska, which used electrocution as the sole method of execution, the other eight states gave the inmate the choice of lethal injection. (See Table 5.4.) As of September 2005, the Death Penalty Information Center's (DPIC) Execution Database listed the May 2004 execution of James Neil Tucker of South Carolina as the last electrocution that occurred in the United States.

Lethal Gas

In 1921 Nevada became the first state to authorize the use of lethal gas for capital punishment. In 1924 Nevada executed Jon Gee using cyanide gas. This was the first time lethal gas was used for execution in the United States. The Nevada statute called for the condemned man to be executed in his cell, without warning, while asleep. Prison officials, unable to figure out a practical way to carry out the execution, ended up constructing a gas chamber. In 1994 a U.S. district judge in California ruled that lethal gas was an inhumane method of execution, a decision upheld by the U.S. Ninth Circuit Court of Appeals in 1995. The U.S. Supreme Court declined to rule on the case and remanded it back to the circuit court in 1996. In 2003 four states continued to authorize the use of lethal gas. (See Table 5.4.) As of September 2005, according to the DPIC's Execution Database (http://www.deathpenaltyinfo.org/executions.php), the last execution using lethal gas was carried out in Arizona in March 1999.

Hanging

In *Capital Punishment, 2003* the Bureau of Justice statistics reported that Delaware, New Hampshire, and Washington had authorized hanging as a method of execution that year. The state of Washington gave the condemned person the choice of death by lethal injection, while New Hampshire authorized hanging only if, for some reason, lethal injection could not be administered. (See Table 5.4.) On July 8, 2003, Delaware dismantled its gallows because it no longer had an inmate eligible to choose the option of hanging (only those whose capital offense had occurred before June 13, 1986, were eligible). For Delaware convicts whose offenses occurred on or after June 13, 1986, lethal injection is the sole method of execution.

As of September 2005, the DPIC Execution Database showed that Washington last hanged two inmates in 1993 and 1994, while Delaware hanged its last death row inmate in 1996. It was Delaware's first hanging in fifty years. New Hampshire's last hanging occurred in 1939.

WITNESSES TO EXECUTIONS

Death penalty states have statutes or policies (or both) that specify which witnesses may be present at an execution. Witnesses usually include prison officials, physicians, the condemned person's relatives, the victim's relatives, spiritual advisers, selected state citizens, and reporters. In celebrated cases, however, such as that of the Rosenbergs, who were convicted spies (1953), the notorious California killer Caryl Chessman (1960), and convicted Oklahoma City bomber Timothy McVeigh (2001), the witnesses made up a larger group.

Robert Jay Lifton and Greg Mitchell, in *Who Owns Death? Capital Punishment, the American Conscience, and the End of Executions* (New York: William Morrow, 2000), reported that the number of witnesses allowed at an execution varies from state to state. For example, Pennsylvania and North Carolina allow six official witnesses, New Hampshire allows twelve, and other states have different required numbers. The authors observed, however, that as the number of executions rises, some prison authorities have resorted to going on the Internet to recruit witnesses. Others telephone the public to invite them to witness executions.

Victims' Families as Witnesses at Executions

As of 2005 the laws of twenty-one states—Alabama, Arizona, Arkansas, California, Colorado, Delaware, Georgia, Kentucky, Louisiana, Maryland, Mississippi, Missouri, Nevada, Ohio, Oklahoma, North Carolina, Oregon (also specified by policy), Pennsylvania, South Carolina, Tennessee, and Washington—allowed victims' families to be present at executions.

According to the National Center for Victims of Crime in *FYI: Rights of Survivors of Homicide* (1999), the statutes of the different states vary in the procedural requirements that victims' relatives have to follow in order to request notification and/or attendance. For example, the Nevada statute defines immediate family as those "who are related by blood, adoption or marriage, within the second degree of consanguinity (blood relationship) or affinity (relationship by marriage or adoption rather than by blood)." The victims' relatives may write the director of the prison department if they wish notification of the execution. Requests to view the execution also have to be submitted in writing.

The Oklahoma statute puts no limit on the number of immediate family members who may view the execution. Each family member has to be eighteen years or older and may be "the spouse, a child by birth or adoption, a stepchild, a parent, a grandparent, or a sibling of the deceased victim." The family views the execution in an area separate from the other witnesses. If a separate room for direct viewing is not available, a closed-circuit television is provided. However, in Delaware and Louisiana, only a single family member or representative is allowed to attend the execution.

Six other states—Florida, Illinois, Montana, Texas, Utah, and Virginia—allow victims' families to be present at executions by policy. Only one state, New Jersey, prohibits "any person who is related by either blood or marriage to the sentenced person or to the victim to be present at the execution."

The federal government also allows victims' families to witness an execution. This practice was brought into question during the execution of Timothy McVeigh, who was sentenced to die in 2001 for the bombing of the federal building in Oklahoma City that killed 168 people in 1995. The Justice Department reported that 232 survivors and family members would view the execution. The prison facility could not accommodate the hundreds of victims' relatives who would wish to witness the execution. On June 11, 2001, the day of the execution, ten survivors of the bombing and members of victims' families chosen by lottery watched McVeigh die in Terre Haute, Indiana, behind tinted glass, unseen by the condemned. In addition, ten journalists, four people selected by McVeigh, and several government officials witnessed the execution. Survivors and family members of the victims not chosen by lottery were allowed to witness the execution on closed-circuit television in a federal prison in Oklahoma City.

Media Witnesses

Prior to 1996, witnesses could watch an entire execution procedure in California from the moment the inmate was led to the gas chamber (or gallows before 1936) until death was pronounced. On February 23, 1996, William Bonin became the first person in California to be executed by lethal injection. Based on the state's new public witness procedure (Procedure 770), officials at San Quentin Prison opened the curtain to the observation room only after the condemned had been strapped to the gurney and the intravenous (IV) solution had been inserted and was running.

In April 1996 the Society of Professional Journalists' Northern California Chapter and the California First Amendment Coalition filed a lawsuit claiming that Procedure 770 violated their First Amendment right to view the entire execution procedure. The journalists argued that because they were not allowed to see the guards preparing the condemned for execution, the journalists could not inform the public of the whole process of execution.

San Quentin Prison officials maintained that it could take the execution team as long as twenty minutes to prepare the condemned. They were concerned that the prolonged "exposure to witnesses will increase the likelihood of an identification of execution team members." This would in turn subject the staff and their families to possible repercussions that might affect their safety, such as gang violence, as well as affect prison security.

On May 1, 1996, the U.S. District Court issued an injunction forbidding prison officials from limiting media access to the entire execution. On May 3, 1996, reporters were able to witness Keith Daniel Williams's execution in its entirety. In February 1997 the U.S. District Court for the Northern District of California, in *California First Amendment Coalition v. Calderon* (956 F. Supp. 883 [N.D. Cal. 1997]), ruled that "the First Amendment requires prison officials to allow the public and the media to witness lethal injection from the time just before the prisoner is strapped down to a gurney until after death." A long history of access to executions has helped inform the public "on whether the state's 'awesome' power to commit executions was properly exercised."

Prison officials appealed their case to the U.S. Court of Appeals for the Ninth Circuit in July 1998. In *California First Amendment Coalition v. Calderon* (150 F.3d 976, 983, 9th Cir. 1998), the court ruled that Procedure 770 does not violate the First Amendment rights of the press and the case was sent back to the U.S. district court so it could determine whether or not the concerns of the prison officials were justified.

On July 26, 2000, in *California First Amendment Coalition v. Woodford* (No. C-96-1291-VRW), U.S. District Judge Vaughn Walker concluded that the prison officials' practice of restricting witness observation was "an exaggerated response to [their own] safety con-

cerns." The judge ruled that media witnesses should view the entire execution procedure.

In March 2001, prior to Robert Lee Massie's execution, the state filed an emergency motion before the Ninth Circuit and, subsequently, before the U.S. Supreme Court to overturn the rulings that allowed the media full access to the execution proceedings. On March 26, 2001, both the appellate and high courts denied the motion. The next day witnesses saw Massie's entire execution. On August 2, 2002, in the latest court ruling on California's Procedure 770, the U.S. Court of Appeals for the Ninth Circuit upheld Judge Walker's ruling. In *California First Amendment Coalition v. Woodford* (No. 00-16752), the court stated,

> We hold that Procedure 770 is an exaggerated, unreasonable response to prison officials' legitimate concerns about the safety of prison staff and thereby unconstitutionally restricts the public's First Amendment right to view executions from the moment the condemned is escorted into the execution chamber. . . . An informed public debate is the main purpose for granting a right of access to governmental proceedings.
>
> [T]here exists a ready, low-cost alternative that would fully accommodate the public's First Amendment right of access and adequately address defendants' security concerns as well. [T]he district court found that "[t]he use of surgical garb is a practical alternative to restricting access to witness lethal injection executions in order to conceal the identity of such execution staff should security concerns warrant such concealment."

MORATORIUMS, CHALLENGES, AND CONTROVERSIES SURROUNDING STATE DEATH PENALTY LAWS
Illinois

On January 31, 2000, Illinois became the first state to declare a moratorium on the death penalty. Governor George H. Ryan, a death penalty supporter, suspended all executions because he believed the state's death penalty system was "fraught with errors." The *Chicago Tribune* had issued a report showing that thirteen inmates in Ryan's state had been released from death row since 1976. The reasons for the exoneration of these inmates ranged from DNA evidence showing innocence to false testimonies by jailhouse informants to coercion of so-called witnesses by prosecution and police.

Governor Ryan then appointed a commission to investigate the thirteen cases, as well as all capital cases in Illinois. On April 15, 2002, the *Report of the Governor's Commission on Capital Punishment* was released. The fourteen-member panel issued eighty-five recommendations it thought would help reform the state's death penalty process. The recommended reforms included videotaping of capital suspects during interrogation at police facilities, banning the death penalty in cases where the conviction is based on a single-eyewitness testimony, and thorough examination of a jailhouse-informant testimony at a pretrial hearing to determine whether to use that testimony during trial.

John J. Kinsella, First Assistant State's Attorney of DuPage County, Illinois, was asked to appear before the U.S. Senate Judiciary Committee in 2002 to express his views as a prosecutor concerning Governor Ryan's moratorium and his Commission on capital punishment. Kinsella noted that the governor had only one active prosecutor among the fourteen commission members. While many of the commission recommendations involve how the police should perform their jobs, not one police officer was invited to be a part of the commission. No victim rights groups were also represented. Furthermore, most of the members were death penalty opponents.

On January 10, 2003, the day before leaving office, Governor Ryan pardoned four inmates who had been on death row in Illinois at least twelve years. Governor Ryan claimed the men were innocent of the murders for which they had been convicted. He found that the police had tortured the men into making false confessions. Three of the men had been released. The fourth inmate remained in prison because of a separate conviction. The following day Governor Ryan commuted 167 death sentences to life imprisonment without the possibility of parole, emptying death row.

Rod Blagojevich entered office on January 12, 2003, and as of June 1, 2005, the Illinois moratorium had not been lifted. However, the Illinois death row did not remain empty. In February 2003 Anthony Mertz was sent to death row for a 2001 rape and murder, and by 2005 ten inmates were under sentence of death in Illinois.

Kansas

The Kansas Supreme Court in *State v. Marsh* (278 Kan. 520, 102 P.3d 445) ruled Kansas's death penalty statute unconstitutional in 2004. Michael Marsh was sentenced to death for murdering Marry Pusch and her nineteenth-month-old daughter in 1996. According to Kansas statute, if a sentencing jury weighs the evidence for and against the death sentence and both arguments seem equally valid, then the jury should choose the death sentence. Marsh took the case to the Kansas Supreme Court, claiming that the state statute was unconstitutional under the Eighth and Fourteenth Amendments. In a 5–4 vote, the justices of the Kansas high court agreed with Marsh and vacated his sentence as well as the sentences of six other inmates on death row. The court believed that no U.S. Supreme Court precedent existed to back their ruling. The state prosecutor took the case to the U.S. Supreme Court, which agreed to hear the case and scheduled arguments for December 7, 2005.

Louisiana

In August 1995 Louisiana enacted a law allowing the death penalty for rape when the victims are under age twelve. In December 1995 Anthony Wilson was charged by a grand jury with the aggravated rape of a five-year-old girl. (A grand jury differs from a regular jury in that the former, typically consisting of up to twenty-three jurors determines whether the criminal complaint brought by the prosecutor warrants an indictment, and eventually a trial.) Patrick Dwayne Bethley was charged with raping three girls, one of whom was his daughter. At the time of the rape, the girls were five, seven, and nine years old. The two defendants moved to quash their indictments. They claimed that the death penalty, when imposed for rape, constitutes "cruel and unusual punishment" and, therefore, is unconstitutional under the Eighth Amendment and Article I, Section 20, of the Louisiana Constitution. On December 13, 1996, the Louisiana Supreme Court, in *State v. Wilson* (685 So.2d 1063), held by a 5–2 vote that the state death penalty statute was constitutional. The Louisiana Supreme Court concluded,

> Given the appalling nature of the crime, the severity of the harm inflicted upon the victim, and the harm imposed on society, the death penalty is not an excessive penalty for the crime of rape when the victim is a child under the age of twelve years old.

In 1998 Bethley entered into a plea agreement with prosecutors in which he received a life sentence for rape. In turn, the state of Louisiana did not seek the death penalty against him. In 1999, upon appeal, Wilson was found mentally retarded and, therefore, unable to assist in his defense.

In August 2003, for the first time in Louisiana, a jury imposed the death penalty for the rape of a child. Patrick O. Kennedy had been convicted of repeatedly raping his eight-year-old stepdaughter in 1998. Some experts believe Kennedy's case might be heard by the U.S. Supreme Court because the Court's decision in *Coker v. Georgia* (433 U.S. 584, 1977), outlawing capital punishment for rape, addressed only the rape of an adult woman. Others observed that, partly in light of the growing number of Catholic priests found guilty of abusing children, states might pursue such cases more vehemently.

Maryland

In July 2001 a *de facto* (in practice, as opposed to *de jure*, meaning in law) moratorium occurred in Maryland pending the resolution by the state's high court of an appeal by inmate Steven Oken challenging the constitutionality of Maryland's capital punishment laws. Oken was sentenced to death in 1991 for the 1987 murder of Dawn Marie Garvin. He had also received life sentences for killing his sister-in-law and a motel desk clerk in Maine.

In May 2002 Maryland's governor, Parris Glendening, imposed a moratorium to allow for the completion of a study on capital punishment. Newly elected governor Robert Ehrlich, Jr., lifted the ban on executions in January 2003.

Maryland again imposed a moratorium in February 2003 after the state's highest court stayed the execution of Oken, who was scheduled to die the following month. The Maryland Court of Appeals granted the temporary reprieve to hear Oken's case at a future date. On May 1, 2003, during his fourth review by the state's appellate court, Oken argued that the state's death penalty is unconstitutional in light of the 2000 Supreme Court ruling, *Apprendi v. New Jersey* (530 U.S. 466), which held that jurors must use the higher standard of "beyond a reasonable doubt" in considering evidence during the sentencing phase of a trial.

The Maryland Court of Appeals (*Oken v. State*, No. 117, November 17, 2003) upheld the death sentence of Steven Oken. The court did not address Oken's *Apprendi* argument and ruled only on his claim that *Ring v. Arizona* implicated the state's death penalty law. The court rejected that claim.

In 2003 Erlich signed Oken's death warrant, and Maryland's moratorium ended on July 17, 2004, with the execution of Oken by lethal injection.

New Hampshire

In May 2000 the New Hampshire legislature passed a bill abolishing the death penalty. Governor Jeanne Shaheen, however, vetoed the bill. A similar bill introduced in the House of Representatives in January 2001 was defeated three months later. Although the death penalty is in the statute books, New Hampshire has not sentenced anyone to death since reinstating capital punishment in 1991. The state had not had an execution since 1939. As of September 2005, New Hampshire had no inmates on death row.

New York

GUILTY PLEAS. Until 1998 New York's death penalty statute prohibited the imposition of a death sentence when a defendant entered a guilty plea. The maximum penalty in such a case would be life imprisonment without parole. However, a defendant who pleaded not guilty would have to stand trial and face the possibility of a death sentence. The law provided two levels of penalty for the same offense, imposing the death penalty only on those who claimed innocence.

Defendants in two capital cases challenged the plea provisions of New York's death penalty statute, claiming these provisions violated their Fifth Amendment right against self-incrimination and the Sixth Amendment right to a jury trial. This was the first major constitutional challenge to New York's death penalty law. On December 22, 1998, the New York Court of Appeals (New York's highest court), in *Hynes v. Tomei* (including *Relin v. Mateo*, 92 N.Y. 2d. 613, 706 N.E. 2d. 1201, 684 N.Y.S. 2d. 177), unanimously agreed, striking down these plea-bargaining provisions as unconstitutional. The court, relying on the U.S. Supreme Court decision in *United States v. Jackson* (390 U.S. 570, 1968), observed that "the Supreme Court in *Jackson* prohibited statutes that 'needlessly' encourage guilty pleas, which are not constitutionally protected, by impermissibly burdening constitutional rights." The ruling left the death penalty intact, but the court could no longer give preference to those who entered a guilty plea.

JURY DEADLOCK INSTRUCTIONS. In 2004 the New York Court of Appeals agreed to hear another challenge to the constitutionality of New York's death penalty. Stephen LaValle was sentenced to death in 1999 by a New York jury for the rape and murder of Cynthia Quinn. Under New York law, a jury can sentence a defendant convicted of murder to life in prison without parole or to death. All jurors must vote unanimously. In the event of a hung jury, the court sentences a guilty defendant to life imprisonment with parole eligibility after serving a minimum of twenty to twenty-five years, leaving room for the convict to be released.

LaValle claimed that this "jury deadlock instruction" violated his constitutional rights because it would encourage members of the jury who do not favor the death penalty to vote for the death penalty if they are in the minority. LaValle even presented a study showing that most jurors would choose the death penalty if given the choice of the death penalty or imprisonment with a chance of parole. In *People v. LaValle* (783 NYS 2d, 485, 2004), the New York Court of Appeals agreed with LaValle and vacated his sentence. The state high court stated that this jury instruction was cruel and unusual punishment in violation of the Eighth and Fourteenth Amendments, citing the U.S. Supreme Court's decision in *Woodson v. North Carolina* (428 U.S. 280, 1976). The nation's highest court held in *Woodson* that a mandatory death sentence for a capital offense was unconstitutional and forced jurors to charge the defendant with a lesser charge if they did not want to see the defendant sentenced to death. (See Chapter 2.)

This decision by the New York court effectively put a moratorium on the New York death penalty until the New York state legislature changed the death penalty statutes. Roughly a year later, the New York State Assembly Codes Committee (the state legislative committee in charge of changing death penalty statutes) defeated a bill to reinstate the death penalty, claiming that the system was riddled with flaws. As of September 2005, the unofficial moratorium on the death penalty remained in effect.

Washington

CONTROVERSY OVER GREEN RIVER KILLER PLEA BARGAIN. A plea agreement between a serial killer and King County, Washington, prosecutor Norm Maleng caused controversy over the fair application of the death penalty. Gary Leon Ridgway escaped the death penalty by agreeing to provide information about the forty-eight women he had murdered. Ridgway, known as the Green River Killer because he dumped the bodies of his victims, many of them prostitutes and runaways, along the Green River near Seattle, Washington, committed his crimes between 1980 and 1998. Authorities say this is the largest number of murders ever committed by a serial killer. In November 2001 authorities linked Ridgway's DNA to samples found on some of the victims. In December 2003 Ridgway received forty-eight consecutive life terms without the possibility of parole. He was also ordered to pay $10,000 for each victim.

Both sides of the death penalty issue have used the Ridgway case to bolster their causes. Opponents of the death penalty argue that if a case involving the largest number of serial killings did not warrant the death penalty, then others involving fewer murders certainly do not deserve the ultimate punishment. Some have noted that if the criminal justice system did not sentence a white mass murderer to death, then it should think twice about imposing the death penalty on a black person who has killed just one person or a few. Proponents of capital punishment use the case as an example of how murderers can manipulate the system, and they call for shortening the time between death sentencing and execution. Still others think the prosecutor took the right course by not acting on his initial plan to seek the death sentence. He believed that victims' families could find closure through the information Ridgway could provide about their loved ones' deaths.

In the *Seattle Times* (November 8, 2003), Washington Superior Court Judge David A. Nichols called for the abolition of the death penalty in his state. He pointed out that it is a "mockery of all reasonable notions of justice" that a mass murderer is able to avoid the death penalty because he has something to offer in exchange for the deal, while another murderer gets the death sentence because he has nothing to offer. However, the case did not result in overturning the death penalty in Washington, which was still in effect in 2005.

STATES CONSIDER RESTORING THE DEATH PENALTY

Several states without the death penalty have considered reinstating it. In 2003 Hawaii, Massachusetts, Minnesota, and Wisconsin lawmakers introduced bills in their state legislatures that would reinstitute the death penalty. Michigan entertained reviving the death penalty in 2004. However, none of these legislative measures passed.

CHAPTER 6
EXECUTIONS—HISTORICAL STATISTICS

NUMBER OF EXECUTIONS

Until 1930 the U.S. government did not keep any record of the number of people executed under the death penalty. According to the Bureau of Justice Statistics in *Capital Punishment, 2003*, from 1930 through 2003 a total of 4,744 executions were conducted under civil authority in the United States. Military authorities carried out an additional 160 executions between 1930 and 1961, the date of the last military execution.

From 1930 to 1939 a total of 1,667 inmates were executed, the highest number of persons put to death in any decade. (See Table 6.1.) The number of executions generally declined between the 1930s and the 1960s. In 1930, 155 executions took place, reaching a high of 199 in 1935. By 1950 executions were down to eighty-two, further dropping to forty-nine each in 1958 and 1959, and then rising slightly to fifty-six in 1960. In 1967 a ten-year moratorium (temporary suspension) of the death penalty began as states waited for the U.S. Supreme Court to determine a constitutionally acceptable procedure for carrying out the death penalty. (See Figure 1.1 in Chapter 1.)

The moratorium ended in 1976, but no executions occurred that year. The first execution following the moratorium occurred in Utah in January 1977. In 1999, ninety-eight inmates were put to death, the most in one year since the death penalty was reinstated. In 2000 the number of executions (eighty-five) declined 13% from the previous year, further dropping 22% to sixty-six executions in 2001. In 2002 the number of executions rose slightly to seventy-one and then declined again to fifty-nine in 2004. Thirty-eight people were executed in the fist five months of 2005. Between 1976 and mid-2005, nearly 1,000 people were put to death.

LOCATIONS OF EXECUTIONS

According to the "Facts about the Death Penalty," released by the Death Penalty Information Center (DPIC)

in Washington, D.C., as of August 30, 2005, approximately four out of every five executions (804 out of 980 civil executions) took place in the South between 1976 and August 30, 2005. As of 2003, the South had the highest murder rate of any region of the country (6.9 murders per 100,000 population) and a higher rate than the national average of 5.7 per 100,000. (See Figure 6.1.)

Overall, thirty-two states carried out executions from 1976 to August 2005. The federal government executed three men. The largest number (348) of executions in a single state occurred in Texas, followed by Virginia (ninety-four), Oklahoma (seventy-nine), Missouri (sixty-four), and Florida (sixty). Together, these five states carried out 66% of all executions during this twenty-eight-year period.

In 2000 Texas accounted for the largest number of executions (forty), the most in a single year in any state since 1976, according to the DPIC. That same year Tennessee executed its first inmate since 1960, while Arkansas put to death a female inmate, the first woman ever executed in that state.

Oklahoma led the nation in executions (eighteen) in 2001, followed by Texas (seventeen). In 2002 Texas resumed its lead, executing thirty-three inmates, almost five times as many as the next leading state, Oklahoma (seven inmates). (See Table 6.1.) The DPIC reported that between 1993 and October 1, 2003, the number of executions in Texas (256) comprised 38% of the total number during that ten-year period, with the rest of the states accounting for 62% (432 executions). (See Figure 6.2.)

GENDER

The National Association for the Advancement of Colored People Legal Defense and Educational Fund (LDF) publishes the quarterly *Death Row USA*, which not only reports the number of death row inmates but also

TABLE 6.1

Number of prisoners executed, by region and jurisdiction, 1930–2003

Region and jurisdiction	Total	1930 to 1934	1935 to 1939	1940 to 1944	1945 to 1949	1950 to 1954	1955 to 1959	1960 to 1964	1965 to 1969	1970 to 1979	1980 to 1984	1985	1986	1987	1988
United States	**4,744**	**776**	**891**	**645**	**639**	**413**	**304**	**181**	**10**	**3**	**29**	**18**	**18**	**25**	**11**
Federal	36	1	9	7	6	6	3	1	—	—	—	—	—	—	—
State	4,708	775	882	638	633	407	301	180	10	3	29	18	18	25	11
Northeast	611	155	145	110	74	56	51	17	—	—	—	—	—	—	—
Connecticut	21	2	3	5	5	—	5	1	—	—	—	—	—	—	—
Maine	X	X	X	X	X	X	X	X	X	X	X	X	X	X	X
Massachusetts	27	7	11	6	3	—	—	—	—	—	—	X	X	X	X
New Hampshire	1	—	1	—	—	—	—	—	—	—	—	—	—	—	—
New Jersey	74	24	16	6	8	8	9	3	—	X	—	—	—	—	—
New York	329	80	73	78	36	27	25	10	—	—	—	X	X	X	X
Pennsylvania	155	41	41	15	21	19	12	3	—	—	—	—	—	—	—
Rhode Island	—	—	—	—	—	—	—	—	—	—	X	X	X	X	X
Vermont	4	1	—	—	1	2	—	—	—	—	—	—	—	—	—
Midwest	498	105	113	42	64	42	16	16	5	—	1	1	—	—	—
Illinois	102	34	27	13	5	8	1	2	—	—	—	—	—	—	—
Indiana	52	11	20	2	5	2	—	1	—	—	1	1	—	—	—
Iowa	18	1	7	3	4	1	—	2	X	X	X	X	X	X	X
Kansas	15	X	—	3	2	5	—	1	4	X	X	X	X	X	X
Michigan	—	—	—	—	—	—	—	—	X	X	X	X	X	X	X
Minnesota	X	X	X	X	X	X	X	X	X	X	X	X	X	X	X
Missouri	123	16	20	6	9	5	2	3	1	—	—	—	—	—	—
Nebraska	7	—	—	—	2	1	1	—	—	—	—	—	—	—	—
North Dakota	—	—	—	—	—	—	—	—	—	—	X	X	X	X	X
Ohio	180	43	39	15	36	20	12	7	—	—	—	—	—	—	—
South Dakota	1	X	—	—	1	—	—	—	—	—	—	—	—	—	—
Wisconsin	X	X	X	X	X	X	X	X	X	X	X	X	X	X	X
South	3,031	419	524	413	419	244	183	102	2	1	28	16	18	24	10
Alabama	163	19	41	29	21	14	6	4	1	—	1	—	1	1	—
Arkansas	143	20	33	20	18	11	7	9	—	—	—	—	—	—	—
Delaware	25	2	6	2	2	—	—	—	—	—	—	—	—	—	—
District of Columbia	40	15	5	3	13	3	1	—	—	X	X	X	X	X	X
Florida	227	15	29	38	27	22	27	12	—	1	9	3	3	1	2
Georgia	400	64	73	58	72	51	34	14	—	—	3	3	1	5	1
Kentucky	105	18	34	19	15	8	8	1	—	—	—	—	—	—	—
Louisiana	160	39	19	24	23	14	13	1	—	—	6	1	—	8	3
Maryland	71	6	10	26	19	2	4	1	—	—	—	—	—	—	—
Mississippi	160	26	22	34	26	15	21	10	—	—	1	—	—	2	—
North Carolina	293	51	80	50	62	14	5	1	—	—	2	—	1	—	—
Oklahoma	129	25	9	6	7	4	3	5	1	—	—	—	—	—	—
South Carolina	190	37	30	32	29	16	10	8	—	—	—	1	1	—	—
Tennessee	94	16	31	19	18	1	7	1	—	—	—	—	—	—	—
Texas	610	48	72	38	36	49	25	29	—	—	4	6	10	6	3
Virginia	181	8	20	13	22	15	8	6	—	—	2	2	1	1	1
West Virginia	40	10	10	2	9	5	4	—	X	X	X	X	X	X	X
West	568	96	100	73	76	65	51	45	3	2	—	1	—	1	1
Alaska*	X	X	X	X	X	X	X	X	X	X	X	X	X	X	X
Arizona	60	7	10	6	3	2	6	4	—	—	—	—	—	—	—
California	302	51	57	35	45	39	35	29	1	—	—	—	—	—	—
Colorado	48	16	9	6	7	1	2	5	1	—	—	—	—	—	—
Hawaii*	X	X	X	X	X	X	X	X	X	X	X	X	X	X	X
Idaho	4	—	—	—	—	2	1	—	—	—	—	—	—	—	—
Montana	8	1	4	1	—	—	—	—	—	—	—	—	—	—	—
Nevada	38	5	3	5	5	9	—	2	—	1	—	1	—	—	—
New Mexico	9	2	—	—	2	2	1	1	—	—	—	—	—	—	—
Oregon	21	1	1	6	6	4	—	1	X	—	—	—	—	—	—
Utah	19	—	2	3	1	2	4	1	—	1	—	—	—	1	1
Washington	51	10	13	9	7	4	2	2	—	—	—	—	—	—	—
Wyoming	8	3	1	2	—	—	—	—	1	—	—	—	—	—	—

the number of inmates executed since January 1, 1976. The spring 2005 LDF report showed that between 1976 and April 1, 2005, 946 men and ten women had been executed. (See Table 6.2.)

Victor L. Streib of the Claude W. Pettit College of Law of Ohio Northern University has been compiling information on female offenders and the death penalty in the United States since 1984. In *Death Penalty for Female Offenders: January 1, 1973, through June 30, 2005* (July 2005), Streib reported that between 1632 and June 30, 2005, 566 documented executions of women had been reported. Of this number, forty-nine women were put to death between 1900 and 2005. (See Table 6.3.)

TABLE 6.1

Number of prisoners executed, by region and jurisdiction, 1930–2003 [CONTINUED]

Region and jurisdiction	1989	1990	1991	1992	1993	1994	1995	1996	1997	1998	1999	2000	2001	2002	2003
United States	**16**	**23**	**14**	**31**	**38**	**31**	**56**	**45**	**74**	**68**	**98**	**85**	**66**	**71**	**65**
Federal	—	—	—	—	—	—	—	—	—	—	—	—	2	—	1
State	16	23	14	31	38	31	56	45	74	68	98	85	64	71	64
Northeast	—	—	—	—	—	—	2	—	—	—	1	—	—	—	—
Connecticut	—	—	—	—	—	—	—	—	—	—	—	—	—	—	—
Maine	X	X	X	X	X	X	X	X	X	X	X	X	X	X	X
Massachusetts	X	X	X	X	X	X	X	X	X	X	X	X	X	X	X
New Hampshire	—	—	—	—	—	—	—	—	—	—	—	—	—	—	—
New Jersey	—	—	—	—	—	—	—	—	—	—	—	—	—	—	—
New York	X	X	X	X	X	X	—	—	—	—	—	—	—	—	—
Pennsylvania	—	—	—	—	—	—	2	—	—	—	1	—	—	—	—
Rhode Island	X	X	X	X	X	X	X	X	X	X	X	X	X	X	X
Vermont	—	—	X	X	X	X	X	X	X	X	X	X	X	X	X
Midwest	1	5	1	1	4	3	11	9	10	5	12	5	10	9	7
Illinois	—	1	—	—	—	1	5	1	2	1	1	—	—	—	—
Indiana	—	—	—	—	—	1	—	1	1	1	1	—	2	—	2
Iowa	X	X	X	X	X	X	X	X	X	X	X	X	X	X	X
Kansas	X	X	X	X	X	X	—	—	—	—	—	—	—	—	—
Michigan	X	X	X	X	X	X	X	X	X	X	X	X	X	X	X
Minnesota	X	X	X	X	X	X	X	X	X	X	X	X	X	X	X
Missouri	1	4	1	1	4	X	6	6	6	3	9	5	7	6	2
Nebraska	—	—	—	—	—	1	—	1	1	—	—	—	—	—	—
North Dakota	X	X	X	X	X	X	X	X	X	X	X	X	X	X	X
Ohio	—	—	—	—	—	—	—	—	—	—	1	—	1	3	3
South Dakota	—	—	—	—	—	—	—	—	—	—	—	—	—	—	—
Wisconsin	X	X	X	X	X	X	X	X	X	X	X	X	X	X	X
South	13	17	13	26	30	26	41	29	60	55	74	76	50	61	57
Alabama	4	1	—	2	—	—	2	1	3	1	2	4	—	2	3
Arkansas	—	2	—	2	—	5	2	1	4	1	4	2	1	—	1
Delaware	—	—	—	1	2	1	1	3	—	—	2	1	2	—	—
District of Columbia	X	X	X	X	X	X	X	X	X	X	X	X	X	X	X
Florida	2	4	2	2	3	1	3	2	1	4	1	6	1	3	3
Georgia	1	—	1	—	2	1	2	2	—	1	—	—	4	4	3
Kentucky	—	—	—	—	—	—	—	—	1	—	1	—	—	—	—
Louisiana	—	1	1	—	1	—	1	1	1	—	1	1	—	1	—
Maryland	—	—	—	—	—	1	—	—	1	1	—	—	—	2	—
Mississippi	1	—	—	—	—	—	—	—	—	—	—	—	—	2	—
North Carolina	—	—	1	1	—	1	2	—	—	3	4	1	5	2	7
Oklahoma	—	1	—	2	—	—	3	2	1	4	6	11	18	7	14
South Carolina	—	1	1	—	—	—	1	6	2	7	4	1	—	3	—
Tennessee	—	—	—	—	—	—	—	—	—	—	—	1	—	—	—
Texas	4	4	5	12	17	14	19	3	37	20	35	40	17	33	24
Virginia	1	3	2	4	5	2	5	8	9	13	14	8	2	4	2
West Virginia	X	X	X	X	X	X	X	X	X	X	X	X	X	X	X
West	2	1	—	4	4	2	2	7	4	8	11	4	4	1	—
Alaska*	X	X	X	X	X	X	X	X	X	X	X	X	X	X	X
Arizona	—	—	—	1	2	—	1	2	2	4	7	3	—	—	—
California	—	—	—	1	1	—	—	2	—	1	2	1	1	1	—
Colorado	—	—	—	—	—	—	—	—	1	—	—	—	—	—	—
Hawaii*	X	X	X	X	X	X	X	X	X	X	X	X	X	X	X
Idaho	—	—	—	—	—	1	—	—	—	—	—	—	—	—	—
Montana	—	—	—	—	—	—	1	—	—	1	—	—	—	—	—
Nevada	2	1	—	—	—	—	—	1	—	1	1	—	1	—	—
New Mexico	—	—	—	—	—	—	—	—	—	—	—	—	1	—	—
Oregon	—	—	—	—	—	—	—	1	1	—	—	—	—	—	—
Utah	—	—	—	1	—	—	—	1	—	—	1	—	—	—	—
Washington	—	—	—	—	1	1	—	—	—	—	1	—	1	—	—
Wyoming	—	—	—	1	—	—	—	—	—	—	—	—	—	—	—

*As states, Alaska and Hawaii are included in the series beginning Jan. 1, 1960.

—represents zero

Note: In three states, Maine, Minnesota, and Wisconsin, there were no death penalty statutes in effect for the entire period covered by the table. Alaska and Hawaii have not had the death penalty since 1960, when they were first included as states. For other states, the death penalty may have been abolished or declared unconstitutional, and/or subsequently reinstated. In these cases, an X appears to indicate years when the death penalty was not in effect.

SOURCE: Kathleen Maguire and Ann L. Pastore, eds., "Table 6.82. Prisoners Executed under Civil Authority, by Region and Jurisdiction, 1930–2003," in *Sourcebook of Criminal Justice Statistics 2003*, U.S. Department of Justice, Bureau of Justice Statistics, 2003, http://www.albany.edu/sourcebook/pdf/t682.pdf (accessed June 1, 2005)

FIGURE 6.1

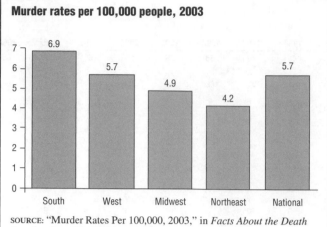

Murder rates per 100,000 people, 2003

SOURCE: "Murder Rates Per 100,000, 2003," in *Facts About the Death Penalty, June 30, 2005*, Death Penalty Information Center, June 2005, http://www.deathpenaltyinfo.org/FactSheet.pdf (accessed June 1, 2005)

FIGURE 6.2

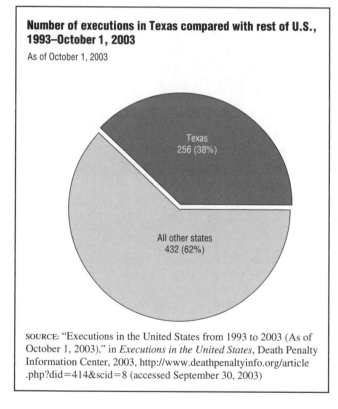

Number of executions in Texas compared with rest of U.S., 1993–October 1, 2003

As of October 1, 2003

Texas 256 (38%)

All other states 432 (62%)

SOURCE: "Executions in the United States from 1993 to 2003 (As of October 1, 2003)," in *Executions in the United States*, Death Penalty Information Center, 2003, http://www.deathpenaltyinfo.org/article .php?did=414&scid=8 (accessed September 30, 2003)

TABLE 6.2

Total number of executions, by demographic characteristics, 1976–April 1, 2005

1977	1978	1979	1980	1981	1982	1983	1984	1985	1986
1	0	2	0	1	2	5	21	18	18

1987	1988	1989	1990	1991	1992	1993	1994	1995	1996
25	11	16	23	14	31	38	31	56	45

1997	1998	1999	2000	2001	2002	2003	2004	2005	
74	68	98	85	66	71	65	59	12	

Gender of defendants executed

Total number 956

Female	10 (1.05%)
Male	946 (98.95%)

Race of defendants executed

White	553 (57.85%)
Black	322 (33.68%)
Latino/a	60 (6.28%)
Native American	14 (1.46%)
Asian	7 (.73%)

Gender of victims

Total number 1428

Female	706 (49.44%)
Male	722 (50.56%)

Race of victims

White	1,152 (80.67%)
Black	192 (13.45%)
Latino/a	56 (3.92%)
Native American	5 (.35%)
Asian	23 (1.61%)

SOURCE: "Execution Update (As of April 1, 2005)," in *Death Row USA, Spring 2005*, NAACP Legal Defense and Educational Fund, Inc., 2005, http://www.naacpldf.org/content/pdf/pubs/drusa/DRUSA_Spring_2005.pdf (accessed June 1, 2005)

In 1984 Margie Velma Barfield was executed in North Carolina for poisoning her boyfriend. Karla Faye Tucker of Texas was convicted of beating two people to death with a pickax. In February 1998 Tucker became the first woman to be executed in Texas since the Civil War. (In 1863 Chipita Rodriguez, the last woman to be executed in Texas, was put to death by hanging. She had been convicted of the axe murder of a horse trader.) In Florida Judias Buenoano was convicted of poisoning her husband with arsenic. She was also convicted of drowning her paraplegic son and of trying to kill her boyfriend. In March 1998 Buenoano became the first woman to be executed in Florida since 1848, when a freed slave named Celia was hanged for killing her former owner. (See Table 6.4.)

In February 2000 Betty Lou Beets was executed in Texas for killing her fifth husband. (See Table 6.4.) Christina Marie Riggs, convicted of killing her two children, was executed in Arkansas in May 2000. The last woman put to death in Arkansas prior to Riggs—Lavinia Burnett—was hanged in 1845 for being an accessory to murder.

In 2001 Oklahoma executed three female inmates. In January 2001 Wanda Jean Allen became the first woman to be executed in Oklahoma since 1903. She was also the first black woman to be put to death in the United States since 1954. Allen was convicted of murdering her gay lover in 1988. In May 2001 Marilyn Kay Plantz was executed for the 1988 murder of her husband. Plantz had hired two men to kill her husband. One of the men, William Bryson, was executed in June 2000 for the murder, and the other, Clinton McKimble, received a life

TABLE 6.3

Execution of female offenders by state, January 1, 1900–June 30, 2005

State	Date of execution	Name	Race	Age at crime
Alabama	01-24-1930	Gilmore, Selena	Black	adult
	09-04-1953	Dennison, Earle	White	54
	10-11-1957	Martin, Rhonda Belle	White	48
	05-10-2002	Block, Linda Lyon	White	45
Arizona	02-21-1930	Dugan, Eva	White	49
Arkansas	05-02-2000	Riggs, Christina Marie	White	26
California	11-21-1941	Spinelli, Ethel Leta Juanita	White	52
	04-11-1947	Peete, Louise	White	58
	06-03-1955	Graham, Barbara	White	32
	08-08-1962	Duncan, Elizabeth Ann	White	58
Delaware	06-07-1935	Carey, May H.	White	52
Florida	03-30-1998	Buenoano, Judias	White	28
	10-09-2002	Wuornos, Aileen	White	33
Federal				
(New York)	06-19-1953	Rosenberg, Ethel*	White	32
(Missouri)	12-18-1953	Heady, Bonnie Brown	White	41
Georgia	03-05-1945	Baker, Lena	Black	44
Illinois	01-28-1938	Porter, Marie	White	38
Louisiana	02-01-1929	LeBoeuf, Ada	White	38
	02-08-1935	Moore, Julia (aka Powers; aka Williams)	?	adult
	11-28-1942	Henri, Toni Jo (aka Annie)	White	26
Mississippi	01-13-1922	Perdue, Pattie	Black	adult
	10-13-1922	Knight, Ann	Black	adult
	04-29-1937	Holmes, Mary	Black	32
	05-19-1944	Johnson, Mildred Louise (aka James)	Black	34
New York	03-29-1909	Farmer, Mary	White	29
	01-12-1928	Snyder, Ruth Brown	White	33
	08-09-1934	Antonio, Anna	White	27
	06-27-1935	Coo, Eva	White	40
	07-16-1936	Creighton, Mary Francis	White	36
	11-16-1944	Fowler, Helen	Black	37
	03-08-1951	Beck, Martha	White	29
North Carolina	01-01-1943	Phillips, Rosana Lightner	Black	25
	12-29-1944	Williams, Bessie May	Black	19
	11-02-1984	Barfield, Velma	White	52
Ohio	12-07-1938	Hahn, Anna Marie	White	32
	01-15-1954	Dean, Dovie Smarr	White	55
	06-12-1954	Butler, Betty	Black	25
Oklahoma	07-17-1903	Wright, Dora	Black	adult
	01-11-2001	Allen, Wanda Jean	Black	29
	05-01-2001	Plantz, Marilyn Kay	White	27
	12-04-2001	Smith, Lois Nadeen	White	41
Pennsylvania	02-23-1931	Schroeder, Irene	White	22
	10-14-1946	Sykes, Corrine	Black	22
South Carolina	01-15-1943	Logue, Sue Stidham	White	43
	01-17-1947	Stinette, Rose Marie	Black	49
Texas	02-03-1998	Tucker, Karla Faye	White	38
	02-24-2000	Beets, Betty Lou	White	46
Vermont	12-08-1905	Rogers, Mary Mabel	White	21
Virginia	08-16-1912	Christian, Virginia	Black	17

*Ethel Rosenberg's capital crime was espionage, the only one of these 20th and 21st century executions of female offenders which was imposed for a crime other than murder.

SOURCE: Victor L. Streib, "Table 1. Executions of Female Offenders by State, January 1, 1900, Through June 30, 2005," in *Death Penalty for Female Offenders, January 1, 1973, through June 30, 2005*, Ohio Northern University, The Claude W. Pettit College of Law, July 2005, http://www.law.onu.edu/faculty/streib/documents/FemDeathJune2005_000.pdf (accessed July 15, 2005)

sentence in exchange for his testimony against Plantz and Bryson. Lois Nadean Smith, executed in December 2001, was convicted of killing her son's girlfriend in 1982. (See Table 6.4.)

Lynda Lyon Block and her husband, George Sibley, Jr., murdered a police officer in 1993. In May 2002 Alabama executed Block, making her the first woman to be executed in the state in forty-five years. As of June 30, 2005, Sibley remained on death row. Aileen Carol Wuornos, convicted of killing six men in Florida, was put to death by lethal injection in October 2002. (See Table 6.4.)

RACE AND ETHNICITY

According to the Bureau of Justice Statistics in the *Sourcebook of Criminal Justice Statistics, 2003*, 2,246 (52%) of the 4,359 prisoners executed between 1930

TABLE 6.4

Execution of female offenders, January 1, 1973–June 30, 2005

Date of execution	Date of crime	State	Name	Race	Age at crime	Age at execution
11-02-1984	02-01-1978	N. Carolina	Barfield, Velma	White	52	58
02-03-1998	06-13-1983	Texas	Tucker, Karla Faye	White	23	38
03-30-1998	09-16-1971	Florida	Buenoano, Judias	White	28	54
02-24-2000	08-06-1983	Texas	Beets, Betty Lou	White	46	62
05-02-2000	11-04-1997	Arkansas	Riggs, Christina	White	26	29
01-11-2001	12-01-1988	Oklahoma	Allen, Wanda Jean	Black	29	41
05-01-2001	08-26-1988	Oklahoma	Plantz, Marilyn Kay	White	27	40
12-04-2001	07-04-1982	Oklahoma	Smith, Lois Nadean	White	41	61
05-10-2002	10-04-1993	Alabama	Block, Linda Lyon	White	45	54
10-09-2002	1989–1990	Florida	Wuornos, Aileen	White	33	46

• Only ten (1.0%) of the 972 total executions since 1973 have been of female offenders. This execution pace has changed recently, with only one (0.2%) of the 434 executions from 1973 to 1997 being a female offender. Since 1998, nine (1.7%) of the 538 total executions have been of female offenders.

• This recent (1998–mid-2005) execution pace matches almost exactly that beginning in 1900, so it appears that the 1973–1997 lull in executions of female offenders was atypical and that we have now returned to our normal rate.

SOURCE: Victor L. Streib, "Table 2. Executions of Female Offenders by States During Current Era, January 1, 1973, through June 30, 2005," in *Death Penalty for Female Offenders, January 1, 1973, through June 30, 2005*, Ohio Northern University, The Claude W. Pettit College of Law, July 2005, http://www.law.onu.edu/faculty/streib/documents/FemDeathJune2005_000.pdf (accessed July 15,2005)

and 1998 were black, 2,064 (47%) were white, and forty-nine (1%) were categorized as of "other" race. (See Table 6.5.) Data compiled by the NAACP Legal Defense and Educational Fund in *Death Row USA, Spring 2005* show that of the 956 prisoners executed from 1976 to April 1, 2005, 57.9% were white (553), 33.7% were black (322), 6.3% were Hispanic (who may be of any race; sixty), 1.5% were Native American (fourteen), and less than 1% were Asian (seven). (See Table 6.2.)

LDF maintains statistics not only on the race of the executed prisoners, but also on their victims. These types of statistics have been used in court cases to decide the constitutionality of the death penalty. The courts have to consider whether whites who murdered blacks got lighter sentences than blacks who murdered whites and whether those sentences violated the equal protection rights of the Constitution.

From 1976 through April 1, 2005, 54.6% (522) of those executed were whites who had murdered other whites, while 1.3% (twelve) were whites who had murdered blacks. Twenty-one percent (199) of those executed were blacks who had murdered whites, and 10.4% (ninety-nine) were blacks who had murdered other blacks. (See Table 6.2.)

CRIMES WARRANTING THE DEATH PENALTY

According to the Bureau of Justice Statistics in the *Sourcebook of Criminal Justice Statistics, 2003*, the vast majority of executions from 1930 through 1998 were for murder (85.7%), followed by rape (10.4%). The remaining 1% of executions included twenty-five cases for armed robbery, twenty for kidnapping, eleven for burglary, six for sabotage, six for aggravated assault, and two for espionage. Since 1965 all those executed have been convicted on murder charges. (See Table 6.5.)

The last executions for rape occurred in 1964. Six executions for rape occurred in three states that year—Arkansas (one), Missouri (two), and Texas (three). In 1977 in *Coker v. Georgia* (433 U.S. 584), the Supreme Court ruled that rape did not warrant the death penalty. The case concerned the rape of an adult woman. The Court did not address the rape of a child. In December 1996, however, the Louisiana Supreme Court ruled that death is a just and constitutional punishment for the rape of a child under twelve years of age. As of July 1, 2005, no one had been executed under Louisiana's statute.

METHOD OF EXECUTION

According to the Bureau of Justice Statistics in *Capital Punishment, 2003*, among the 885 prisoners executed between 1977 and 2003, a little over 81% (718) received lethal injection, followed by electrocution (17%, or 151). Eleven executions were carried out by lethal gas, three by hanging, and two by firing squad. Texas, the state with the largest number of prisoners executed, used lethal injection in all 313 cases. Virginia executed sixty-two inmates by lethal injection and twenty-seven inmates by electrocution. Florida put to death forty-four prisoners by electrocution and thirteen prisoners by lethal injection. (See Table 6.6.)

TABLE 6.5

Prisoners executed under civil authority, by race and offense, 1930–1998

	Total				White				Black				Other			
	Total	Murder	Rape	Other offenses[a]	Total	Murder	Rape	Other offenses	Total	Murder	Rape	Other offenses	Total	Murder	Rape	Other offenses
1930–98	**4,359**	**3,734**	**455**	**70**	**2,064**	**1,977**	**48**	**39**	**2,246**	**1,810**	**405**	**31**	**49**	**47**	**2**	**—**
1998	68	68	—	—	48	48	—	—	18	18	—	—	2	2	—	—
1997	74	74	—	—	45	45	—	—	27	27	—	—	2	2	—	—
1996	45	45	—	—	31	31	—	—	14	14	—	—	—	—	—	—
1995	56	56	—	—	33	33	—	—	22	22	—	—	1	1	—	—
1994	31	31	—	—	20	20	—	—	11	11	—	—	—	—	—	—
1993	38	38	—	—	23	23	—	—	14	14	—	—	1	1	—	—
1992	31	31	—	—	19	19	—	—	11	11	—	—	1	1	—	—
1991	14	14	—	—	7	7	—	—	7	7	—	—	—	—	—	—
1990	23	23	—	—	16	16	—	—	7	7	—	—	—	—	—	—
1989	16	16	—	—	8	8	—	—	8	8	—	—	—	—	—	—
1988	11	11	—	—	6	6	—	—	5	5	—	—	—	—	—	—
1987	25	25	—	—	13	13	—	—	12	12	—	—	—	—	—	—
1986	18	18	—	—	11	11	—	—	7	7	—	—	—	—	—	—
1985	18	18	—	—	11	11	—	—	7	7	—	—	—	—	—	—
1984	21	21	—	—	13	13	—	—	8	8	—	—	—	—	—	—
1983	5	5	—	—	4	4	—	—	1	1	—	—	—	—	—	—
1982	2	2	—	—	1	1	—	—	1	1	—	—	—	—	—	—
1981	1	1	—	—	1	1	—	—	—	—	—	—	—	—	—	—
1980	—	—	—	—	—	—	—	—	—	—	—	—	—	—	—	—
1979	2	2	—	—	2	2	—	—	—	—	—	—	—	—	—	—
1978	—	—	—	—	—	—	—	—	—	—	—	—	—	—	—	—
1977[b]	1	1	—	—	1	1	—	—	—	—	—	—	—	—	—	—
1967	2	2	—	—	1	1	—	—	1	1	—	—	—	—	—	—
1966	1	1	—	—	1	1	—	—	—	—	—	—	—	—	—	—
1965	7	7	—	—	6	6	—	—	1	1	—	—	—	—	—	—
1964	15	9	6	—	8	5	3	—	7	4	3	—	—	—	—	—
1963	21	18	2	1	13	12	—	1	8	6	2	—	—	—	—	—
1962	47	41	4	2	28	26	2	—	19	15	2	2	—	—	—	—
1961	42	33	8	1	20	18	1	1	22	15	7	—	—	—	—	—
1960	56	44	8	4	21	18	—	3	35	26	8	1	—	—	—	—
1959	49	41	8	—	16	15	1	—	33	26	7	—	—	—	—	—
1958	49	41	7	1	20	20	—	—	28	20	7	1	1	1	—	—
1957	65	54	10	1	34	32	2	—	31	22	8	1	—	—	—	—
1956	65	52	12	1	21	20	—	1	43	31	12	—	1	1	—	—
1955	76	65	7	4	44	41	1	2	32	24	6	2	—	—	—	—
1954	81	71	9	1	38	37	1	—	42	33	8	1	1	1	—	—
1953	62	51	7	4	30	25	1	4	31	25	6	—	1	1	—	—
1952	83	71	12	—	36	35	1	—	47	36	11	—	—	—	—	—
1951	105	87	17	1	57	55	2	—	47	31	15	1	1	1	—	—
1950	82	68	13	1	40	36	4	—	42	32	9	1	—	—	—	—
1949	119	107	10	2	50	49	—	1	67	56	10	1	2	2	—	—
1948	119	95	22	2	35	32	1	2	82	61	21	—	2	2	—	—
1947	153	129	23	1	42	40	2	—	111	89	21	1	—	—	—	—
1946	131	107	22	2	46	45	—	1	84	61	22	1	1	1	—	—
1945	117	90	26	1	41	37	4	—	75	52	22	1	1	1	—	—
1944	120	96	24	—	47	45	2	—	70	48	22	—	3	3	—	—
1943	131	118	13	—	54	54	—	—	74	63	11	—	3	1	2	—
1942	147	115	25	7	67	57	4	6	80	58	21	1	—	—	—	—
1941	123	102	20	1	59	55	4	—	63	46	16	1	1	1	—	—
1940	124	105	15	4	49	44	2	3	75	61	13	1	—	—	—	—
1939	160	145	12	3	80	79	—	1	77	63	12	2	3	3	—	—
1938	190	154	25	11	96	89	1	6	92	63	24	5	2	2	—	—
1937	147	133	13	1	69	67	2	—	74	62	11	1	4	4	—	—
1936	195	181	10	4	92	86	2	4	101	93	8	—	2	2	—	—
1935	199	184	13	2	119	115	2	2	77	66	11	—	3	3	—	—
1934	168	154	14	—	65	64	1	—	102	89	13	—	1	1	—	—
1933	160	151	7	2	77	75	1	1	81	74	6	1	2	2	—	—
1932	140	128	10	2	62	62	—	—	75	63	10	2	3	3	—	—
1931	153	137	15	1	77	76	1	—	72	57	14	1	4	4	—	—
1930	155	147	6	2	90	90	—	—	65	57	6	2	—	—	—	—

Note: "—" represents zero.
[a]Includes 25 executed for armed robbery, 20 for kidnaping, 11 for burglary, 6 for sabotage, 6 for aggravated assault, and 2 for espionage.
[b]There were no executions from 1968 through 1976.

SOURCE: Kathleen Maguire and Ann L. Pastore, eds., "Table 6.83. Prisoners Executed under Civil Authority, by Race and Offense, United States, 1930–1998" in *Sourcebook of Criminal Justice Statistics 2003*, U.S. Department of Justice, Bureau of Justice Statistics, 2003, http://www.albany.edu/sourcebook/pdf/t683.pdf (accessed June 1, 2005)

TABLE 6.6

Executions, by state and method, 1977–2003

State	Number executed	Lethal injection	Electrocution	Lethal gas	Hanging	Firing squad
Total	885	718	151	11	3	2
Federal system	3	3	0	0	0	0
Alabama	28	4	24	0	0	0
Arizona	22	20	0	2	0	0
Arkansas	25	24	1	0	0	0
California	10	8	0	2	0	0
Colorado	1	1	0	0	0	0
Delaware	13	12	0	0	1	0
Florida	57	13	44	0	0	0
Georgia	34	11	23	0	0	0
Idaho	1	1	0	0	0	0
Illinois	12	12	0	0	0	0
Indiana	11	8	3	0	0	0
Kentucky	2	1	1	0	0	0
Louisiana	27	7	20	0	0	0
Maryland	3	3	0	0	0	0
Mississippi	6	2	0	4	0	0
Missouri	61	61	0	0	0	0
Montana	2	2	0	0	0	0
Nebraska	3	0	3	0	0	0
Nevada	9	8	0	1	0	0
New Mexico	1	1	0	0	0	0
North Carolina	30	28	0	2	0	0
Ohio	8	8	0	0	0	0
Oklahoma	69	69	0	0	0	0
Oregon	2	2	0	0	0	0
Pennsylvania	3	3	0	0	0	0
South Carolina	28	23	5	0	0	0
Tennessee	1	1	0	0	0	0
Texas	313	313	0	0	0	0
Utah	6	4	0	0	0	2
Virginia	89	62	27	0	0	0
Washington	4	2	0	0	2	0
Wyoming	1	1	0	0	0	0

SOURCE: Thomas P. Bonczar and Tracy L. Snell, "Appendix Table 5. Executions, by Jurisdiction and Method, 1977–2003," in *Capital Punishment, 2003*, U.S. Department of Justice, Bureau of Justice Statistics, November 2004, http://www.ojp.usdoj.gov/bjs/pub/pdf/cp03.pdf (accessed June 1, 2005)

CHAPTER 7
UNDER SENTENCE OF DEATH

The Bureau of Justice Statistics reported in *Capital Punishment, 2003* that, at year-end 2003, a total of 3,374 prisoners were held under sentence of death in federal and state prisons. That was 188 fewer inmates than on December 31, 2002 (3,562). (See Table 7.1.) Between 1976, when the U.S. Supreme Court reinstated the death penalty, and the year 2000, the number of prisoners on death row increased each year. The year 2001 was the first time since 1976 that the total number of death row inmates declined. (See Figure 7.1.)

During the calendar year 2003, twenty-five state prisons received 142 persons under sentence of death. The federal Bureau of Prisons received two inmates. According to the BJS, death row admissions have declined fairly steadily between 1998 and 2003. In 1998 state and federal prisons received 307 inmates. The number entering death row dropped to 282 in 1999, 234 in 2000, 165 in 2001, and then rose slightly to 168 in 2002. The 2003 admission of 144 inmates was the lowest number since 1973, when forty-four people entered death row. (See Table 7.2.)

A number of prisoners are removed from death row for reasons other than execution—resentencing, retrial, commutation (replacement of the death sentence with a lesser sentence), or death while awaiting execution (natural death, murder, or suicide). As Table 7.3 shows, 7,403 persons received the death sentence between 1973 and 2003. Of these, 885 were executed, 279 died while awaiting execution, 2,498 had their sentences or convictions overturned, and 335 had their sentences commuted. As of December 31, 2003, about half (3,374 inmates) were still on death row awaiting execution.

In 2003, 143 of the 144 prisoners admitted to death row had been convicted of murder and one had been convicted of raping a child (Louisiana). A total of 257 prisoners from twenty-six states and the federal Bureau of Prisons had their death sentences overturned or removed. By far the largest number of sentences (61%) was vacated January 2003 when outgoing Illinois Governor George Ryan cleared his state's death row by commuting the death sentences of 167 convicts, mostly to life in prison. Pennsylvania came in a distant second with sixteen sentences overturned and removed. In previous years far fewer death sentences in the United States were vacated—eighty-three in 2002, ninety in 2001, and fifty-eight in 2000. Florida typically reported the highest number of vacated sentences during these years with fourteen in 2002, eleven in 2001, and nine in 2000.

The NAACP Legal Defense and Educational Fund (LDF) is a major source of death row statistics. While the Bureau of Justice Statistics' annual report counts only those on death row awaiting execution, the LDF statistics include persons who have been sentenced to death and are awaiting transfer to prison. As of April 1, 2005, the LDF report, *Death Row USA, Spring 2005* showed 3,459 prisoners under sentence of death in the United States. Seven of these criminals were sentenced to death in more than one state, so the actual number of prisoners under sentence of death was 3,452. (See Table 7.4.)

GEOGRAPHIC DISTRIBUTION

The LDF reported that, as of April 1, 2005, more than half (54.9%) of the state prisoners awaiting execution were in the South, which is made up of fifteen states. An additional 27.3% were in the eleven western states, and 9.2% were in the seven Midwestern states. The northeastern states of Connecticut, New Jersey, New York, and Pennsylvania accounted for 7.4%. Over 42% of the condemned were awaiting execution in three states—California (644), Texas (441), and Florida (384). Of the thirty-eight jurisdictions with statutes authorizing the death penalty, only New Hampshire had no one under a capital sentence, while Colorado,

TABLE 7.1

Persons under sentence of death, by region, state, and race, 2002–2003

Region and state	Prisoners under sentence of death, 12/31/02			Received under sentence of death			Removed from death row (excluding executions)[a]			Executed			Prisoners under sentence of death, 12/31/03		
	Total[b]	White[c]	Black[c]	Total[b]	White	Black	Total[b]	White	Black	Total[b]	White	Black	Total[b]	White	Black
U.S. total	3,562	1,939	1,551	144	92	44	267	109	157	65	44	20	3,374	1,878	1,418
Federal[d]	23	6	17	2	0	1	1	0	1	1	0	1	23	6	16
State	3,539	1,933	1,534	142	92	43	266	109	156	64	44	19	3,351	1,872	1,402
Northeast	266	97	158	7	4	3	17	7	10	0	0	0	256	94	151
Connecticut	7	4	3	0	0	0	0	0	0	0	0	0	7	4	3
New Hampshire	0	0	0	0	0	0	0	0	0	0	0	0	0	0	0
New Jersey	14	8	6	0	0	0	0	0	0	0	0	0	14	8	6
New York	5	4	1	1	0	1	1	1	0	0	0	0	5	3	2
Pennsylvania	240	81	148	6	4	2	16	6	10	0	0	0	230	79	140
Midwest	486	230	253	14	11	3	178	65	113	7	6	1	315	170	142
Illinois	159	57	102	2	2	0	159	57	102	0	0	0	2	2	0
Indiana	37	26	11	1	1	0	1	0	1	2	2	0	35	25	10
Kansas	5	3	2	1	1	0	0	0	0	0	0	0	6	4	2
Missouri	66	34	32	3	1	2	15	6	9	2	2	0	52	27	25
Nebraska	7	6	1	0	0	0	0	0	0	0	0	0	7	6	1
Ohio	207	99	105	7	6	1	2	1	1	3	2	1	209	102	104
South Dakota	5	5	0	0	0	0	1	1	0	0	0	0	4	4	0
South	1,892	1,020	848	85	58	24	54	25	29	57	38	18	1,866	1,015	825
Alabama	191	100	90	6	5	1	2	1	1	3	3	0	192	101	90
Arkansas	42	17	25	0	0	0	1	0	1	1	0	1	40	17	23
Delaware	14	10	4	2	2	0	0	0	0	0	0	0	16	12	4
Florida[e]	366	234	132	11	11	0	10	5	5	3	2	1	364	238	126
Georgia	115	58	56	1	1	0	2	0	2	3	3	0	111	56	54
Kentucky	36	28	8	0	0	0	1	0	1	0	0	0	35	28	7
Louisiana	90	27	62	1	0	1	4	0	4	0	0	0	87	27	59
Maryland	15	5	10	0	0	0	4	1	3	0	0	0	11	4	7
Mississippi	65	29	35	3	2	1	2	0	2	0	0	0	66	31	34
North Carolina	206	80	118	6	2	4	10	4	6	7	3	3	195	75	113
Oklahoma	112	64	42	9	4	3	5	4	1	14	8	6	102	56	38
South Carolina[e]	72	38	34	5	3	2	6	3	3	0	0	0	71	38	33
Tennessee	96	57	38	6	4	1	6	6	0	0	0	0	96	55	39
Texas	449	260	184	29	20	9	1	1	0	24	17	7	453	262	186
Virginia	23	13	10	6	4	2	0	0	0	2	2	0	27	15	12
West	895	586	275	36	19	13	17	12	4	0	0	0	914	593	284
Arizona	117	100	12	9	5	2	3	2	1	0	0	0	123	103	13
California	613	369	220	19	6	11	3	2	1	0	0	0	629	373	230
Colorado	5	2	2	1	1	0	3	2	0	0	0	0	3	1	2
Idaho	20	20	0	1	1	0	2	2	0	0	0	0	19	19	0
Montana	6	5	0	0	0	0	1	1	0	0	0	0	5	4	0
Nevada	82	48	33	4	4	0	2	0	2	0	0	0	84	52	31
New Mexico	2	2	0	0	0	0	0	0	0	0	0	0	2	2	0
Oregon	27	25	1	2	2	0	1	1	0	0	0	0	28	26	1
Utah	11	8	2	0	0	0	1	1	0	0	0	0	10	7	2
Washington	10	5	5	0	0	0	0	0	0	0	0	0	10	5	5
Wyoming	2	2	0	0	0	0	1	1	0	0	0	0	1	1	0

Note: Some figures shown for yearend 2002 are revised. The revised figures include 15 inmates who were either reported late to the National Prisoner Statistics program or were not in custody of state correctional authorities on 12/31/02 (3 each in Louisiana and Pennsylvania; 2 each in Arkansas and Ohio; and 1 each in Florida, Georgia, Indiana, Oregon, and Tennessee) and exclude 13 inmates who were relieved of a death sentence before 12/31/02 (4 in Pennsylvania; 3 in Arizona; and 1 each in Florida, Mississippi, Texas, California, Nevada, and the federal system). Data for 12/31/02 also include 2 inmates in Georgia and 1 inmate in Louisiana who were erroneously reported as being removed from under sentence of death.
[a]Includes 6 deaths from natural causes (2 each in Tennessee and California; and 1 each in Ohio and Utah); and 4 deaths from suicide (1 each in South Dakota, Georgia, Tennessee, and Montana).
[b]Totals include persons of races other than white and black.
[c]White and black inmates include Hispanics.
[d]Excludes persons held under Armed Forces jurisdiction with a military death sentence for murder.
[e]Race has been changed from black to white for 1 inmate.

SOURCE: Thomas P. Bonczar and Tracy L. Snell, "Table 4. Persons under Sentence of Death, by Region, State, and Race, 2002 and 2003," in *Capital Punishment, 2003*, U.S. Department of Justice, Bureau of Justice Statistics, November 2004, http://www.ojp.usdoj.gov/bjs/pub/pdf/cp03.pdf (accessed June 1, 2005)

Montana, New Mexico, New York, South Dakota, and Wyoming had four or fewer. (See Table 7.4.)

RACE

As of April 1, 2005, *Death Row USA, Spring 2005* reported that 46% of all death row inmates were white,

and 42% were African-American. Hispanic prisoners (who may be of any race) accounted for 10% of those under a death sentence. Native Americans and Asian Americans represented 1% each of death row inmates. Nearly nine in ten (89.1%) of the Hispanics on death row were imprisoned in five states—California, Texas, Florida, Arizona, and Pennsylvania. (See Table 7.4.)

FIGURE 7.1

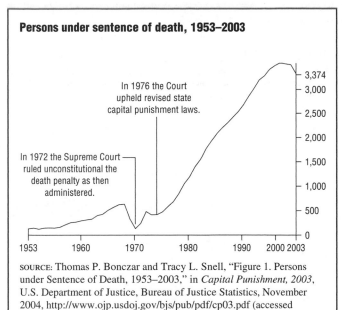

Persons under sentence of death, 1953–2003

In 1976 the Court upheld revised state capital punishment laws.

In 1972 the Supreme Court ruled unconstitutional the death penalty as then administered.

SOURCE: Thomas P. Bonczar and Tracy L. Snell, "Figure 1. Persons under Sentence of Death, 1953–2003," in *Capital Punishment, 2003*, U.S. Department of Justice, Bureau of Justice Statistics, November 2004, http://www.ojp.usdoj.gov/bjs/pub/pdf/cp03.pdf (accessed June 1, 2005)

TABLE 7.2

Inmates received under sentence of death, 1994–2003

1994	327
1995	327
1996	323
1997	281
1998	307
1999	282
2000	234
2001	165
2002	168
2003	144

SOURCE: Thomas P. Bonczar and Tracy L. Snell, "Inmates Received under Sentence of Death," in *Capital Punishment, 2003*, U.S. Department of Justice, Bureau of Justice Statistics, November 2004, http://www.ojp.usdoj .gov/bjs/pub/pdf/cp03.pdf (accessed June 1, 2005)

GENDER

Death Row USA, Spring 2005 reported that as of April 1, 2005, 98.5% (3,399) of all prisoners under sentence of death were males. Some fifty-three females were awaiting execution. Of the male inmates, seventy-two were juveniles.

In *Death Penalty for Female Offenders: January 1, 1973, through June 30, 2005* (July 1, 2005), Victor L. Streib of the Claude W. Pettit College of Law of Ohio Northern University reported on female offenders on death row. Between 1973 and June 30, 2005, 152 females had been sentenced to death in the United States. (See Table 7.5.) Nearly two-thirds (64.5%; ninety-eight inmates) were white, and more than one-fourth (26.3%; forty inmates) were African-American. Ten women were

Hispanic, and four were Native American. Of the twenty-five states with women on death row, California, North Carolina, Florida, Texas, and Ohio accounted for almost half (48.7%; 74 inmates). (See Table 7.6.)

CHARACTERISTICS OF PRISONERS

The Bureau of Justice Statistics collects additional information on death row inmates. In 2003 the median age of those under sentence of death was forty years (this means that half of the inmates were younger than forty and half were older than that age). Two-thirds (64%) were ages twenty-five to forty-four, and one-third (33.9%) were between thirty and thirty-nine years old. One inmate was under age twenty, and 110 inmates were sixty and older. The youngest inmate was nineteen years old and was sentenced to death in August 2002. The oldest was eighty-eight, having been sentenced in June 1983 at the age of sixty-eight. Almost half (49.1%) of all inmates under sentence of death were ages twenty to twenty-nine when they were arrested for their capital offense. (See Table 7.7.)

Among those for whom information about education was available as of December 31, 2003, more than half (52.3%) had not graduated from high school, and only one in eleven had any college education. The median level of education was the eleventh grade. Most had never married (54%), and about one-fourth (23.5%) were separated, divorced, or widowed. (See Table 7.8.)

CRIMINAL HISTORY OF DEATH ROW INMATES

The Bureau of Justice Statistics reported in *Capital Punishment, 2003* that, as of December 31, 2003, among prisoners on death row, nearly two-thirds (64.5%) had prior felony convictions. Almost one in twelve (8.2%) had been previously convicted of murder or manslaughter. About two of five (40.3%) had an active criminal justice record at the time of the murder for which they were condemned. Almost half of those with an active criminal record were out on parole when they committed their crime, and one-fourth were on probation. The others had charges pending, were in prison, had escaped from prison, or had some other criminal justice status. (See Table 7.9.)

Criminal history patterns varied slightly by race and Hispanic origin. African-Americans (69.8%) had somewhat more prior felony convictions than whites (61.8%) and Hispanics (58.7%). African-Americans (8.5%) and whites (8.3%) had a higher proportion of prior homicide convictions than Hispanics (6.9%). Hispanics (21.6%) and African-Americans (17.7%) were more likely than whites (14.4%) to be on parole when arrested for their capital crime. (See Table 7.9.)

TABLE 7.3

Number sentenced to death and number of removals, by jurisdiction and reason for removal, 1973–2003

Jurisdiction	Total sentenced to death, 1973–2003	Number of removals, 1973–2003					Under sentence of death, 12/31/03
		Executed	Died	Sentence or conviction overturned	Sentence commuted	Other removals	
U.S. total	7,403	885	279	2,498	335	34	3,374
Federal	34	3	0	7	1	0	23
Alabama	348	28	17	109	2	0	192
Arizona	248	22	12	84	6	1	123
Arkansas	101	25	2	32	2	0	40
California	814	10	39	121	15	0	629
Colorado	20	1	2	13	1	0	3
Connecticut	8	0	0	1	0	0	7
Delaware	50	13	0	21	0	0	16
Florida	883	57	35	407	18	2	364
Georgia	301	34	10	138	7	1	111
Idaho	41	1	1	17	3	0	19
Illinois	296	12	14	98	158	12	2
Indiana	98	11	2	46	2	2	35
Kansas	7	0	0	1	0	0	6
Kentucky	75	2	3	34	1	0	35
Louisiana	218	27	4	92	7	1	87
Maryland	52	3	2	32	4	0	11
Massachusetts	4	0	0	2	2	0	0
Mississippi	176	6	3	98	0	3	66
Missouri	170	61	9	46	2	0	52
Montana	15	2	1	6	1	0	5
Nebraska	27	3	3	12	2	0	7
Nevada	139	9	11	31	4	0	84
New Jersey	51	0	3	26	0	8	14
New Mexico	28	1	1	19	5	0	2
New York	10	0	0	5	0	0	5
North Carolina	508	30	13	262	8	0	195
Ohio	376	8	12	136	11	0	209
Oklahoma	322	69	10	140	1	0	102
Oregon	53	2	1	22	0	0	28
Pennsylvania	360	3	15	107	5	0	230
Rhode Island	2	0	0	2	0	0	0
South Carolina	183	28	4	77	3	0	71
South Dakota	5	0	1	0	0	0	4
Tennessee	209	1	13	94	3	2	96
Texas	954	313	28	110	49	1	453
Utah	26	6	1	8	1	0	10
Virginia	142	89	5	11	9	1	27
Washington	38	4	1	23	0	0	10
Wyoming	11	1	1	8	0	0	1
Percent	100%	12.0%	3.8%	33.7%	4.5%	0.5%	45.6%

Note: For those persons sentenced to death more than once, the numbers are based on the most recent death sentence.

SOURCE: Thomas P. Bonczar and Tracy L. Snell, "Appendix Table 4. Number Sentenced to Death and Number of Removals by Jurisdiction and Reason for Removal, 1973–2003," in *Capital Punishment, 2003*, U.S. Department of Justice, Bureau of Justice Statistics, November 2004, http://www.ojp.usdoj.gov/bjs/pub/pdf/cp03.pdf (accessed June 1, 2005)

Since 1988 the Bureau of Justice Statistics has been collecting information on the number of death sentences imposed on the offenders entering the prison system. Among the 4,156 individuals admitted under sentence of death between 1988 to 2003, nearly one in seven (14%) was admitted with two or more death sentences.

A LONG WAIT

It can be a long wait on death row. Between 1977 and 2003 a total of 7,061 offenders were under sentence of death for varying lengths of time, according to *Capital Punishment, 2003*. Of these, 885 (12.5%) were actually executed. Another 2,802 (39.7%) were removed from under a death sentence because of appellate court decisions and reviews or commutations, or they had died while awaiting execution.

For those executed from 1977 to 2003, the average time between the imposition of the most recent death sentence and the execution was about ten years and four months. White prisoners had waited an average of ten years and one month, and African-American prisoners, ten years and nine months, before their execution. In 2003 the sixty-five inmates executed were under sentence of death for an average of ten years and eleven months. (See Table 7.10.)

TABLE 7.4

Number of prisoners on death row, by state and race, April 1, 2005

State	Total	Black		White		Latino/a		Native American		Asian		Unknown	
AL	195	92	47%	101	52%	2	1%	0	—	0	—	0	—
AZ	129	13	10%	91	71%	21	16%	3	2%	1	.8%	0	—
AR	38	22	58%	16	42%	0	—	0	—	0	—	0	—
CA	644	232	36%	252	39%	126	20%	14	2%	20	3%	0	—
CO	3	2	67%	0	—	1	33%	0	—	0	—	0	—
CT	9	3	33%	4	44%	2	22%	0	—	0	—	0	—
DE	19	6	32%	10	53%	3	16%	0	—	0	—	0	—
FL	384	130	34%	218	57%	34	9%	1	.3%	1	.3%	0	—
GA	112	55	49%	53	47%	3	3%	0	—	1	.9%	0	—
ID	22	0	—	22	100%	0	—	0	—	0	—	0	—
IL	10	2	20%	6	60%	2	20%	0	—	0	—	0	—
IN	33	9	27%	24	73%	0	—	0	—	0	—	0	—
KS	7	2	29%	5	71%	0	—	0	—	0	—	0	—
KY	37	8	22%	28	76%	1	3%	0	—	0	—	0	—
LA	91	59	65%	29	32%	2	2%	0	—	1	1%	0	—
MD	9	6	67%	3	33%	0	—	0	—	0	—	0	—
MS	70	36	51%	33	47%	0	—	0	—	1	1%	0	—
MO	56	24	43%	32	57%	0	—	0	—	0	—	0	—
MT	4	0	—	4	100%	0	—	0	—	0	—	0	—
NE	9	1	11%	5	56%	3	33%	0	—	0	—	0	—
NV	86	34	40%	42	49%	9	10%	0	—	1	1%	0	—
NJ	15	7	47%	8	53%	0	—	0	—	0	—	0	—
NM	2	0	—	2	100%	0	—	0	—	0	—	0	—
NY	2	1	50%	1	50%	0	—	0	—	0	—	0	—
NC	197	109	55%	72	37%	4	2%	10	5%	2	1%	0	—
OH	198	98	49%	94	47%	2	1%	2	1%	2	1%	0	—
OK	98	39	40%	52	53%	1	1%	6	6%	0	—	0	—
OR	32	2	6%	26	81%	2	6%	1	3%	0	—	1	3%
PA	230	140	61%	70	30%	18	8%	0	—	2	.9%	0	—
SC	77	39	51%	38	49%	0	—	0	—	0	—	0	—
SD	4	0	—	4	100%	0	—	0	—	0	—	0	—
TN	107	42	39%	60	56%	1	.9%	2	2%	2	2%	0	—
TX	441	179	41%	136	31%	121	28%	0	—	5	1%	0	—
UT	10	2	20%	6	60%	1	10%	1	10%	0	—	0	—
VA	23	13	57%	10	43%	0	—	0	—	0	—	0	—
WA	11	5	45%	6	55%	0	—	0	—	0	—	0	—
WY	2	0	—	2	100%	0	—	0	—	0	—	0	—
US govt	36	23	64%	12	33%	0	—	1	3%	0	—	0	—
Military	7	5	71%	1	14%	0	—	0	—	1	14%	0	—
Total	**3,459**	**1,440**	**42%**	**1,578**	**46%**	**359**	**10%**	**41**	**1%**	**40**	**1%**	**1**	**.03%**

Note: 7 prisoners were sentenced to death in more than one state. They are included in the chart above for each state in which they were sentenced to death.

SOURCE: "Summary of State Lists of Prisoners on Death Row (As of April 1, 2005)," in *Death Row USA, Spring 2005*, NAACP Legal Defense and Educational Fund, Inc., 2005, http://www.naacpldf.org/content/pdf/pubs/drusa/DRUSA_Spring_2005.pdf (accessed June 1, 2005)

GETTING OFF DEATH ROW

Prisoners can get off death row by different means. The Bureau of Justice Statistics breaks down the outcome of the sentences for the 7,403 inmates condemned to death for the period 1973 through 2003. During this period, 885 were executed. One-third (2,498 inmates) of those who left death row were sentenced in states where the death penalty statute was later overturned or had their sentences or convictions overturned by an appellate or higher court. Some 333 had their sentences commuted, while another 279 died while awaiting execution. (See Table 7.11.)

Using a single year as an example, of the 318 persons sentenced to death in 1995, thirty-three were executed, twelve died while in confinement, and forty-three had their convictions or sentences overturned. Of those prisoners sentenced to death in 1995, 218 remained on death row as of December 31, 2003.

AUTOMATIC REVIEW OF DEATH SENTENCES

In all states, a death sentence is automatically reviewed by a state appellate court or supreme court for possible constitutional or legal errors that may have taken place in the initial trial. At year-end 2003, among the thirty-eight states with capital punishment statutes, thirty-seven states provided for automatic review of all death sentences, regardless of the defendant's wishes. The remaining state, South Carolina, allowed the defendant to dispense with the sentence review if the court found him competent to decide for himself (per the Supreme Court decision in *State v. Torrence*, 473 S.E.2d. 703 [S.C. 1996]). The federal death penalty procedures, however, did not provide for automatic review after a death sentence was imposed.

Although most of the thirty-seven states authorized an automatic review of both conviction and sentence, Idaho, Indiana, Kentucky, Oklahoma, South Dakota,

TABLE 7.5

Death sentences imposed on female offenders, January 1, 1973–June 30, 2005

Year	Total death sentences	Death sentences for females	Portion of total
1973	42	1	2.4%
1974	149	1	0.7%
1975	298	8	2.3%
1976	233	3	1.3%
1977	137	1	0.7%
1978	185	4	2.1%
1979	151	4	2.6%
1980	173	2	1.1%
1981	224	3	1.3%
1982	265	5	1.8%
1983	252	4	1.6%
1984	285	8	2.8%
1985	266	5	1.8%
1986	300	3	1.0%
1987	289	5	1.7%
1988	290	5	1.7%
1989	259	11	4.2%
1990	252	7	2.7%
1991	267	6	2.2%
1992	287	10	3.5%
1993	289	6	2.0%
1994	315	5	1.6%
1995	318	7	2.2%
1996	320	2	0.6%
1997	276	2	0.7%
1998	300	7	2.3%
1999	279	5	1.8%
2000	231	7	3.1%
2001	163	2	1.3%
2002	159	5	3.2%
2003	144	2	1.4%
2004	125	5	2.3%
2005[a]	60[b]	1	1.7%
Totals:	**7,523[b]**	**152**	**2.0%**

[a]As of June 30, 2005
[b]Estimates

SOURCE: Victor L. Streib, "Table 3. Death Sentences Imposed on Female Offenders, January 1, 1973, through June 30, 2005," in *Death Penalty for Female Offenders, January 1, 1973, through June 30, 2005*, Ohio Northern University, The Claude W. Pettit College of Law, July 2005, http://www.law .onu.edu/faculty/streib/documents/FemDeathJune2005_000.pdf (accessed July 15, 2005)

TABLE 7.6

Number of female offenders sentenced to death, by state and race, January 1, 1973–June 30, 2005

Rank	Sentencing state	Race of offender				Total females sentenced
		White	Black	Latin	American Indian	
(1)	California	8	3	6	0	17
(2)	North Carolina	10	4	0	2	16
	Texas	10	6	0	0	16
(4)	Florida	11	3	1	0	15
(5)	Ohio	4	6	0	0	10
(6)	Alabama	6	3	0	0	9
(7)	Oklahoma	7	1	0	0	8
(8)	Illinois	1	4	2	0	7
	Mississippi	5	2	0	0	7
(10)	Georgia	5	1	0	0	6
	Pennsylvania	3	3	0	0	6
(12)	Missouri	4	0	1	0	5
(13)	Indiana	2	2	0	0	4
(14)	Arizona	3	0	0	0	3
	Kentucky	3	0	0	0	3
	Maryland	1	0	0	2	3
(17)	New Jersey	3	0	0	0	3
(18)	Arkansas	2	0	0	0	2
	Idaho	2	0	0	0	2
	Louisiana	1	1	0	0	2
	Nevada	1	1	0	0	2
	Tennessee	2	0	0	0	2
(23)	Delaware	1	0	0	0	1
	Federal (Iowa)	1	0	0	0	1
	South Carolina	1	0	0	0	1
	Virginia	1	0	0	0	1
	Totals	**98**	**40**	**10**	**4**	**152**

SOURCE: Victor L. Streib, "Table 4. State-by-State Breakdown of Death Sentences for Female Offenders," January 1, 1973, through June 30, 2005," in *Death Penalty for Female Offenders, January 1, 1973, through June 30, 2005*, Ohio Northern University, The Claude W. Pettit College of Law, July 2005, http://www.law.onu.edu/faculty/streib/documents/ FemDeathJune2005_ 000.pdf (accessed July 15, 2005)

and Tennessee required review of the sentence only. In Idaho inmates who wanted their convictions reviewed had to file an appeal or lose the right to do so. In Indiana and Kentucky defendants were allowed to waive review of their convictions.

Generally, the state's highest court of appeals conducts the review regardless of whether the defendant requests it. If the appellate court vacates (annuls) the conviction or the sentence, the case could be returned to the trial court for additional proceedings or for retrial. Subsequent to the resentencing or retrial, the death sentence could be reinstated.

RIGHT TO COUNSEL

The Sixth Amendment to the U.S. Constitution guarantees the "assistance of counsel for defense" in federal criminal prosecution. In 1963 the U.S. Supreme Court extended the right to counsel to state criminal prosecution of indigent (poor) persons charged with felonies (*Gideon v. Wainwright*, 372 U.S. 335). In 1972 the high court held that poor persons charged with any crime that carries a sentence of imprisonment have the right to counsel (*Argersinger v. Hamlin*, 407 U.S. 25).

The Court later ruled in *Strickland v. Washington* (466 U.S. 688, 1984) that the lawyers provided for poor defendants must abide by certain professional standards in criminal cases. Some of these standards include: demonstrating loyalty to the client, avoiding conflicts of interest, keeping the defendant informed of important developments in the trial, and conducting reasonable factual and legal investigations that may aid the client's case.

Ineffective Counsel

The release near the end of the twentieth century of several inmates who were said to be innocent after serving time on death row called attention to the ineffective representation of defendants unable to afford private counsel. Death penalty experts claimed that some lawyers who defend capital cases were inexperienced, ill trained,

TABLE 7.7

Age at time of arrest for capital offense and age of prisoners under sentence of death, December 31, 2003

	Prisoners under sentence of death			
	At time of arrest		On December 31, 2003	
Age	Number*	Percent	Number	Percent
Total number under sentence of death on 12/31/03	3,117	100%	3,374	100%
17 or younger	67	2.1	0	
18–19	341	10.9	1	—
20–24	843	27.0	133	3.9
25–29	687	22.0	400	11.9
30–34	512	16.4	565	16.7
35–39	333	10.7	582	17.2
40–44	177	5.7	613	18.2
45–49	97	3.1	477	14.1
50–54	38	1.2	297	8.8
55–59	16	0.5	196	5.8
60–64	3	0.1	67	2.0
65 or older	3	0.1	43	1.3
Mean age	28 yrs.		40 yrs.	
Median age	27 yrs.		40 yrs.	

Note: The youngest person under sentence of death was a white male in Texas, born in April 1984 and sentenced to death in August 2002. The oldest person under sentence of death was a white male in Arizona, born in September 1915 and sentenced to death in June 1983. Detail may not add to total due to rounding.
—Less than 0.05%.
*Excludes 257 inmates for whom the date of arrest for capital offense was not available.

SOURCE: Thomas P. Bonczar and Tracy L. Snell, "Table 7. Age at Time of Arrest for Capital Offense and Age of Prisoners under Sentence of Death at Yearend 2003," in *Capital Punishment, 2003*, U.S. Department of Justice, Bureau of Justice Statistics, November 2004, http://www.ojp.usdoj.gov/bjs/pub/pdf/cp03.pdf (accessed June 1, 2005)

TABLE 7.8

Demographic characteristics of prisoners under sentence of death, 2003

	Prisoners under sentence of death, 2003		
Characteristic	Yearend	Admissions	Removals
Total number under sentence of death	3,374	144	332
Gender			
Male	98.6%	98.6%	98.2%
Female	1.4	1.4	1.8
Race			
White	55.7%	63.9%	46.1%
Black	42.0	30.6	53.3
All other races*	2.3	5.5	0.6
Hispanic origin			
Hispanic	12.5%	27.0%	6.2%
Non-Hispanic	87.5	73.0	93.8
Education			
8th grade or less	15.2%	18.3%	11.6%
9th–11th grade	37.1	41.7	40.4
High school graduate/GED	38.3	35.0	37.2
Any college	9.3	5.0	10.8
Median	11th	11th	11th
Martial status			
Married	22.5%	29.1%	21.9%
Divorced/separated	20.7	17.1	20.2
Widowed	2.8	4.3	3.1
Never married	54.0	49.6	54.8

Note: Calculations are based on those cases for which data were reported. Missing data by category were as follows:

	Prisoners under sentence of death, 2003		
Characteristic	Yearend	Admissions	Removals
Hispanic origin	416	55	44
Education	483	24	55
Marital status	333	27	40

*At yearend 2002, other races consisted of 29 American Indians, 35 Asians, and 14 self-identified Hispanics. During 2003, 3 American Indians, 3 Asians, and 2 self-identified Hispanics were admitted; 1 Asian was removed; and 1 American Indian was executed.

SOURCE: Thomas P. Bonczar and Tracy L. Snell, "Table 5. Demographic Characteristics of Prisoners under Sentence of Death, 2003," in *Capital Punishment, 2003*, U.S. Department of Justice, Bureau of Justice Statistics, November 2004, http://www.ojp.usdoj.gov/bjs/pub/pdf/cp03.pdf (accessed June 1, 2005)

or incompetent. They pointed to cases where the defense lawyers fell asleep during trial, drank to excess the night before, or even showed up in the courtroom intoxicated. They also cited the well-publicized cases of inmates exonerated as a result of college students finding evidence that defense lawyers had failed to uncover.

Several studies have revealed that attorneys who took on capital murder cases involving poor defendants were often incompetent. In a November 1999 five-part series, "The Failure of the Death Penalty in Illinois" (*Chicago Tribune*), Ken Armstrong and Steve Mills examined all 285 death penalty cases since Illinois reinstated the death penalty in 1977. The journalists reported that at least thirty-three defendants sentenced to death in Illinois had lawyers who were later suspended or disbarred, "sanctions reserved for conduct so incompetent, unethical, or even criminal the lawyer's license [was] taken away." A similar three-part series entitled "Uncertain Justice" by Lise Olsen (*Seattle Post-Intelligencer*, August 6, 2001) revealed that one-fifth of the eighty-four people who faced possible execution in Washington state between 1981 and 2001 were represented by attorneys who had been disbarred, suspended, or arrested sometime prior to or after the murder trial. These lawyers were some of the worst in Washington state.

A December 2004 American Bar Association report entitled "Gideon's Broken Promise: America's Continuing Quest for Equal Justice" provided some insight into why poor defendants received such inadequate counsel. The study analyzed the indigent defense system in twenty-two states and found that lawyers who took on poor defendants received lousy pay and that judges tended to let legal protocols slide in order to clear overcrowded dockets. In non-capital cases involving lesser offenses, prosecutors and judges sometimes forced defendants to plead guilty before receiving counsel in order to move them through the system. In addition, the indigent defense systems lacked the basic accountability and oversight needed to ensure decent legal representation or correct these problems.

States generally vary in fulfilling *Gideon*. Some states have undertaken the establishment and funding of

TABLE 7.9

Criminal history profile of prisoners under sentence of death, by race and Hispanic origin, 2003

	Number of prisoners under sentence of death				Percent of prisoners under sentence of death[a]			
	All[b]	White[c]	Black[c]	Hispanic	All[b]	White[c]	Black[c]	Hispanic
U.S. total	3,374	1,541	1,404	369	100%	100%	100%	100%
Prior felony convictions								
Yes	2,007	879	899	200	64.5%	61.8%	69.8%	58.7%
No	1,103	544	389	141	35.5	38.2	30.2	41.3
Not reported	264							
Prior homicide convictions								
Yes	272	125	117	25	8.2%	8.3%	8.5%	6.9%
No	3,032	1,387	1,252	339	91.8%	91.7	91.5	93.1
Not reported	70							
Legal status at time of capital offense								
Charges pending	239	120	101	17	7.9%	8.7%	8.0%	5.1%
Probation	327	132	151	38	10.8	9.5	12.0	11.4
Parole	501	199	222	72	16.5	14.4	17.7	21.6
Prison escapee	42	23	12	6	1.4	1.7	1.0	1.8
Incarcerated	95	52	33	8	3.1	3.8	2.6	2.4
Other status	17	7	7	2	0.6	0.5	0.6	0.6
None	1,809	850	730	191	59.7	61.5	58.1	57.2
Not reported	344							

[a]Percentages are based on those offenders for whom data were reported. Detail may not add to total because of rounding.
[b]Includes American Indians and Asians.
[c]Excludes persons of Hispanic origin.

SOURCE: Thomas P. Bonczar and Tracy L. Snell, "Table 8. Criminal History Profile of Prisoners under Sentence of Death, by Race and Hispanic Origin, 2003," in *Capital Punishment, 2003*, U.S. Department of Justice, Bureau of Justice Statistics, November 2004, http://www.ojp.usdoj.gov/bjs/pub/pdf/cp03.pdf (accessed June 1, 2005)

TABLE 7.10

Time under sentence of death and execution, by race, 1977–2003

Year of execution	Number executed			Average elapsed time from sentence to execution for:		
	All races[a]	White[b]	Black[b]	All races[a]	White[b]	Black[b]
Total	885	568	303	124 mo	121 mo	129 mo
1977–83	11	9	2	51 mo	49 mo	58 mo
1984	21	13	8	74	76	71
1985	18	11	7	71	65	80
1986	18	11	7	87	78	102
1987	25	13	12	86	78	96
1988	11	6	5	80	72	89
1989	16	8	8	95	78	112
1990	23	16	7	95	97	91
1991	14	7	7	116	124	107
1992	31	19	11	114	104	135
1993	38	23	14	113	112	121
1994	31	20	11	122	117	132
1995	56	33	22	134	128	144
1996	45	31	14	125	112	153
1997	74	45	27	133	126	147
1998	68	48	18	130	128	132
1999	98	61	33	143	143	141
2000	85	49	35	137	134	142
2001	66	48	17	142	134	166
2002	71	53	18	127	130	120
2003	65	44	20	131	135	120

Note: Average time was calculated from the most recent sentencing date.
[a]Includes American Indians and Asians.
[b]Includes Hispanics.

SOURCE: Thomas P. Bonczar and Tracy L. Snell, "Table 11. Time Under Sentence of Death and Execution, by Race, 1977–2003," in *Capital Punishment, 2003*, U.S. Department of Justice, Bureau of Justice Statistics, November 2004, http://www.ojp.usdoj.gov/bjs/pub/pdf/cp03.pdf (accessed June 1, 2005)

TABLE 7.11

Prisoners sentenced to death and outcome of the sentence, by year of sentencing, 1973–2003

Year of sentence	Number sentenced to death	Execution	Other death	Appeals or higher courts overturned — Death penalty statute	Conviction	Sentence	Sentence commuted	Other or unknown reasons	Under sentence of death 12/31/2003
1973	42	2	0	14	9	8	9	0	0
1974	149	11	4	65	15	30	22	1	1
1975	298	6	4	171	24	67	21	2	3
1976	233	14	5	136	17	43	15	0	3
1977	137	19	3	40	26	32	7	0	10
1978	185	36	6	21	36	65	8	0	13
1979	151	28	13	2	28	59	6	1	14
1980	173	45	13	3	30	50	12	0	20
1981	223	54	13	0	42	78	12	1	23
1982	266	58	18	0	38	73	12	1	66
1983	252	61	17	1	27	63	14	2	67
1984	284	59	14	2	44	65	12	8	80
1985	266	43	9	1	42	75	12	4	80
1986	299	61	20	0	46	57	13	5	97
1987	289	49	20	5	39	62	4	7	103
1988	291	47	13	1	33	61	13	0	123
1989	258	37	10	0	32	52	11	1	115
1990	251	41	9	0	35	43	15	1	107
1991	267	31	10	0	33	35	10	0	148
1992	286	32	11	0	24	43	17	0	159
1993	289	32	13	0	18	31	16	0	179
1994	314	39	10	0	24	35	11	0	195
1995	318	33	12	0	15	28	12	0	218
1996	320	19	9	0	21	39	10	0	222
1997	276	8	5	0	20	26	5	0	212
1998	302	11	7	1	17	20	8	0	238
1999	276	3	6	2	12	15	10	0	228
2000	232	5	3	1	6	13	8	0	196
2001	164	0	1	0	2	7	2	0	152
2002	168	1	1	0	0	2	6	0	158
2003	144	0	0	0	0	0	0	0	144
Total, 1973–2003	**7,403**	**885**	**279**	**466**	**755**	**1,277**	**333**	**34**	**3,374**

Note: For those persons sentenced to death more than once, the numbers are based on the most recent death sentence.

SOURCE: Thomas P. Bonczar and Tracy L. Snell, "Appendix Table 2. Prisoners Sentenced to Death and Outcome of the Sentence, by Year of Sentencing, 1973–2003," in *Capital Punishment, 2003,* U.S. Department of Justice, Bureau of Justice Statistics, November 2004, http://www.ojp.usdoj.gov/bjs/pub/pdf/cp03.pdf (accessed June 1, 2005)

an indigent defense system; others have passed the responsibility on to individual counties. Across the United States, different jurisdictions use one or a combination of three systems to provide counsel to poor defendants. The first system used by some jurisdictions has public defenders that are usually government employees. Under the second system, the court-assigned counsel system, a judge appoints private lawyers to represent the poor. A third system involves contract lawyers who bid for the job of providing indigent defense.

Court-assigned lawyers belong to a list of private lawyers who accept clients on a case-by-case basis. In jurisdictions that employ these lawyers, judges appoint lawyers from a list of private bar members and determine their pay. In most cases the pay is very low. Beth A. Wilkinson, co-chair of the Constitution Project's Death Penalty Initiative, testified before the U.S. Senate Judiciary Committee hearing (June 27, 2001) that many jurisdictions paid their court-appointed lawyers very low

hourly rates for capital defense. For example, Alabama paid $20 to $40 an hour, with a limit of $2,000. This means that a lawyer spending six hundred hours preparing for a capital case earned a little over $3 an hour. (The American Civil Liberties Union estimated that defending a capital case at the trial level takes about seven hundred to one thousand hours.) Wilkinson added that while Tennessee paid $20 to $30 an hour, Mississippi had a $1,000 limit. According to the December 2004 American Bar Association report, salaried defense attorneys did not fare much better. In Massachusetts, for instance, salaries started at $35,000 for public defenders and were increased to $50,000 after ten years. Moreover, courts often refused to authorize the needed funds for investigating cases and using expert testimony. In contrast, the prosecution usually had unlimited funds at its disposal.

Some states, such as Alabama and Mississippi, have no statewide public defender system and have taken few steps to put one in place. Other states have taken strides since the late-1990s to improve their systems. Colorado and New York have both public defender offices and capital defender offices that specialize in death penalty cases. When New York brought back capital punishment in 1995, the death penalty statute required the establishment of a capital defender office with a $15 million allotment to train trial lawyers and investigators. Until 2001, of Texas's 254 counties, only three had a public defender program. In June 2001 the state passed the Texas Fair Defense Act requiring state funding for indigent defense. The act required that indigent defendants receive counsel no later then five days after arrest and authorized $20 million in state money to help judges pay more for defense attorneys and investigations. In 2003 Nevada raised its maximum pay for defense counsel in a death penalty case from $12,000 to $20,000 and changed the hourly rate from $25 to $75. Georgia also enacted legislation in 2003 to reform its defense system. The legislation called for the establishment of defender offices within each judicial circuit to give representation in felony cases by 2005. Virginia established the Virginia Defense Commission in 2004. This governmental body was created to oversee both assigned counsel and public defender programs throughout the state.

To remedy some of the problems inherent in death penalty trials, the U.S. Congress passed and President Bush signed the Innocence Protection Act of 2004 (P.L. 108-405). This act launched a program in which state governments received grants from the federal government to improve the quality of legal representation for poor defendants in state capital cases. In order to receive such a grant, a state's capital defense system had to meet a number of requirements, which included establishing minimum standards for defense attorneys and monitoring the performance of those attorneys.

Postconviction Review

While death row inmates have the right to seek review of their conviction and sentence, they do not have the right to counsel for postconviction proceedings (*Murray v. Giarratano*, 492 U.S. 1, 1989). Since most of those awaiting execution are poor, they must find lawyers willing to handle appeals for free. In 1995 Congress discontinued federal funding of private organizations (called resource centers) that represented death row inmates in postconviction proceedings. As a result, private organizations and law firms, both proponents and opponents of the death penalty, concerned with the increasing problems in capital cases, now volunteer their services. Some hold training seminars on the complex process of appellate review, while others provide research and investigation.

Some private organizations, however, cannot keep up with the large numbers of death row inmates. For example, the Equal Justice Initiative of Alabama (EJI), comprising seven lawyers, has been representing a majority of Alabama inmates seeking appeals. According to their Web site in September 2005 (http://www.e-ji.org/), the EJI counted 190 death row inmates in the state, with 300 more facing trials involving capital murder. Under state law, lawyers appointed to represent indigent inmates could not be paid more than $1,000 per case.

ARE INNOCENT PEOPLE BEING EXECUTED?

In 1993 the Subcommittee on Civil and Constitutional Rights of the U.S. House Judiciary Committee used data on death row exonerations provided by the Death Penalty Information Center (DPIC) in Washington, D.C., for its hearing on "Innocence and the Death Penalty: Assessing the Danger of Mistaken Executions." Since then, the DPIC has periodically updated its "List of Inmates Released" from death row.

According to the DPIC, from 1973 to February 9, 2005, 118 death row inmates in twenty-five states were exonerated and freed from death row. Between 1973 and 1998 a total of seventy-four inmates were released, an average of three inmates each year. This average rose to eight between the years of 1999 and 2003, with the highest number of exonerations (twelve) occurring in 2003. Only six inmates were freed from death row in 2004. (See Figure 7.2.)

Between 1973 and March 15, 2005, Florida accounted for the greatest number of exonerations (twenty-one), followed by Illinois (eighteen), Louisiana (eight), and Texas (eight). Arizona and Oklahoma each released seven inmates from death row. (See Figure 7.3.) Of the inmates released, sixty were African-American and forty-six were white. Twelve were Hispanic, and one was of "other" race. The inmates had spent an average of 9.3 years on death row.

According to the DPIC:

> The definition of innocence that DPIC uses in placing defendants on the list is that they had been convicted and sentenced to death, and subsequently either a) their conviction was overturned and they were acquitted at a retrial, or all charges were dropped; or b) they were given an absolute pardon by the governor based on new evidence of innocence.

Those who are concerned with the administration of the death penalty often refer to the increasing number of death row exonerations on the DPIC list. However, some death penalty supporters and researchers have challenged what they call the "death penalty innocents." In 2002 Ward A. Campbell, California Supervising Deputy Attorney General, investigated the 102 cases of exonerated death row inmates on the DPIC list at that time. In his report, *Critique of DPIC List "Innocence: Freed from*

FIGURE 7.2

Death row exonerations by year, 1973–February 9, 2005

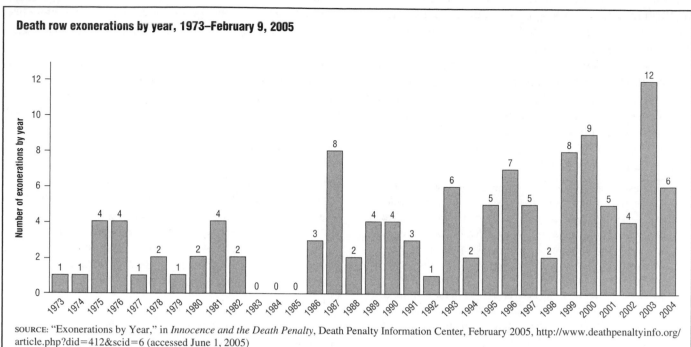

SOURCE: "Exonerations by Year," in *Innocence and the Death Penalty*, Death Penalty Information Center, February 2005, http://www.deathpenaltyinfo.org/article.php?did=412&scid=6 (accessed June 1, 2005)

FIGURE 7.3

Death row exonerations by state, 1973–February 9, 2005

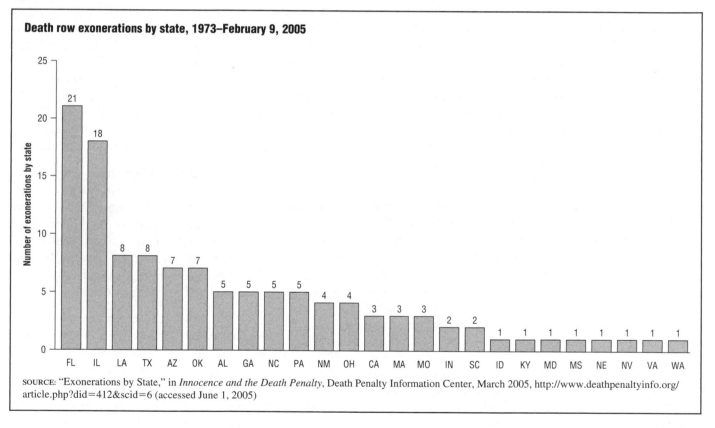

SOURCE: "Exonerations by State," in *Innocence and the Death Penalty*, Death Penalty Information Center, March 2005, http://www.deathpenaltyinfo.org/article.php?did=412&scid=6 (accessed June 1, 2005)

Death Row" (http://www.prodeathpenalty.com/DPIC.htm), Campbell concluded that at least sixty-eight of the 102 inmates on the list should not have been included. Campbell found that "many defendants on the List were not 'actually innocent' [meaning prosecution found the defendant innocent of the crime]." Some had pleaded guilty to lesser charges and had their sentences commuted. Campbell noted that "an acquittal because the prosecution has not proven guilt beyond a reasonable doubt does not mean that the defendant did not actually commit the crime."

On October 16, 2002, Senator Orrin Hatch (R-UT) confirmed Campbell's findings on the DPIC list of exonerees during the U.S. Senate Committee on the Judiciary's hearing on the Innocence Protection Act of 2002 (S. 486). Senator Hatch mentioned the example of twenty-three Florida inmates released from death row included on the list. On June 20, 2002, the Florida Commission on Capital Cases released the results of its investigation into these cases (*Case Histories: A Review of 23 Individuals Released from Death Row*). The commission concluded,

> Of these twenty-three inmates, none were found "innocent" even when acquitted, because no such verdict exists. A defendant is found guilty or not guilty, never innocent. The guilt of only four defendants, however, was ever truly doubted. . . . An analysis of the remaining nineteen inmates can be divided into three categories that account for their releases: (1) six cases were remanded due to evidence issues, (2) an additional seven were remanded in light of witness issues, and (3) the remaining six were remanded as a result of issues involving court officials.

A Case of Innocence

Anthony Porter of Illinois was convicted of two 1982 murders and sentenced to death in 1983. He was convicted based on the testimony of two eyewitnesses who separately claimed they saw Porter commit the crimes. By 1998 Porter had exhausted all his appeals. On September 21, 1998, two days before Porter's scheduled execution, the defense lawyer filed an emergency petition with the Illinois Supreme Court, arguing that the defendant was mentally retarded (he had an IQ of fifty-one) and did not understand what was about to happen to him. The court granted Porter a stay of execution to determine his mental competency.

In the meantime, an investigative journalism class taught by David Protess (Northwestern University, Medill School of Journalism, Evanston, IL) had chosen Porter's case to review. The professor, his students, and a private investigator, Paul Ciolino, uncovered evidence of Porter's innocence. The first eyewitness (the second one had died) confessed to giving false testimony. The group tracked down the wife of the real murderer in Milwaukee (the couple had moved soon after Porter's arrest) and were able to convince her to confess to being present when her husband shot the victims. Next, the investigator succeeded in obtaining a videotaped confession from the murderer, Alstory Simon. On March 11, 1999, Porter's conviction was reversed; he had been on death row for seventeen years.

DNA TESTING

Before DNA testing became available as proof of identity, the U.S. Supreme Court held the view that the nation's appellate courts could not reverse a murder conviction based on newly discovered post-trial evidence. The National Commission on the Future of DNA Evidence mentioned this in their report *Postconviction DNA Testing: Recommendations for Handling Requests* (Washington, DC: National Institute of Justice, September 1999). According to the commission, the nation's highest court ruled in *Herrera v. Collins* (506 U.S. 390, 1993) that newly discovered evidence does not constitute grounds for a federal *habeas* relief if there is no evidence of a constitutional violation occurring during state criminal proceedings. (In this case, Leonel Torres Herrera, ten years after his initial trial, alleged that he was innocent of a double murder, presenting "actual evidence" that his brother, who had since died, had committed the crime.) The commission, however, stated that today, with the availability of DNA testing, "the possibility of demonstrating actual innocence has moved from the realm of theory to the actual."

The science of deoxyribonucleic acid (DNA) testing is improving rapidly. When DNA testing was first used in criminal trials starting in the mid-1980s, DNA samples had to be not only fresh but contain thousands of cells. As DNA technology has become more sophisticated, scientists are able to test a single cell for DNA patterns that could link suspects to hair or semen found on a victim. Today a crime laboratory can identify unique DNA patterns in a tiny sample of less than fifty cells. DNA testing has played a substantial role in proving the innocence of a number of persons wrongly convicted. The DPIC reported in "Innocence: Freed from Death Row" that as of August 2005 fourteen of the 121 inmates released from death row since 1973 were exonerated by DNA evidence.

When biological material has been left at the scene of the crime, DNA testing could, in some cases, establish with near certainty a defendant's innocence or guilt. DNA, which stores the genetic code of the human body, is found in saliva, skin tissue, bones, blood, semen, and the roots of hair. Biological samples that were difficult to test in the 1980s may yield more accurate information where previous results had proved inconclusive.

By the mid-1990s, DNA evidence was being used in efforts to prove that certain prisoners on death row had been wrongly convicted. In 1996 David Protess and another group of students at Northwestern University's Medill School of Journalism helped uncover new evidence that proved the innocence of four African-American men who were convicted for a 1978 gang rape and double murder. Two received life imprisonment while the other two were sentenced to death. DNA tests helped prove the men's innocence. In March 1999 the four men received a $36 million settlement from Cook County, Illinois, to resolve a lawsuit charging police misconduct. In a Florida case, Frank Lee Smith was sentenced to death in 1986 for the rape and murder of an eight-year-old girl. DNA testing performed in 2000 proved Smith's innocence. However, Smith had died of cancer the previous year while awaiting execution.

Backlog of DNA Testing

Given the high price of analyzing DNA samples, DNA evidence from crime scenes often goes untested. Such testing, however, could exonerate death row inmates that had been falsely accused. In December 2000 Congress authorized the U.S. Department of Justice to provide state crime laboratories more than $30 million to analyze the backlog of DNA samples that had been collected but never tested. Under the DNA Analysis Backlog Reduction Act of 2000 (P.L. 106-546), states would receive funding to conduct tests on about half a million samples collected from criminals and crime scenes that had never been analyzed. Each test costs about $2,000 to perform. Of this number, about 180,000 rape kits nationwide had not been tested. In August 2001 U.S. Attorney General John Ashcroft announced that, in addition to the state initiative, the Department of Justice had authorized the collection of DNA samples from about twenty to thirty thousand federal, military, and District of Columbia offenders.

As of 2003, the backlog was nowhere near being cleared. *The Report to the Attorney General on Delays in Forensic DNA Analysis* (National Institute of Justice [NIJ], Washington, D.C., March 2003) revealed that a task force assembled by the NIJ found a continuing backlog in the testing of DNA samples collected at crime scenes. While an estimated 350,000 rape and homicide DNA samples needed testing, just 10% of the samples were in forensic crime laboratories. Most of the evidence samples were in the custody of law enforcement agencies because most laboratories lacked the proper storage facilities for preventing damage to the evidence.

Even if the laboratories had the proper storage facilities, the analysis of DNA samples could not take place because of the shortage of trained forensic scientists. Newly hired scientists need on-the-job training that requires an experienced scientist to spend time working one-on-one with new hires. The task force found that even when these problems were confronted, public crime laboratories could not retain their staff because of their lower compensation, compared with that paid by private companies.

Most States Provide Postconviction DNA Testing

At the hearing on the Innocence Protection Act of 2002 before the U.S. Senate Committee on the Judiciary on October 16, 2002, Senator Orrin Hatch reported that virtually every state with the death penalty provided access to DNA testing for postconviction defendants. Of the thirty-eight states that have the death penalty, twenty-six had enacted specific statutory provisions for DNA testing. Seven states—Colorado, Connecticut, Mississippi, Montana, Nevada, South Carolina, and South Dakota—relied on general postconviction state laws and/or case law in offering DNA testing, while Alabama and Ohio provided for the testing through an administrative policy or program. Georgia, New Hampshire, Wyoming, and the federal government had no statute or other means of providing postconviction DNA testing.

To disprove the claim that numerous death row inmates were in desperate need of getting access to DNA testing to prove their innocence, Senator Hatch presented a detailed chart illustrating the total number of death row inmates in each state and the number of those who had requested DNA testing and been denied. The chart showed that out of 3,554 death row inmates nationwide, just eighteen had requested and been denied DNA testing. This translated to 0.51% of all death row state inmates. Furthermore, of the twenty-three federal defendants currently on death row, not one sought a DNA test to prove his or her innocence. (See Table 7.12.)

As of December 31, 2004, a total of thirty-four death penalty states had statutes that provided DNA testing to felons and death row defendants. In 2003 Colorado, Connecticut, Georgia, Ohio, Montana, and Nevada passed legislation providing for postconviction DNA testing. New Hampshire passed a general postconviction DNA testing bill in 2004, which allowed for "testing of biological material under certain circumstances." South Dakota did not enact any postconviction DNA testing law but offered testing pursuant to court decisions. In Mississippi, South Carolina, and Alabama, bills for DNA testing failed to pass in 2004. As of 2005, Wyoming did not have legislation or a court decision that provided for postconviction DNA testing.

The federal Innocence Protection Act of 2004 became law on October 30, 2004. The law established the conditions under which a federal prisoner who pleaded not guilty could receive postconviction DNA testing. If a trial defendant were to face conviction, the act called for the preservation of the defendant's biological evidence. A five-year, $25 million grant program was also established to help eligible states pay for postconviction testing.

FAIRNESS AND THE DEATH PENALTY
Racial Questions

Death penalty cases raise a fairness issue. Opponents of the death penalty claim that minorities and poor defendants are more likely to be convicted and receive the death penalty than white or wealthy defendants. In 1986 lawyers appealing the case of Warren McCleskey, a convicted murderer, brought before the Supreme Court

TABLE 7.12

Denials of DNA testing to death row inmates, as of December 31, 2001

Federal/ state	Post-conviction DNA testing procedure	No. of death row inmates As of 12/31/01	Denied DNA test
Federal	No policy because no inmate has ever requested a DNA test	23	0
Alabama	Administrative policy	181	0
Arkansas	ACA § 16-112-201-205; 207	40	0
Arizona	Az. St §13-4240	121	0
California	Ca. Pen. Code § 1405	606	1
Colorado	Case by case basis	6	0
Connecticut	Conn. Gen. Stat. § 52-582 (2001)	7	0
Delaware	Del. Code. Ann. Tit. 11 § 4504	15	0
Florida	Fl. St. § 925.11	370	0
Georgia	No statute	121	0
Idaho	Id. St. 1949.02 and 1927.19	22	1
Illinois	Il. St. Ch. 725 § 5/116-3	160	1
Indiana	In. 35-38-7-5	36	0
Kansas	KSA 21-25-12	4	0
Kentucky	KRS Ch. 422 HB 4	37	0
Louisiana	La. C.Cr.P. Art. 926.1	90	0
Maryland	Md. Crim. Proc. § 8-201	14	0
Missouri	Rev. St. Mo. 547.035	70	1
Mississippi	Judicially created standard in *Ellis v. State*, 97-M-01326.	66	0
Montana	Can be provided by MCA 46-21-102	6	0
Nebraska	Ne. St. § 29-4120	7	0
New Hampshire	No statute or provision	0	0
New Jersey	NJ St. 2a:84A-32a	14	0
New Mexico	NM St § 31-1A-1	3	0
New York	NY C. Cr. P. § 440.30	5	0
North Carolina	NC Gen. Stat. 15A-269	215	0
Nevada	By court order	87	3*
Ohio	Voluntary AG program	204	0
Oklahoma	OK Stat. Tit. 22 § 1371	103	1
Oregon	OR St. T. 14 Ch. 138	25	0
Pennsylvania	42 P.A.C.S. 9543.1	244	0
South Carolina	Case by case basis	73	1
South Dakota	Judicially created standard in *Jenner v. State*, 590 N.W.2d 463 (S.D. 1999).	5	1
Tennessee	Tn. Code Ann. 40-30-401	95	0
Texas	Tx. Code Crim. Pro. 64.01-05	431	8
Utah	Ut. Code Ann 78-35A § 301-304	11	0
Virginia	Va. Code § 19.2-327.1	24	0
Washington	R.C.W. 10.73.170	11	0
Wyoming	No statute	2	0
Total		**3554**	**18**
			(.51%)

*Estimate.

SOURCE: Orrin Hatch, "Attachment D. Denials of DNA Testing to Death Row Inmates," in *Minority Views on S.486* (The Innocence Protection Act of 2002), U.S. Senate Committee on the Judiciary, October 16, 2002, http://www.prodeathpenalty.com/Articles/MINORVIEWS.PDF (accessed July 21, 2005)

the Baldus study (by Professors David C. Baldus, Charles Pulaski, and George Woodworth), an analysis of two thousand cases in Georgia in the 1970s.

This study showed that African-American defendants who were convicted of killing whites were more likely to receive death sentences than white murderers or African-Americans who had killed African-Americans. The justices, in *McCleskey v. Kemp* (481 U.S. 279, 1987), rejected the study, declaring that "apparent disparities . . .

are an inevitable part of our criminal justice system" and that there were enough safeguards built into the legal system to protect every defendant.

In 1998 Dr. Baldus and others, expanding on the Baldus study, found evidence of race-of-victim disparities in twenty-six out of twenty-nine death penalty states ("Racial Discrimination and the Death Penalty in the Post-*Furman* Era: An Empirical and Legal Analysis with Recent Findings from Philadelphia," *Cornell Law Review*, Vol. 83). The researchers found that the race of the victim was related to whether capital punishment was imposed. A defendant was more likely to receive the death penalty if the victim was white than if the victim was African-American.

These studies were consistent with a 1990 U.S. government study of capital punishment. The U.S. General Accounting Office (GAO), in *Death Penalty Sentencing: Research Indicates Pattern of Racial Disparities*, reviewed twenty-eight studies on race and the death penalty. The GAO reported that "in 82% of the studies, the race of the victim was found to influence the likelihood of being charged with capital murder or receiving the death penalty." The GAO found that when the victim was white, the defendant, whether white or African-American, was more likely to get the death sentence.

GAO added that in the small number of horrendous murders, death sentences were more likely to be imposed, regardless of race. Nevertheless, when the offender killed a person while robbing him or when the murderer had a previous record, the race of the victim played a role. The studies also showed that for crimes of passion, the convicted person (regardless of race) rarely received the death penalty.

In testimony before the Illinois House of Representatives' hearing on the state's system of capital punishment in September 1999, Richard C. Dieter, Executive Director of the Death Penalty Information Center, noted,

Ten out of twelve people who have been released from Illinois's death row are members of a minority. Most are African-American. That doesn't prove bias, but it should raise concerns. Illinois's death row is made up of approximately 156 individuals, ninety-seven of whom are African-American—that's 62% in a state where the African-American population is less than 15%. Again, those figures do not prove any racial bias, but such a glaring disproportion is evidence that something is wrong at some level of society. If race is playing a role in who is sentenced to death, then it can also be playing a role in who is wrongly convicted.

Some people have claimed that district attorneys, who decide which cases to try as death penalty cases, may be motivated by politics or racial prejudice to impose the death penalty on minority defendants. Profes-

TABLE 7.13

Race of district attorneys[a] in death penalty states, 1998

State	White DAs	Black DAs	Hispanic DAs
Alabama	39	1	0
Arizona	15	0	1
Arkansas	24	0	0
California	55	0	3
Colorado	21	0	1
Connecticut	12	0	0
Delaware	3	0	0
Florida	19	0	1
Georgia	45	1	0
Idaho	44	0	0
Illinois	102	0	0
Indiana	90	1	0
Kansas	104	1	0
Kentucky	56	0	0
Louisiana	39	1	0
Maryland	23	2	0
Mississippi	21	1	0
Missouri	115	0	0
Montana[b]	56	0	0
Nebraska	89	0	0
Nevada	17	0	0
New Hampshire	10	0	0
New Jersey	20	1	0
New Mexico	9	0	5
New York	61	1	0
North Carolina	37	2	0
Ohio	87	1	0
Oklahoma[b]	26	0	0
Oregon	36	0	0
Pennsylvania	67	0	0
South Carolina	15	1	0
South Dakota	66	0	0
Tennessee	31	0	0
Texas	137	0	11
Utah	29	0	0
Virginia	113	8	0
Washington	39	0	0
Wyoming	22	0	0
Total	**1794**	**22**	**22**
	97.5%	1.2%	1.2%

[a]The title for this official differs from state to state. The chief prosecuting official with discretionary power to determine charging levels is referred to as the "District Attorney."
[b]Montana and Oklahoma have one Native American District Attorney each.

SOURCE: Richard Dieter, "Figure 9. Race of District Attorneys in Death Penalty States," in *The Death Penalty in Black and White: Who Lives, Who Dies, Who Decides*, Death Penalty Information Center, June 1998, http://www.deathpenaltyinfo.org/article.php?scid=45&did=539 (accessed June 1, 2005)

sor Jeffrey Pokorak of St. Mary's University School of Law, in "Probing the Capital Prosecutor's Perspective: Race of the Discretionary Actors" (*Cornell Law Review* 83, 1998), found that 1,794 out of 1,838 prosecutors (97.5%) in the thirty-eight states with capital punishment were white. Only 1.2% each were African-American or Hispanic. (See Table 7.13.)

Racial Justice Legislation

In 1998 Kentucky became the first state to enact a racial justice law (Racial Justice Act, SB171), prohibiting the execution of a convicted person when evidence shows racial discrimination in prosecution or sentencing. Other states that have considered similar legisla-

tion include Florida, Georgia, Indiana, Nebraska, New Mexico, North Carolina, Ohio, Oregon, and Texas. As of June 1, 2005, however, no other state had passed such legislation.

FIRST FEDERAL STUDY OF RACIAL AND ETHNIC BIAS

In July 2000 President Bill Clinton ordered the Department of Justice to review the administration of the federal death penalty system. This order came in the aftermath of a request for clemency by Raul Juan Garza, who was granted a stay by President Clinton, but who was ultimately executed in June 2001. Garza's lawyer contended that it was unfair to execute his client because the federal death penalty discriminated against members of minorities.

On September 12, 2000, the Justice Department released *The Federal Death Penalty System: A Statistical Survey (1988–2000)*, providing information on the federal death penalty since the passage of the first federal capital punishment law in 1988 (the Anti-Drug Abuse Act). From 1988 to 1994 prosecutors in the ninety-four federal districts were required to submit to the U.S. attorney general for review and approval only those cases that the attorney general deemed worthy for the death penalty. During this period the prosecutors sought the death penalty in fifty-two cases and received authorization from the attorney general in forty-seven cases.

In 1995 the Justice Department adopted a new protocol, requiring U.S. attorneys to submit for review all cases in which a defendant was charged with a crime subject to the death penalty, regardless of whether they intended to seek authorization to pursue the death penalty. These cases were first reviewed by the attorney general's Review Committee on Capital Cases, a committee of senior Justice Department lawyers.

The period 1995–2000, which provides a more extensive picture of the Justice Department's internal decision process as it pertains to the federal death penalty, showed that between January 27, 1995, and July 20, 2000, at every phase of the federal process, minority defendants were overrepresented. Of the 682 defendants whose cases were submitted for review by federal prosecutors, 19.6% were white, 47.5% were African-American, and 28.6% were Hispanic. The prosecutors recommended seeking the death penalty for 183 of 682 cases submitted for review. Of these 183 cases, about two-thirds (44.3% African-Americans and 21.3% Hispanics) were members of minorities. The attorney general reviewed 588 of the cases and authorized the U.S. attorneys to seek the death penalty in 159 cases. Of the 159 defendants, 44.7% were

TABLE 7.14

Distribution of defendants within each stage of the federal death penalty process, 1995–2000

State	Total #	Total %	White #	White %	Black #	Black %	Hispanic #	Hispanic %	Other #	Other %
Submitted by U.S. attorneys	682	100.0%	134	19.6%	324	47.5%	195	28.6%	29	4.3%
No recommendation	5	100.0%	1	20.0%	1	20.0%	3	60.0%	0	0.0%
Recommendation not to seek death penalty (DP)	494	100.0%	85	17.2%	242	49.0%	153	31.0%	14	2.8%
Recommendation to seek DP	183	100.0%	48	26.2%	81	44.3%	39	21.3%	15	8.2%
Considered by review committee	618	100.0%	119	19.3%	301	48.7%	172	27.8%	26	4.2%
No recommendation	15	100.0%	4	26.7%	6	40.0%	4	26.7%	1	6.7%
Recommendation not to seek DP	420	100.0%	68	16.2%	215	51.2%	125	29.8%	12	2.9%
Recommendation to seek DP	183	100.0%	47	25.7%	80	43.7%	43	23.5%	13	7.1%
Considered by attorney general (AG)	588	100.0%	115	19.6%	287	48.8%	160	27.2%	26	4.4%
Decision deferred or pending	12	100.0%	3	25.0%	4	33.3%	4	33.3%	1	8.3%
Authorization not to seek DP	417	100.0%	68	16.3%	212	50.8%	124	29.7%	13	3.1%
Authorization to seek DP	159	100.0%	44	27.7%	71	44.7%	32	20.1%	12	7.5%
Authorized by AG to seek DP	159	100.0%	44	27.7%	71	44.7%	32	20.1%	12	7.5%
DP notice withdrawn—plea agreement	51	100.0%	21	41.2%	18	35.3%	9	17.6%	3	5.9%
DP notice withdrawn—subsequent AG decision	11	100.0%	1	9.1%	3	27.3%	5	45.5%	2	18.2%
DP notice dismissed or trial terminated	4	100.0%	0	0.0%	1	25.0%	3	75.0%	0	0.0%
Pending trial or completion of trial	51	100.0%	11	21.6%	23	45.1%	13	25.5%	4	7.8%
Not convicted of capital charge	1	100.0%	0	0.0%	1	100.0%	0	0.0%	0	0.0%
Convicted of capital charge	41	100.0%	11	26.8%	25	61.0%	2	4.9%	3	7.3%
Convicted of capital charge	41	100.0%	11	26.8%	25	61.0%	2	4.9%	3	7.3%
Jury verdict—DP not recommended	21	100.0%	7	33.3%	12	57.1%	0	0.0%	2	9.5%
Jury verdict—DP recommended	20	100.0%	4	20.0%	13	65.0%	2	10.0%	1	5.0%
Sentenced to death	20	100.0%	4	20.0%	13	65.0%	2	10.0%	1	5.0%
DP recommended by jury but not yet imposed	2	100.0%	0	0.0%	0	0.0%	2	100.0%	0	0.0%
DP vacated by court, further action pending	4	100.0%	1	25.0%	3	75.0%	0	0.0%	0	0.0%
Death sentence pending	14	100.0%	3	21.4%	10	71.4%	0	0.0%	1	7.1%

SOURCE: "Table 1A. Distribution of Defendants within Each Stage of the Federal Death Penalty Process (1995–2000)," in *The Federal Death Penalty System: A Statistical Survey (1988–2000)*, U.S. Department of Justice, September 12, 2000, http://www.usdoj.gov/dag/pubdoc/_dp_survey_final.pdf (accessed October 20, 2003)

African-American and 20.1% were Hispanic. Only about 28% were white. (See Table 7.14.)

Racial Disparity in Plea Bargaining

It should be noted that the attorney general's decision to seek the death penalty may be changed up until the jury has returned a sentencing verdict. This change may be sought by the defense lawyer, the U.S. attorney, the Review Committee, or by the attorney general. A plea agreement is one avenue that may result in the withdrawal of the death penalty. This means that the defendant enters into an agreement with the U.S. attorney resulting in a guilty plea, saving him or her from the death penalty. From 1995 to 2000, after the attorney general sought the death penalty for 159 defendants, fifty-one defendants entered into plea agreements. Almost twice as many white defendants (48%, or twenty-one out of forty-four) as African-Americans (25%, or eighteen of seventy-one) received a plea agreement. About 28% (nine of thirty-two) of Hispanics entered into a plea agreement. (See Table 7.14.)

Government Defends Data

The National Institute of Justice observed in their solicitation entitled "Research into the Investigation and Prosecution of Homicide: Examining the Federal Death Penalty System" (Washington, DC, July 2001) that, "generally speaking, once submitted for review [to obtain a death penalty authorization], minorities proceeded to the next stages in the death penalty process at lower rates than whites." The institute claimed that the attorney general authorized the death penalty for a larger proportion of whites being considered (38%, or forty-four of 115), compared with 25% (seventy-one of 287) of African-American defendants and 20% (thirty-two of 160) of Hispanic defendants. (See Table 7.14.)

SECOND FEDERAL STUDY OF RACIAL AND ETHNIC BIAS

On June 6, 2001, the Justice Department released a supplement to the September 2000 report—*The Federal Death Penalty System: Supplementary Data, Analysis and Revised Protocols for Capital Case Review*. That same day Attorney General John Ashcroft told the Judiciary Committee of the U.S. House of Representatives that the report confirmed that the subsequent study of the administration of the federal death penalty showed no indication of racial or ethnic bias.

The follow-up study had been ordered by his predecessor, Attorney General Janet Reno. In addition to the 682 cases submitted by federal prosecutors for review in the first study of the federal death penalty, another 291 cases were analyzed, for a total of 973 cases. These included cases that should have been submitted for review for the first report but were not, those in which the defendant eventually entered into a plea agreement for a lesser sentence, and cases in which the death penalty could have been sought but was not. Among the 973 defendants, 17% (166) were white, 42% (408) were African-American, and 36% (350) were Hispanic.

According to the supplement, from 1995 to 2000, of the 973 defendants eligible for capital charges, federal prosecutors requested authorization to pursue the death penalty against 81% of whites, 79% of African-Americans, and 56% of Hispanics. The attorney general ultimately authorized seeking the death penalty for 27% of the white defendants, 17% of the African-American defendants, and 9% of the Hispanic defendants.

Critics of the supplementary report pointed out that the second federal review failed to address many issues. Following the release of the September 2000 survey, Attorney General Reno ordered a study to find out how death penalty cases are taken into the federal system when there is joint state and federal jurisdiction. The June report did not cover this issue. Instead, the report described a National Institute of Justice (NIJ) meeting on January 10, 2001, in which researchers and practitioners agreed that such a study "would entail a highly complex, multi-year research initiative" and that "even if such a study were carried out, it could not be expected to yield definitive answers concerning the reasons for disparities in federal death penalty."

Testifying before the Senate Judiciary Committee on June 11, 2001, David C. Baldus of the University of Iowa reported that he was one of the researchers at the NIJ January 2001 meeting. Baldus claimed that, while it was true he and others at the meeting agreed that the study ordered by Attorney General Reno would likely take two years to complete, the consensus was that "such a study would provide the best possible evidence on the question." Baldus further pointed out that quite some time had elapsed since that meeting and the first report, and still the Justice Department had not taken any steps to initiate such a study.

On July 20, 2001, the NIJ published the above-mentioned solicitation for research of the federal death penalty, including the decision-making factors that determine whether a homicide case is prosecuted in the federal or state system, as well as issues of race/ethnicity and geography in the imposition of the death penalty. This allows researchers to apply for government grants in order to complete the requested research, but such research has yet to be undertaken.

The American Civil Liberties Union (ACLU) noted that, unlike the September 2000 report, the new Justice Department report did not include information on whether the supplemental 291 cases were from all or just some districts and, therefore, whether or not they represented all of the death penalty–eligible cases between 1995 and 2000. The ACLU also pointed out that, while the report found that federal prosecutors were less likely to submit cases of African-American and Hispanic defendants to the attorney general for death penalty authorizations and that the attorney general authorized capital punishment for a higher proportion of whites than African-Americans and Hispanics, there was no information about the decision-making process behind prosecuting on the federal level and of offering plea agreements.

STUDIES ANALYZING THE ERROR RATE IN THE U.S. DEATH PENALTY SYSTEM

Liebman Study

James S. Liebman, Jeffrey Fagan, and Valerie West conducted the first study of its kind—a statistical study of modern American capital appeals—for the U.S. Senate Judiciary Committee. The study, called *A Broken System: Error Rates in Capital Cases, 1973–1995* (June 12, 2000), examined all death penalty sentences (5,760) imposed in the United States over a twenty-three-year period.

On direct appeal, the state high courts reviewed 4,578 death sentences. The study found that 68% of the death sentences reviewed by courts across the country were found to have serious errors. For every one hundred death sentences, forty-one were returned to the courts during state appeal because of serious errors. Of the fifty-nine death sentences that reached the second state appeal, another six went back to court because of errors. At the third level of appeal—with the federal courts—twenty-one more cases were remanded to the lower courts because of errors found. All in all, of the original one hundred death penalty sentences, sixty-eight had serious errors that required retrial. Of the sixty-eight defendants who were retried, 82% (fifty-six) were found not deserving of the death penalty. Another five inmates were found not guilty of the capital crime for which they received the death sentence.

THE LIEBMAN STUDY IS ANALYZED. Critics have challenged the results of the Liebman study. Appearing before the U.S. Senate Committee on the Judiciary hearing on "Reducing the Risk of Executing the Innocent: The Report of the Illinois Governor's Commission on Capital Punishment" (June 12, 2002), Senator Strom Thurmond (R-SC) warned,

> A Columbia University report known as the Liebman study is often cited as proof that capital punishment in this country is deeply flawed. This study . . . alleged that from 1973 to 1995, 70% of death penalty convictions were reversed on appeal. The implication is that 70% of the time, innocent people were sentenced to death. This study should be viewed carefully because during the time period addressed by this study, the Supreme Court issued a series of retroactive rules that nullified a number of verdicts. These reversals were not based on the actual innocence of defendants, but rather were based on procedural rules.

Nevada Attorney General Frankie Sue Del Papa also took issue with Liebman's conclusions. According to the attorney general, Liebman claimed that, in Nevada, of the 108 death sentences, thirty-four were reversed, accounting for an error rate of 38%. (The correct percentage is 31.5%.) The attorney general's researchers found 152 cases with thirty death sentence reversals for an error rate of 19.7%. Liebman also used a two-year period to determine the reversal rate of federal *habeas appeals*. He reached an overall error rate of 50% after finding two reversals out of four that underwent federal review. Del Papa's office found seventeen federal reviews with four reversals for a 23.5% error rate. According to Del Papa,

> Liebman creates the impression that the reversals are due to innocence, but most are attorney or judge procedural errors. Some are cases where juries followed the existing law, but later the Supreme Court changed it, and constitutional changes are applied retroactively on death cases, to give the defendant every benefit. Liebman also failed to report that after a new trial or penalty hearing, in twelve of those thirty-one cases death sentences were imposed again. In thirteen cases, inmates received "life-in-prison" sentences. Those were not inmates found to be innocent of their murders!

Latzer Study

Barry Latzer and James N. G. Cauthen noted that their reexamination of the Liebman study found that about one-fourth (27%)—and not two-thirds (68%)—of capital convictions were reversed between 1973 and 1995. In "Capital Appeals Revisited" (*Judicature* 84, no. 2, September-October 2000), the authors noted that the Liebman study did not differentiate between reversals of convictions and reversals of death sentences.

Latzer and Cauthen conducted their own investigation, based on the theory that many of the appeals resulted in reversed sentences but not reversed convictions. The study covered the period 1990–99, using reversal data in the same twenty-six states studied by Liebman and his collea-

TABLE 7.15

Capital case reversals by state courts, 1990–1999

State reversals	Conviction reversals		Sentence only	
Alabama	19	(.76)	6	(.24)
Arizona	15	(.45)	18	(.55)
Arkansas	7	(.44)	9	(.56)
California	8	(.57)	6	(.43)
Florida	66	(.28)	173	(.72)
Georgia	18	(.67)	9	(.33)
Idaho	0	(.00)	3	(1.00)
Illinois	35	(.58)	25	(.42)
Indiana	3	(.16)	16	(.84)
Kentucky	7	(.64)	4	(.36)
Louisiana	10	(.50)	10	(.50)
Maryland	7	(.47)	8	(.53)
Mississippi	25	(.45)	31	(.55)
Missouri	10	(.45)	12	(.54)
Montana	0	(.00)	3	(1.00)
Nebraska	1	(1.00)	0	(.00)
Nevada	6	(.33)	12	(.67)
North Carolina	28	(.29)	68	(.71)
Oklahoma	27	(.42)	37	(.58)
Pennsylvania	15	(.41)	22	(.59)
South Carolina	9	(.45)	11	(.55)
Tennessee	3	(.14)	19	(.86)
Texas	2	(.40)	3	(.60)
Utah	3	(1.00)	0	(.00)
Virginia	4	(.57)	3	(.43)
Wyoming	0	(.00)	1	(1.00)
Total	**328**	**(.39)**	**509**	**(.61)**

Notes: Includes all capital case reversals of conviction or sentence by state courts of last resort on direct appeal or post-conviction review decided between January 1, 1990 and December 31, 1999. Numbers in parentheses are proportions for each state and, at the bottom of the table, for all states.

SOURCE: Barry Latzer and James N. G. Cauthen, "Table 1. Capital Case Reversals by State Courts, 1990–1999," in "Capital Appeals Revisited," *Judicature*, vol. 84, no. 2, September–October 2000, pp. 64–71, http://www.lib.jjay.cuny.edu/docs/latzer.pdf (accessed June 1, 2005)

gues. Latzer and Cauthen wanted more recent data of the death penalty system that would provide more complete reversal rate differences.

The authors found that, of the 837 death penalty reversals in state-level direct appeal or postconviction review, 61% were sentence reversals, and 39% were conviction reversals (reversals addressing the guilt or innocence of the defendant). Using Liebman's conclusion that five of ten capital judgments were reversed at either the direct-appeal phase or postconviction review phase, Latzer and Cauthen applied this finding to their study and concluded that, of the five reversals, three were sentence reversals and two were conviction reversals. (See Table 7.15.)

The authors also investigated reversals at the federal level—the third stage of death penalty judgment review—using data from the Ninth Circuit Court of Appeals, the largest of the circuit courts. Of the twenty-nine capital cases reversed by the court during the ten-year period, twenty-one (72.4%) were sentence reversals, and eight (27.7%) were conviction reversals. This was consistent with the authors' findings regarding direct-appeal and

FIGURE 7.4

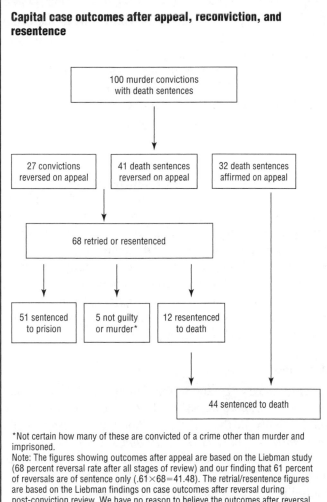

Capital case outcomes after appeal, reconviction, and resentence

100 murder convictions with death sentences

27 convictions reversed on appeal

41 death sentences reversed on appeal

32 death sentences affirmed on appeal

68 retried or resentenced

51 sentenced to prision

5 not guilty or murder*

12 resentenced to death

44 sentenced to death

*Not certain how many of these are convicted of a crime other than murder and imprisoned.
Note: The figures showing outcomes after appeal are based on the Liebman study (68 percent reversal rate after all stages of review) and our finding that 61 percent of reversals are of sentence only (.61×68=41.48). The retrial/resentence figures are based on the Liebman findings on case outcomes after reversal during post-conviction review. We have no reason to believe the outcomes after reversal at other stages of review are any different from the outcomes after reversal on post-conviction review.

SOURCE: Barry Latzer and James N. G. Cauthen, "Figure 1. Capital Case Outcomes after Appeal, Reconviction, and Resentence," in "Capital Appeals Revisited," *Judicature*, vol. 84, no. 2, September–October 2000, pp. 64–71, http://www.lib.jjay.cuny.edu/docs/latzer.pdf (accessed June 1, 2005)

postconviction sentence reversals at the state level. Using Liebman's finding that sixty-eight of one hundred capital judgments were reversed, Latzer and Cauthen concluded, "If sixty-eight of one hundred capital decisions are reversed after direct, postconviction, and federal *habeas corpus* review, and 39% of these are conviction reversals, then convictions in 26.5 (39% of sixty-eight) of one hundred capital decisions are reversed." Figure 7.4 presents Latzer and Cauthen's findings on the capital case outcomes for a typical group of a hundred murder convictions with death sentences.

DEATH ROW AND MURDER RATES

In "Explaining Death Row's Population and Racial Composition" (*Journal of Empirical Legal Studies* 1, no. 1, March 2004), John Blume, Theodore Eisenberg, and Martin T. Wells, compared twenty-three years of death row statistics to state murder rates. They found that between 1977 and 1999 the number of death row inmates in most states, including those with a reputation for sending a high number of defendants to death row, was nearly proportional to the number of murders in that state.

Overall, the number of inmates on death row in each state was between 0.4% (Colorado) and 6% (Nevada) of murders in that state, and the mean "death sentencing rate" among all states was 2.2%. Despite having the highest number of executions per year, Texas came in below this average with a death row to murder ratio of 2%. While Texas juries sentenced 776 people to death row, a total of 37,879 murders had been committed during the study period. Florida, which had a total death row population of 735 inmates, had experienced 121,837 murders and a death sentencing rate of 3.4%. Nevada, on the other hand, had 124 death row inmates, but only 2,072 murders, giving the state a death sentencing rate three times that of Texas. California, Virginia, Washington, New Mexico, and Maryland all had death sentencing rates below 1.5%.

To explain the slight discrepancy between states, the researchers looked at the states' statutes, politics, and other factors that might influence sentencing rates. They discovered that death sentencing rates were nearly twice as high in states where a judge handed out the sentence as opposed to a jury (4.1% versus 2.1%). State statutes also made a big difference. States with more open-ended statutes that allowed a jury to base their verdicts on subjective standards, such as the heinousness of the murder, had sentencing rates of 2.7%. Sentencing rates dropped to 1.9% in states where specific murders, such as the murder of a pregnant woman or police officer, warranted the death sentence.

The researchers then compared the race of the death row inmates to the number of murders committed by race across the country. Nationwide, African-Americans committed 51.5% of murders between 1977 and 1999, but they only made up 41.3% of death row. The researchers analyzed data from seven states—Georgia, Indiana, Maryland, Nevada, Pennsylvania, South Carolina, and Virginia—to determine why these percentages did not match up.

Generally, what they found was that juries give the death sentence to a far smaller percentage of African-American murderers when the victim was also African-American, rather than white. In South Carolina, for instance, only 0.3% of African-Americans who kill African-Americans received the death penalty, whereas 6.8% of African-Americans who murdered whites were sentenced to death. Since most African-American homicide victims were killed by African-Americans (94%), the percentage of African-Americans on death row tended to be lower than the percentage of African-American murderers. While the researchers speculated that racism may figure into these percentages, they also believed that African-American juries in communities with a great deal of black-on-black crime were less likely to hand out the death sentence.

STATES' IMPOSITION OF THE DEATH PENALTY

Many studies have been conducted to analyze the death penalty systems of individual states. Extensive studies have been performed on Arizona, Connecticut, Delaware, Illinois, Indiana, Kansas, Maryland, Nebraska, Nevada, North Carolina, Ohio, Pennsylvania, Tennessee, Texas, and Virginia. Some of the studies were commissioned by the states, and others were performed by nongovernmental organizations. Among other flaws in the capital punishment system, the studies generally pointed to problems of racial inequality, inadequate legal representation for indigent defendants, and the high cost of the death penalty. The findings and the impacts of some of these studies follow.

Ohio

The Ohio Associated Press published an extensive study on the Ohio death penalty system on May 7, 2005. The news organization reviewed 2,543 reported cases in which prisoners were brought up on capital charges between 1981 and 2002. This number was narrowed to 1,936 after analysts weeded out charges dismissed or erroneously reported. Roughly 270 of the indictments led to a death sentence. The AP analyzed the indictments to find any discrepancies in sentencing involving race, sex, or jurisdiction. The results were presented in the three-part series "Death Penalty Unequal" (Andrew Welsh-Huggins, *Cincinnati Enquirer*, May 7–9, 2005).

With respect to race, those indicted of capital murder in Ohio were much more likely to receive the death sentence if the victim was white. Some 17.9% of indictments led to a death sentence if the victim was white, as opposed to 8.5% if the victim was African-American. However, unlike the Baldus study, these percentages were not dependent on the race of the defendant. In cases where the offender and victim were both white, 18.3% of offenders received the death sentence. Roughly the same number of African-American offenders (17.9%) were sentenced to death if the victim was white. If the victim was African-American, 8.4% of African-American offenders were sentenced to death, compared with 8.7% for white offenders.

Jurisdiction had a bigger impact than race on who received the death sentence in Ohio. The AP looked at indictments by county and compared the numbers with those aspects of each county that might influence death penalty verdicts. The news organization found that the politics of a county played a significant role in determining the percentage of defendants who received the death penalty. Hamilton County (Cincinnati metropolitan area) and Cuyahoga County (Cleveland metropolitan area) are both large counties that paid their defense attorneys reasonably well. Yet, only 8% of all capital cases ended with a death sentence in Democratic Cuyahoga County, as opposed to 43% in the largely Republican Hamilton County.

The Ohio report also found that compensation for lawyers who represent poor defendants varied drastically from county to county. The limits ranged from $3,000 maximum per death penalty case in rural Coshocton County (east-central Ohio) up to $75,000 in the more affluent Montgomery County (Dayton metropolitan area). Generally, death penalty cases place an enormous strain on the resources of a small county court as opposed to a large county court. Rural judges reported having to dedicate all their resources for months on end when capital cases came through their courts.

Maryland

On January 7, 2003, the University of Maryland released a state-commissioned study of the use of the death penalty in the state (Raymond Paternoster et al., *An Empirical Analysis of Maryland's Death Sentencing System with Respect to the Influence of Race and Legal Jurisdiction*). The researchers reviewed 1,311 death-eligible cases out of 6,000 murder cases prosecuted between 1978 and 1999. Of the 1,311 death-eligible cases, state attorneys filed a formal notice to seek the death penalty in 353 cases (27%). Of the 353 cases, state attorneys dropped the death penalty notice in 140 cases (40%). The death penalty notice was retained in 213 cases (60%), out of which 180 cases (84.5%) proceeded to the penalty phase.

The researchers examined the four decision stages in the death penalty sentencing system—the prosecutor's decision to seek the death penalty, the prosecutor's decision to drop or stick with the death penalty notice, the case's proceeding to a penalty trial, and the court's decision to impose the death sentence. The researchers "found no evidence that the race of the defendant matter[ed] in the processing of capital cases in the state." However, the race of the victim had an impact on whether the prosecutor sought the death penalty. Prosecutors were more likely to seek the death penalty for killers of white victims and were more likely to stick with their death penalty notification when the victims were white. However, the researchers found that

> Among the subset of cases where a death notice "sticks" (i.e., is not retracted), the effect of the victim's race on whether the case progresses to a penalty trial is

not statistically significant (although the sign of the effect suggests that white victims are more likely to receive a penalty trial if they make it to this stage). Among the subset of cases where the case actually does reach a penalty trial, the victim's race does not have a significant impact on the imposition of a death sentence.

The study also revealed that jurisdictions affected whether state attorneys sought the death penalty. A defendant in Baltimore County was twenty-six times more likely to be sentenced to death than a defendant in Baltimore City. A defendant was fourteen times more likely to get the death penalty in Baltimore County than in Montgomery County and seven times more likely to get the death penalty in Prince George's County.

North Carolina

On April 16, 2001, Isaac Unah and John Charles Boger released the most comprehensive study of North Carolina's death penalty system in the state's history (*Race and the Death Penalty in North Carolina, an Empirical Analysis: 1993–1997*, University of North Carolina at Chapel Hill and the Common Sense Foundation, NC). The researchers studied all 3,990 homicide cases between 1993 and 1997, including defendants who received death sentences, as well as those sentenced to life imprisonment.

On first analysis of all homicide cases, the researchers found that, overall, the death-sentencing rate where white victims were involved was almost twice as high (3.7%) as the rate where the victims were nonwhite (1.9%). In addition, the death-sentencing rate for nonwhite defendants/white victims (6.4%) was nearly two-and-a-half times higher than the rate for white defendants/white victims (2.6%).

When the researchers confined their investigation to death-eligible cases (those imposing the death penalty, such as a case involving the murder of a police officer), race determined whether the defendant received the death sentence. The death-sentencing rate in all death-eligible cases was much higher in white-victim cases (8%) than in cases in which the victims were nonwhite (4.7%). As with all cases, nonwhite defendants in white-victim homicides received the death sentence at a higher rate (11.6%) than white defendants who murdered whites (6.1%).

After the initial analysis, Unah and Boger performed a more comprehensive investigation involving 502 defendants, collecting 113 factors about each crime. These factors included the circumstances of the homicide, the evidence, the charges brought against the defendant, the character and background of the defendant and the victim, the presence or absence of aggravating or mitigating circumstances as specified under the law, as well as the presence or absence of aggravating or mitigating circumstances not specified under the law. The researchers also looked into other factors that might have influenced the imposition of the death penalty, such as the coming reelection of the district attorney prosecuting the crime. In the end, the researchers found that race—specifically the race of the victim—indeed played a role in the imposition of capital punishment in North Carolina from 1993 to 1997. On average, the odds of receiving the death penalty were increased by a factor of three-and-a-half times when the victim was white.

Texas

On June 14, 2001, Governor Rick Perry signed the Texas Fair Defense Act (Senate Bill 7), providing, for the first time, state funding for indigent defense services. The $12 million yearly appropriation helps establish public defender offices. Two lawyers are provided in capital cases, unless the state indicates in writing that it will not seek the death penalty. The law also limits judges' powers by requiring appointments be made from a rotating list of qualified lawyers. Moreover, courts must pay reasonable fees, including necessary overhead reimbursements.

Under the law, death penalty lawyers have to attend annual training on capital defense in order to remain on the rotating list. In addition, Senate Bill 7 established a Texas Task Force on Indigent Defense to be responsible for setting standards for lawyers. The task force also monitors the operation of the public defender programs in the counties. The task force and the county capital appointment committee review the list of lawyers who handle capital cases.

The Texas Fair Defense Act was passed as a result of findings by Texas Appleseed, a nonpartisan legal advocacy group. On December 12, 2000, Texas Appleseed reported that, unlike other active death penalty states, Texas had been "virtually alone" in not having a statewide program to assist indigent defendants with legal representation (*The Fair Defense Report: Analysis of Indigent Defense Practices in Texas*, Texas Appleseed Fair Defense Project, Austin, TX). As of November 20, 2000, among states that most actively imposed the death penalty, Texas was one of two states that did not fund indigent defense representation (Arizona was the other state). Texas was also the only state that had no statewide oversight commission, public defender agencies, and capital trial unit.

Texas Appleseed pointed out that Texas did not have an oversight commission that could have developed standards for appointment and compensation of lawyers in capital cases. In some states, a similar commission further monitors the performance of defense counsel and the judges' fee decisions.

Many death penalty states have a specialized statewide capital trial unit that assists court-appointed private defense lawyers. In addition, nine states—Colorado, Connecticut, Delaware, Maryland, Missouri, New Hampshire, New Jersey, New Mexico, and Wyoming—have a public defender program, most of which provide public defenders in every county statewide. Texas, however, used private lawyers appointed by judges on a case-by-case basis. These lawyers lacked the support of a public defender system that could have made available the expertise of other lawyers more experienced in capital cases, as well as the training programs that such a system provides.

Nebraska

In May 1999 the Nebraska legislature became the first in the country to pass a bill proposing a two-year moratorium on executions. The bill also called for a study, during the moratorium, to determine the fairness of the administration of the death penalty. Governor Mike Johanns vetoed the bill. The governor also vetoed the proposed study, but the legislature overrode his veto.

On July 25, 2001, the Nebraska Commission on Law Enforcement and Criminal Justice released its findings of the state death penalty (David C. Baldus, George Woodworth, Gary L. Young, and Aaron M. Christ, *The Disposition of Nebraska Capital and Non-Capital Homicide Cases [1973–1999]: A Legal and Empirical Analysis).* The researchers reviewed more than 700 homicide cases that resulted in a conviction. They then closely examined the decision-making process in 177 death-eligible cases, twenty-seven of which received the death sentence. The study did not find racial bias in the use of the death penalty. White defendants (15%) were just as likely as nonwhite defendants (16%) to receive the death penalty. The study also concluded that there was no significant evidence of unfair treatment based on the victim's race—17% of defendants who murdered white victims and 11% of defendants who murdered minority victims were sentenced to death.

The study found, however, that death-eligible defendants who murdered victims of "high socioeconomic status" were nearly four times as likely to receive the death sentence than those who murdered poor victims, even when similar crimes had been committed. In addition, the study found geographic disparities in seeking the death penalty. Prosecutors in rural capital trials were more likely to seek the death penalty than their urban counterparts (31% versus 20%).

COSTS OF THE DEATH PENALTY

Most death penalty opponents advocate life imprisonment without the chance of parole as an alternative to the death sentence. Some people, however, believe that capital punishment costs the taxpayers less than a life sentence without parole. Several studies have found that the death penalty costs more than life imprisonment without parole. Hugo Adam Bedau, in *The Case against the Death Penalty* (Washington, DC: American Civil Liberties Union, 1997), found that a "murder trial normally takes longer when the death penalty is at issue than when it is not. Litigation costs—including the time of judges, prosecutors, public defenders, and court reporters, and the high costs of briefs—are mostly borne by the taxpayer."

In January 2000 the *Palm Beach Post* estimated that the death penalty cost Florida $51 million more than the cost of incarcerating all first-degree murderers without parole. The Department of Legislative Services of Maryland's General Assembly reported that it cost approximately $2.3 million to move a death row defendant through the system. In contrast, keeping the same inmate in prison cost about $19,200 annually, totaling about $768,000 for forty years of confinement.

California

After combing through state and federal records, Rone Tempest of the *Los Angeles Times* reported in "Death Row Often Means a Long Life" (March 6, 2005) that the death penalty system in California cost taxpayers more than $114 million each year. This amount was above and beyond what it would have cost to imprison California's 640 death row inmates for life without parole. The state spent $58 million ($90,000 per prisoner) simply by housing these inmates on death row, where they lived in a private cell and were surrounded by more guards than normal prisoners. Huge costs were also incurred during executions. Since California reinstated its death penalty in 1978, eleven people have been executed. Each of these executions cost taxpayers approximately $250 million. The death penalty also has burdened the courts. According to Ronald George, the Chief Justice of the California Supreme Court, the Supreme Court spent 20% of its resources on capital cases. In the end, the state still did not have enough money to appoint lawyers to 115 death row inmates for their first direct appeal.

Washington

In "Washington State's Death Penalty System: A Review of the Costs, Length, and Results of Capital Cases in Washington State" (November 2004), the Washington Death Penalty Assistance Center (WDPAC) reviewed costs incurred under Washington's capital punishment system between 1999 and 2003. The WDPAC, a not-for-profit organization in Seattle that provides training and resources to capital defense attorneys, found that on average, a non–death penalty trial costs half as much as a death penalty trial. One estimate revealed that a death penalty trial cost about $432,000, and a non–death penalty trial cost approximately $153,000. Capital punishment trials also take much longer than normal criminal trials. A typical death penalty trial lasted roughly twenty months compared with fifteen months for a non–death penalty trial. A death penalty appellate review took on average two years, which was four times longer than a non–death penalty review.

Despite the exorbitant costs of death penalty trials, very few people sentenced to death in Washington have actually been executed. Between 1981—the year Washington reinstated capital punishment—and 2003, thirty-one death sentences were handed down in the state. Twenty-two convicts completed their appellate review by 2003; eight were still awaiting their reviews, and one had been exonerated. Of those convicts who received their review, eighteen had their death sentences reversed after an average of 6.9 years in the appeals processes. Three of the remaining four offenders were executed after effectively waiving their appellate review. Only one person was executed after exhausting all options, which took eleven years.

Kansas

In December 2003 the State of Kansas issued a report entitled "Performance Audit Report: Costs Incurred for Death Penalty Cases." The state found that death penalty murder cases cost an average of $1.26 million from when the murder investigation begins to when the sentence is carried out. Murder cases where the death penalty was neither sought nor given cost $740,000.

The state itemized these costs for each stage of a death penalty case. The cost of investigating a case in which the defendant was sentenced to death was $145,000, compared with $66,000 for a death penalty case in which the defendant received a lesser sentence and $47,000 for a non–death penalty case. The average price tag for a trial that resulted in a death sentence was nearly sixteen times greater than for a non–death penalty trial ($508,000 as opposed to $32,000), and the appeal was twenty-one times greater ($401,000 compared with $19,000). Keeping a convict on death row in Kansas was found to cost roughly half as much as detaining a murderer for whom the death penalty was never sought ($350,000 versus $659,000). Kansas, however, did not have a large death row population. Only seven inmates were on death row as of December 2004, and no one had been executed in Kansas since the death penalty was reinstated in 1994.

Connecticut

Connecticut's Commission on the Death Penalty submitted a report to the state General Assembly on January 8, 2003 ("Study Pursuant to Public Act No. 01-151 of the Imposition of the Death Penalty in Connecticut") that included the cost of prosecuting capital cases. As of January 2002 Connecticut had seven death row inmates and had not executed any. The last execution occurred in 1960. Since Connecticut has not carried out an execution, the commission did not present any comparison between the cost of implementing the death penalty and keeping an inmate in prison without the possibility of parole. Nonetheless, the commission was able to illustrate the defense costs for defendants sentenced to death (following trial and sentencing), compared to the defense costs incurred by defendants receiving life imprisonment without parole (also following trial and sentencing).

The commission reviewed the cases of the seven men on death row from 1973 to 2002. The defense costs ranged from nearly $102,000 to $1.07 million, with an average cost of about $380,000 per case. The prisoners serving life sentences without parole included those incarcerated from 1989 to 2001. Their defense costs ranged from $86,000 to $321,000, with an average cost of about $202,000 per inmate. In 2003–04 the Connecticut Division of Public Defender Services spent approximately $2 million for capital cases (http://www.ocpd.state.ct.us/, "Cost of Public Defender Services: Cost Attributable to the Death Penalty," March 1, 2005).

New York

Daniel Wise investigated the costs of the death penalty in New York since its reinstatement in 1995 ("Capital Punishment Proves to be Expensive," *New York Law Journal* 227, April 30, 2002). Defense costs had amounted to $68.4 million by that time. No national system is in place to track prosecution costs; however, the state Division of Criminal Justice Services paid counties that prosecuted capital cases $5.1 million between 1995 and March 2001. Each year the allocation for the New York Court of Appeals increased by more than $533,000 to allow for the salary of an extra clerk for each of the seven judges. The New York Prosecutors Training Institute, which assists district lawyers in capital cases, costs $1.2 million annually to operate. The defense for Darrel Harris, the first person to be sentenced to death under New York's 1995 law, had spent about $1.7 million, while the Capital Defender Office spent $1.2 million just to prepare the brief. (Harris's conviction was subsequently ruled unconstitutional.) The Department of Correctional Services spent $1.3 million to construct a new death row, allocating another $300,000 annually to guard it.

Federal Death Penalty Costs

Since the passage of the Violent Crime Control and Law Enforcement Act (P.L. 103-322; also known as the Federal Death Penalty Act of 1994), the number of federal prosecutions, including crimes punishable by death, has risen. The Subcommittee on Federal Death Penalty Cases of the Committee on Defender Services of the Judicial Conference of the United States, in *Federal Death Penalty Cases: Recommendations Concerning the Cost and Quality of Defense Representation* (Washington, D.C., 1998), estimated that about 560 federal death penalty cases were filed between 1991 and 1997. The numbers increased each year. In 1991 there were twelve cases, rising nearly tenfold to 118 in 1995, and reaching 159 and 153 cases in 1996 and 1997, respectively.

Although the decision to charge a crime punishable by death is made by the local federal prosecutor, the U.S. attorney general alone authorizes the seeking of the death penalty. Between 1988 and December 1997, the U.S. attorney general authorized seeking capital punishment in 111 cases. The attorney general's decision to authorize seeking the death penalty makes a substantial difference in the cost of representing a defendant. According to the Judicial Conference of the United States, Committee on Defender Services, from 1990 to 1997 the average total cost (for counsel and related services) per representation of a sample of cases in which the defendant was charged with non-capital homicide was $9,159. In contrast, in those cases in which the defendant was charged with an offense punishable by death and the attorney general authorized seeking the death penalty, the average cost was $218,113. This included cases resolved by a guilty plea as well as cases resolved by a trial. In contrast, the average total cost per representation in which the defendant was charged with an offense punishable by death where the attorney general did not authorize seeking the death penalty was $55,773. (See Table 7.16.) According to the Web site of the U.S. Senate Appropriations Committee (http://appropriations.senate.gov/), by fiscal year 2005 the budget for Defender Services had grown to $676.4 million, $78.2 million above the 2004 level.

The decision whether to go to trial or to enter a guilty plea also affects the cost of representing the alleged offender. During the study period 1988 to 1997, of the 111 cases in which the attorney general sought the death sentence, forty-one were tried for capital charges. Cases that ended in capital trials cost an average of $269,139, compared with $192,333 for cases resolved with a guilty plea. (See Table 7.16.)

Since a death penalty case differs from other cases in that a defendant's life is at stake, the defense generally devotes more time to the case. One time-consuming aspect of defense involves prolonged jury selection. While jury selection in non-capital cases may take a couple of days, in capital cases it may take several months. Table 7.17 shows the difference in the number of billable hours in capital and non-capital homicide cases as compiled by the Subcommittee on Federal Death Penalty Cases.

TABLE 7.16

Average amount of non-attorney compensation in capital and non-capital homicide cases, 1997

	Case type	Avg. amount of non-attorney comp.	Avg. total cost of representation (attorney and non-attorney)
Non-capital	Homicides	$ 1,515	$ 9,159
Capital	Auth. denied	$10,094	$ 55,773
	Auth. granted	$51,889	$218,113
	Capital trial	$53,143	$269,139
	Plea	$51,028	$192,333
	Drug cases	$52,218	$244,186

SOURCE: "Average Amount of Non-Attorney Compensation in Capital and Non-Capital Homicide Cases," in *Federal Death Penalty Cases: Recommendations Concerning the Cost and Quality of Defense Representation*, Judicial Conference of the United States, Committee on Defender Services, Subcommittee on Federal Death Penalty Cases, 1998, http://www.uscourts.gov/dpenalty/4REPORT.htm (accessed October 20, 2003)

TABLE 7.17

Average number of attorney hours billed in capital and non-capital homicide cases, 1992–1997

	Case type	In court hours	Out of court hours	Avg. total attorney hours per representation
Non-capital	Homicides	18	100	117
Capital	Auth. denied	38	391	429
	Auth. granted	231	1,233	1,464
	Capital trial	409	1,480	1,889
	Plea	61	1,201	1,262
	Drug cases	277	1,343	1,619

SOURCE: "Average Number of Attorney Hours Billed in Capital and Non-Capital Homicide Cases," in *Federal Death Penalty Cases: Recommendations Concerning the Cost and Quality of Defense Representation*, Judicial Conference of the United States, Committee on Defender Services, Subcommittee on Federal Death Penalty Cases, 1998, http://www.uscourts.gov/dpenalty/4REPORT.htm (accessed October 20, 2003)

Costs of Federal Cases in Non–Death Penalty States

Federal law can be enacted in any U.S. state or territory, even in a jurisdiction that does not have the death penalty. In March 2002 Michigan became the first non–death penalty state in which a federal jury sentenced a person to death. Marvin Gabrion had been convicted of the murder of nineteen-year-old Rachel Timmerman.

In 1997 Timmerman's body, tied with chains and handcuffs and secured to cinder blocks, was found in Oxford Lake in Michigan's Manistee National Forest. Authorities said she was drowned while still alive. Timmerman was scheduled to testify against Gabrion for raping her in 1996. Authorities also believed Gabrion was involved in the disappearance of Timmerman's one-year-old daughter. Since Rachel Timmerman was found on federal property, the government authorized the death penalty.

The federal government's decision to pursue the death penalty meant that taxpayers nationwide had to foot the bill. Ed White of the *Grand Rapids Press* reported on May 24, 2002, that the defense costs amounted to more than $730,000. A major portion of the expenses (over $537,000) went toward attorney fees. According to Chief Justice Robert Holmes Bell of the U.S. District Court of the Western District of Michigan, one of two federal judges who oversaw the budget, defending a federal death penalty case usually costs over $1 million. That price tag does not include the cost of prosecuting the case. However, prosecutors typically do not make an accounting of their expenses. The *Grand Rapids Press* reported that although the U.S. Attorney's Office disclosed it spent at least $316,201, it did not say what the total additional costs were. These included, among other things, staff salaries and Federal Bureau of Investigation expenses.

CHAPTER 8

PUBLIC ATTITUDES TOWARD CAPITAL PUNISHMENT

Like all statistics, those contained in public opinion polls should be viewed cautiously. The way a question is phrased can influence the respondents' answers. Many other factors may also influence a response in ways that are often difficult to determine. Respondents might never have thought of the issue until asked, or they might be giving the pollster the answer they think the pollster wants to hear. Organizations that survey opinions do not claim absolute accuracy. Their findings are approximate snapshots of the attitudes of the nation at a given time.

The surveys presented here have been selected from numerous polls taken on capital punishment. The Gallup Organization and Harris Interactive (formerly Louis Harris and Associates, Inc.), to name two such organizations, are well respected in their fields, and their surveys are accepted as representative of public opinions. A typical, well-conducted survey claims accuracy to about plus or minus three points.

ACCEPTABLE PENALTY FOR MURDER

According to Gallup Poll results from December 1936, about three in five respondents (59%) favored the death penalty at that time. This was the first time the Gallup Organization polled Americans regarding their attitudes toward the death penalty for murder. For the next three decades support for capital punishment fluctuated, dropping to its lowest point in 1966 (42%). Starting in early 1972 support for capital punishment steadily increased, peaking at 80% in 1994. Between 1999 and 2004 support hovered around 70%. (See Figure 8.1 and Figure 8.2.) In May 2005 Gallup found that 74% of Americans favored the death penalty for persons convicted of murder. Twenty-three percent were not in favor, and 3% were undecided.

The lowest proportion of Americans in support of capital punishment for murder was 42% in 1966, a period of civil rights and anti–Vietnam War marches, "flower

children," and the peace movement. It was also the only time in the sixty-nine years of Gallup polling (as of May 2005) that those who opposed capital punishment (47%) outnumbered those who favored it.

An ABC News/*Washington Post* poll of the American public taken April 21–24, 2005, showed that 65% of respondents supported the death penalty for those convicted of murder. On March 29–30, 2005, nearly seven of ten (69%) registered voters surveyed across the nation by the FOX News/Opinion Dynamics Poll said that they favored the death penalty for persons convicted of premeditated murder. Twenty-four percent opposed the death penalty for convicted murderers, while 8% were not sure. These results reflected a decline in support for the death penalty over the previous seven years. In January 1998 a higher proportion (74%) of those surveyed by Fox News indicated they supported the death penalty for convicted killers. In the earlier poll, 18% declared that they were against the death penalty, and 7% were not sure.

DEATH PENALTY VERSUS LIFE IMPRISONMENT WITH NO PAROLE

Some people say they support the death penalty because a person sentenced to life imprisonment may get out on parole at some time in the future. According to a Gallup poll conducted May 2–5, 2005, the number of people favoring the death penalty dropped to 56% when people were asked what the best penalty would be for people convicted of murder. Thirty-nine percent of respondents chose life in prison. As Figure 8.3 shows, these percentages have changed very little since 1985, when 56% of respondents also chose the death penalty. A CBS News poll taken April 13–16, 2005, obtained slightly different results when respondents were asked if they thought murderers deserved life imprisonment without parole, a long sentence with the possibility of parole,

FIGURE 8.1

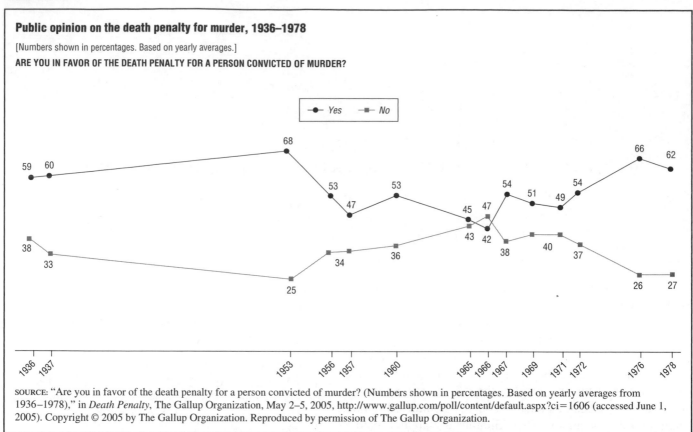

Public opinion on the death penalty for murder, 1936–1978

[Numbers shown in percentages. Based on yearly averages.]

ARE YOU IN FAVOR OF THE DEATH PENALTY FOR A PERSON CONVICTED OF MURDER?

or the death penalty. In this case, the numbers of those favoring the death sentence dropped to 39%. Another 39% chose life without parole for convicted killers, and 6% chose a lengthy jail sentence with a chance for parole.

On January 11, 2003, Governor George Ryan of Illinois commuted 167 death sentences to life imprisonment without the possibility of parole. A January 2003 ABC News/*Washington Post* poll surveyed people in the thirty-eight death penalty states. The respondents were told that Governor Ryan's action was a result of his belief that too many mistakes occurred in capital cases, and were then asked if they would support or oppose a similar blanket commutation by their governor. Thirty-nine percent indicated they would support such an action, while 58% said they would oppose it.

Seven of Ten Texans Favor Life without Parole

As of June 2005, of the thirty-eight states with the death penalty, just two—New Mexico and Texas—do not give the juries the option of sentencing an inmate to imprisonment without the possibility of parole. The federal government and the military also provide this option.

In April 2003 the Texas Senate refused to debate legislation that would have given juries the sentencing option of life without parole. Under the current system, Texas juries have two sentencing options—death or life

in prison with the possibility of parole after forty years. Interestingly, a Scripps Howard Texas poll conducted in February 2003 found that 72% of Texans favored amending the capital law to allow juries the choice of sentencing a convicted murderer to life without parole.

WHO SUPPORTS THE DEATH PENALTY?

According to the *Sourcebook of Criminal Justice Statistics* (Bureau of Justice Statistics, 2003), men (70%) were more likely than women (58%) to support capital punishment in 2003. Whites (67%) tended to favor the death penalty more than African-Americans (39%) or nonwhites in general (52%). Republicans (84%) were more likely than independents (58%) and Democrats (51%) to believe in the death penalty. (See Table 8.1.)

The percentage of those supporting the death penalty varied with income. Middle-income people favored capital punishment the most. More than seven of ten (72%) of persons earning $30,000 to $49,999 favored the death penalty in 2003. Those with incomes under $20,000 demonstrated the least support for the death penalty (52%). Views about the death penalty also varied somewhat with education levels, with those having a postgraduate degree favoring it the least. Regionally,

FIGURE 8.2

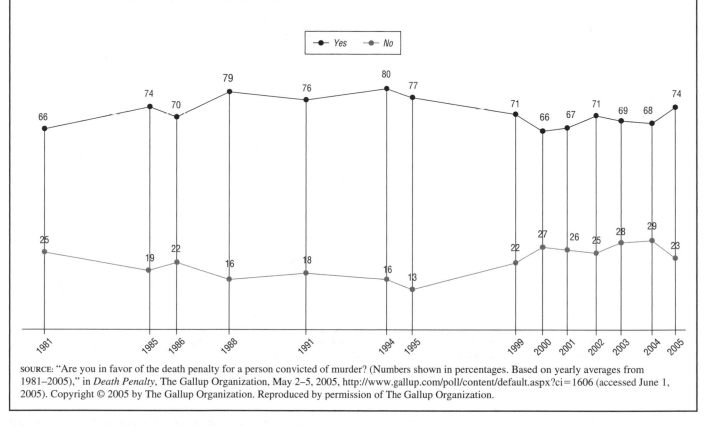

Public opinion on the death penalty for murder, 1981–2005

[Numbers shown in percentages. Based on yearly averages.]

ARE YOU IN FAVOR OF THE DEATH PENALTY FOR A PERSON CONVICTED OF MURDER?

SOURCE: "Are you in favor of the death penalty for a person convicted of murder? (Numbers shown in percentages. Based on yearly averages from 1981–2005)," in *Death Penalty*, The Gallup Organization, May 2–5, 2005, http://www.gallup.com/poll/content/default.aspx?ci=1606 (accessed June 1, 2005). Copyright © 2005 by The Gallup Organization. Reproduced by permission of The Gallup Organization.

people living in the South (71%) and West (69%) were the most likely to favor the death penalty. (See Table 8.1.)

CRIMES DESERVING THE DEATH PENALTY

In June 2000 a *Newsweek* poll conducted by Princeton Survey Research Associates found that, overall, nearly two of five Americans (38%) favored the death penalty for inmates convicted of the most brutal murders, mass murders, and serial killings. More non-Hispanic whites (40%) than nonwhites (33%) supported the death penalty for such heinous crimes. Another 23% of the general public preferred the death penalty for persons convicted of murder, other especially violent crimes, and major drug dealing. A larger proportion of non-Hispanic whites (24%) than nonwhites (15%) favored the death penalty for these crimes. About 12% of respondents thought any murder (be it brutal or less brutal) should be punished by death. However, almost one-fifth (19%) of the American public opposed the death penalty in all cases.

On July 23–24, 2002, 71% of registered voters who responded to a FOX News/Opinion Dynamics Poll said they supported the death sentence as punishment for those guilty of kidnapping and murdering a child.

DEATH PENALTY FOR SELECTED MURDERERS

In early May 2002, Gallup surveyed Americans to determine whether they favored the death penalty for certain types of individuals. Nearly seven out of ten respondents (68%) supported the death penalty for women. A lower proportion (13%) thought mentally retarded murderers should receive the death sentence. Almost one-fifth (19%) favored the death penalty for those who are mentally ill. (See Table 8.2.)

In response to the publicity surrounding the case of Lee Boyd Malvo, the seventeen-year-old convicted of the 2002 sniper attacks in the Washington, D.C., area, the execution of teenage offenders became a hotly debated issue. In May 2002 the Gallup Organization reported that only one-fourth (26%) of Americans favored the death penalty for those who were juveniles when they committed the crime. According to a Gallup poll taken on October 6–8, 2003, however, a majority of adult Americans (59%) still believed that fourteen- to seventeen-year-old juveniles who committed violent crimes should be treated the same as adults. (See Figure 8.4.) In March 2005 the U.S. Supreme Court declared the death penalty for minors unconstitutional.

FIGURE 8.3

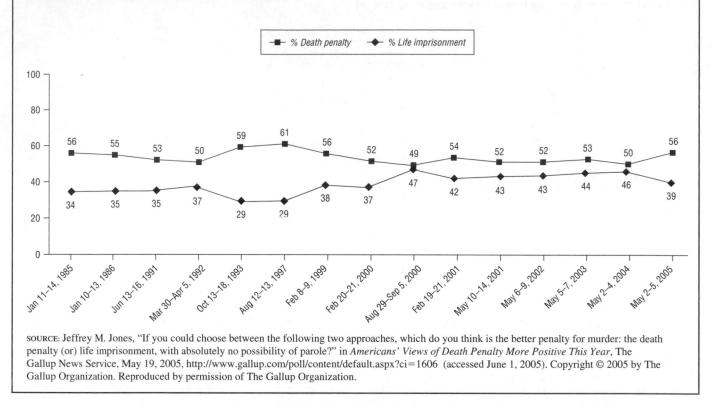

Public opinion on the death penalty over life imprisonment, 1985–2005

IF YOU COULD CHOOSE BETWEEN THE FOLLOWING TWO APPROACHES, WHICH DO YOU THINK IS THE BETTER PENALTY FOR MURDER: THE DEATH PENALTY (OR) LIFE IMPRISONMENT, WITH ABSOLUTELY NO POSSIBILITY OF PAROLE?

SOURCE: Jeffrey M. Jones, "If you could choose between the following two approaches, which do you think is the better penalty for murder: the death penalty (or) life imprisonment, with absolutely no possibility of parole?" in *Americans' Views of Death Penalty More Positive This Year*, The Gallup News Service, May 19, 2005, http://www.gallup.com/poll/content/default.aspx?ci=1606 (accessed June 1, 2005). Copyright © 2005 by The Gallup Organization. Reproduced by permission of The Gallup Organization.

Between 1976, when the United States reinstituted capital punishment, and 2005, Texas executed twelve inmates who were minors when they committed their crimes. Three such executions occurred in 2002. A Scripps Howard Texas poll in February 2003 revealed that 60% of Texans supported the death penalty for those who murdered when they were seventeen years old, a higher percentage than the year before (51%). In 2003, 34% opposed executing offenders who were minors when the crime was committed, slightly lower than in 2002 (37%).

On April 3, 2003, Oklahoma executed Scott Allen Hain, who was seventeen when he and Robert Lambert, age twenty-one, burned two people alive in a car trunk in 1987. A University of Oklahoma poll released after the execution showed that almost 63% of Oklahomans favored a legislative ban on executing offenders who were juveniles at the time of the crime if given the alternative choice of life without parole. As of August 31, 2005, Lambert, with a claim of mental retardation, remained on death row.

REASONS FOR SUPPORTING THE DEATH PENALTY

On May 19–21, 2003, Gallup researchers asked capital punishment supporters why they favored the death penalty for people convicted of murder. Over one-third (37%) believed that the death penalty was the appropriate punishment for murder. Eleven percent believed the death penalty saved taxpayers' money. (Contrary to popular belief, studies show that the death penalty costs more than life imprisonment without parole; see Chapter 7.) Another 11% thought that putting a murderer to death would set an example so that others would not commit similar crimes. Seven percent responded that the best reason for the death penalty was that it prevented murderers from killing again. (See Table 8.3.)

SUPPORT FOR CAPITAL PUNISHMENT VARIES WITH SPECIFIC CASES

Scott Peterson

On December 12, 2004, Scott Peterson was sentenced by a California jury to death row for killing his pregnant wife, Laci Peterson, and dumping her body into the San Francisco Bay. A FOX News/Opinion Dynamics Poll conducted on November 16 to 17, 2004, asked registered U.S. voters whether he should receive the death penalty or not. Only 35% of respondents agreed that Peterson deserved the death penalty. Roughly 50% thought he should get life in prison, and 15% were unsure. Men and women, however, differed in their opinions. Of the women who were polled, some 57%

TABLE 8.1

Support for capital punishment by demographic characteristics, 2003

QUESTION: "ARE YOU IN FAVOR OF THE DEATH PENALTY FOR A PERSON CONVICTED OF MURDER?"

	Yes, in favor	No, not in favor	Don't know/ refused
National	64%	32%	4%
Sex			
Male	70	26	4
Female	58	37	5
Race			
White	67	29	4
Nonwhite	52	42	6
Black	39	54	7
Age			
18 to 29 years	65	34	1
30 to 49 years	65	33	2
50 to 64 years	65	31	4
50 years and older	62	31	7
65 years and older	58	29	13
Education			
College post graduate	47	50	3
College graduate	65	33	2
Some college	68	28	4
High school graduate or less	67	28	5
Income			
$75,000 and over	64	36	0
$50,000 to $74,999	65	31	4
$30,000 to $49,999	72	25	3
$20,000 to $29,999	62	33	5
Under $20,000	52	39	9
Community			
Urban area	60	35	5
Suburban area	67	30	3
Rural area	64	31	5
Region			
East	53	44	3
Midwest	61	36	3
South	71	24	5
West	69	26	5
Politics			
Republican	84	14	2
Democrat	51	42	7
Independent	58	39	3

SOURCE: Kathleen Maguire and Ann L. Pastore, eds., "Table 2.50. Attitudes Towards the Death Penalty for Persons Convicted of Murder, by Demographic Characteristics, United States 2003," in *Sourcebook of Criminal Justice Statistics 2003*, U.S. Department of Justice, Bureau of Justice Statistics, Washington, DC, 2003, http://www.albany.edu/sourcebook/pdf/t250.pdf (accessed June 1, 2005).

said Peterson should spend his life in prison, as opposed to 43% for men. Roughly the same percentage of men (41%) replied that Peterson's death sentence was appropriate. Only 35% of women thought Peterson deserved capital punishment.

John Allen Muhammad and Lee Boyd Malvo

John Allen Muhammad and seventeen-year-old Lee Boyd Malvo, known as the "D.C. snipers," randomly shot and killed ten people around the Washington, D.C., metropolitan area over a three-and-a-half-week

TABLE 8.2

Public opinion on the death penalty for women, the mentally ill, the mentally retarded, and juveniles, 2002

DO YOU FAVOR OR OPPOSE THE DEATH PENALTY FOR—[RANDOM ORDER]? HOW ABOUT FOR—[INSERT NEXT ITEM]?

	Favor	Oppose	No opinion
Women			
2002 May 6–9	68%	29	3
The mentally ill			
2002 May 6–9	19%	75	6
The mentally retarded			
2002 May 6–9	13%	82	5
Juveniles			
2002 May 6–9	26%	69	5

SOURCE: "Do you favor or oppose the death penalty for–[RANDOM ORDER]? How about for–[INSERT NEXT ITEM]?" in *Death Penalty*, The Gallup Organization, May 6–9, 2002, http://www.gallup.com/poll/content/default.aspx?ci=1606 (accessed July 21, 2005). Copyright © 2005 by The Gallup Organization. Reproduced by permission of The Gallup Organization.

FIGURE 8.4

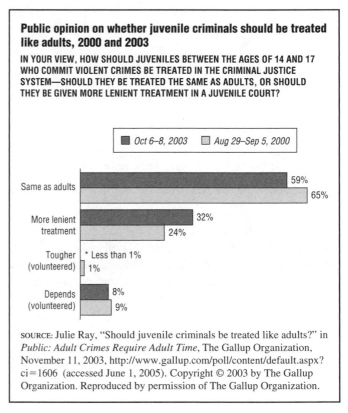

Public opinion on whether juvenile criminals should be treated like adults, 2000 and 2003

IN YOUR VIEW, HOW SHOULD JUVENILES BETWEEN THE AGES OF 14 AND 17 WHO COMMIT VIOLENT CRIMES BE TREATED IN THE CRIMINAL JUSTICE SYSTEM—SHOULD THEY BE TREATED THE SAME AS ADULTS, OR SHOULD THEY BE GIVEN MORE LENIENT TREATMENT IN A JUVENILE COURT?

■ Oct 6–8, 2003 □ Aug 29–Sep 5, 2000

- Same as adults: 59% / 65%
- More lenient treatment: 32% / 24%
- Tougher (volunteered): * Less than 1% / 1%
- Depends (volunteered): 8% / 9%

SOURCE: Julie Ray, "Should juvenile criminals be treated like adults?" in *Public: Adult Crimes Require Adult Time*, The Gallup Organization, November 11, 2003, http://www.gallup.com/poll/content/default.aspx?ci=1606 (accessed June 1, 2005). Copyright © 2003 by The Gallup Organization. Reproduced by permission of The Gallup Organization.

period in October 2002. The snipers' spree ended on October 24, 2002, when police caught the two sleeping at a highway rest stop in eastern Maryland. A judge sentenced Muhammad to death on March 9, 2004, after a Virginia jury convicted him of one of the murders and recommended capital punishment. On the day after Muhammad's sentence was handed down, Malvo was sentenced to life in prison in Virginia without parole.

TABLE 8.3

Public opinion on why people favor the death penalty, selected years, June 1991 to May 2003

WHY DO YOU FAVOR THE DEATH PENALTY FOR PERSONS CONVICTED OF MURDER? [OPEN-ENDED]

[Based on—715—who favor the death penalty for persons convicted of murder]

	May 19–21, 2003	Feb 19–21, 2001	Feb 14–15, 2000	Jun. 13–16, 1991
	%	%	%	%
An eye for an eye/they took a life/ fits the crime	37	48	40	40
They deserve it	13	6	5	5
Save taxpayers money/cost associated with prison	11	20	12	12
Deterrent for potential crimes/ set an example	11	10	8	8
They will repeat crime/keep them from repeating it	7	6	4	4
Biblical reasons	5	3	3	3
Depends on the type of crime they commit	4	6	6	6
Serve justice	4	1	3	2
Fair punishment	3	1	6	6
If there's no doubt the person committed the crime	3	2	—	—
Would help/benefit families of victims	2	1	—	—
Support/believe in death penalty	2	6	—	—
Don't believe they can be rehabilitated	2	2	1	1
Life sentences don't always mean life in prison	1	2	—	—
Relieves prison overcrowding	1	2	—	—
Other	4	3	10	10
No opinion	2	1	3	3

SOURCE: "Why do you favor the death penalty for persons convicted of murder?" in *Death Penalty*, The Gallup Organization, May 19–21, 2003, http://www.gallup.com/poll/content/default.aspx?ci=1606 (accessed July 21, 2005). Copyright © 2005 by The Gallup Organization. Reproduced by permission of The Gallup Organization.

Just after the police captured the snipers, a November 2002 CNN/Time/Harris Interactive poll asked registered voters what punishment Muhammad and Malvo deserved if found guilty. Almost three-quarters of respondents (72%) favored the death penalty for Muhammad, and only one-quarter (23%) thought he deserved life in prison. Despite Malvo being a minor, a majority of respondents (51%) also thought he ought to get the death sentence. Only four of five (43%) of those polled believed Malvo should receive a sentence of life in prison. Americans' ire over the shootings, however, appeared to diminish a bit a year later when a December 2003 ABC News poll asked people what sentence Malvo deserved. According to this poll, only 37% supported the death penalty for Malvo. Some 53% thought he should receive life in prison.

John Walker Lindh

American-born John Walker Lindh was captured by U.S. soldiers in November 2001 in Afghanistan while fighting for the Taliban. ABCNews.com conducted a poll December 5–9, 2001, asking Americans what they thought the United States should do with Lindh. More than half (55%) indicated he should be charged with a crime. Of this group of respondents, one-third (34%) thought Lindh should be tried for treason, which is punishable by death. Sixteen percent chose a lesser charge. In July 2002 Lindh entered into a plea agreement to cooperate with U.S. authorities in investigating al Qaeda, which was responsible for the September 11, 2001, terrorist attacks on the United States. He was sentenced to twenty years in prison.

Andrea Yates

On June 20, 2001, Andrea Pia Yates of Houston, Texas, admitted to police that she drowned her five children. Respondents to a June 28, 2001, Gallup Poll were split over whether Yates should be sentenced to death if convicted of killing her children (44% for and 43% against). Nearly two-thirds (63%) of the respondents believed that the defendant's postpartum depression at the time of the murders should be taken into consideration during her trial.

On October 23 to 31, 2001, a *Houston Chronicle/KHOU-TV* poll of registered voters in Harris County, Texas, revealed that nearly three times as many respondents (57.3% versus 19.4% for the death sentence) thought Andrea Yates should receive a life sentence.

Three of ten Americans (30%) polled by a FOX News/Opinion Dynamics Poll in February 2002, thought Andrea Yates should be sentenced to death. A larger proportion of men (35%) than women (27%) chose the death penalty for the defendant. While the respondents were equally split on a sentence of life in prison (23%) and life in a psychiatric hospital (22%), just 12% said Yates should be sent to a psychiatric hospital until she is well. In March 2002 a Texas jury found Yates guilty of capital murder and sentenced her to life in prison. Her conviction was overturned by a Texas appellate court on January 7, 2005, because of false testimony presented at her original trial. Prosecutors planned to appeal the ruling.

Karla Faye Tucker

In 1998 a *Dallas Morning News* survey found that although most (75%) Texans generally favored capital punishment, less than half (45%) supported the death penalty for Karla Faye Tucker, the second woman to be executed in the nation since the reinstatement of the death penalty in 1976. Tucker, executed by lethal injection in February 1998, was convicted of beating two people to death with a pickax in 1983.

Timothy McVeigh

Timothy McVeigh was executed on June 11, 2001, for the 1995 Oklahoma City bombing that killed 168 people. He was the first federal inmate executed since 1963, when Victor Harry Feguer was hanged in Iowa for kidnapping and murder.

Prior to McVeigh's execution, a June 8–10, 2001, CNN/USA Today/Gallup Poll found that about three of five (59%) respondents favored the death penalty in general and agreed that McVeigh should be put to death. About one of five (19%) respondents opposed the death penalty but believed nevertheless that McVeigh should be executed. A slightly lower proportion (17%) indicated that they were against the death penalty and thought that McVeigh should not be executed.

Earlier, in April 2001 the Gallup Organization polled the American public, asking if they thought the execution of Timothy McVeigh should be televised. Of those polled, 43% indicated that they thought it should not be televised, and 39% thought it should be televised only on closed-circuit television for the victims' families to watch. Seventeen percent of respondents thought the execution should be televised for the general public. The poll also asked if Americans would watch McVeigh's execution if it were televised. Three-quarters (76%) of the respondents said they would not watch, while nearly one-quarter (23%) indicated they would watch.

Juan Raul Garza

In early June 2001 Gallup interviewers also polled Americans on questions regarding drug kingpin Juan Raul Garza. Garza was the second federal inmate since 1963 set for execution for murder. His execution date was June 19, 2001. Fifty percent of respondents who supported the death penalty believed Garza should be executed; 12% of those who opposed the death penalty thought that Garza should be put to death. More than one-fourth (27%) of those who opposed the death penalty believed he should not be executed, which was 10% more than those polled regarding McVeigh.

IS THE DEATH PENALTY IMPOSED TOO OFTEN?

Although the United States leads all Western countries in executions, just one-fifth (20%) of Americans surveyed by the Gallup Organization on May 2–5, 2005, believed the death penalty was imposed too often. More than twice that proportion (53%) thought it was not used often enough, while 24% thought the level of death penalty imposition was about right. (See Figure 8.5.)

Four years before, on May 10–14, 2001, when the Gallup Organization asked the same question, an almost similar proportion (21%) said the death penalty was imposed too often. A smaller percentage (38%) thought the death penalty was not imposed enough. However, more respondents (34%) said the death penalty was imposed the right amount.

FIGURE 8.5

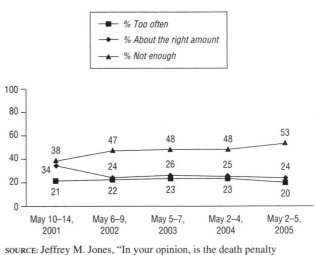

Public opinion on whether the death penalty is imposed too often, 2001–05

IN YOUR OPINION, IS THE DEATH PENALTY IMPOSED: TOO OFTEN, ABOUT THE RIGHT AMOUNT, OR NOT OFTEN ENOUGH?

- ■ % Too often
- ◆ % About the right amount
- ▲ % Not enough

SOURCE: Jeffrey M. Jones, "In your opinion, is the death penalty imposed: too often, about the right amount, or not often enough?" in *Americans' Views of Death Penalty More Positive This Year*, The Gallup News Service, May 19, 2005, http://www.gallup.com/poll/content/default.aspx?ci=1606 (accessed June 1, 2005). Copyright © 2005 by The Gallup Organization. Reproduced by permission of The Gallup Organization.

Only One-Third of Americans Support an Increase in Executions

In December 2003 the Harris Poll reported that about one-third (36%) of Americans favored an increase in the number of executions, one-fourth (21%) favored a decrease, and another one-third (33%) favored no change. These responses had changed very little since 2000 when a similar Harris Poll was conducted, but had fluctuated greatly since 1997. A 1997 Harris Poll revealed that over half (53%) of the public favored an increase in the use of the death penalty, 14% favored a decrease, and 27% wanted no change.

DEATH PENALTY FAVORED EVEN IF SOME ARE INNOCENT

The December 2003 Harris Poll found that virtually all Americans (95%) believed that, on average, for every one hundred people convicted of murder, approximately one in nine (11%) were innocent. Women guessed that this occurred more often (estimate of 13%) than men did (10%). African-Americans estimated that 23% of people convicted of murder were innocent, compared with estimates by Hispanics (16%) and whites (9%). Independents and those with a high school diploma or less were more likely to believe that a higher proportion of innocent people (13% and 13%, respectively) were convicted of murder, as opposed to Republicans and those with a four-year college degree (6% and 7%, respectively).

Though 95% of respondents indicated they believed that at least some of those charged with murder were innocent, the 12% error rate in executions did not seem to qualify as "substantial." When asked if they would still support the death penalty if a "substantial" number of innocent people were convicted of murder, only four in ten (39%) said they would still support the death penalty. Over half (51%) would oppose it under those conditions. Nevertheless, the 39% who continued to support the death penalty were a larger proportion compared to their counterparts in 2001 and a smaller proportion than those in 2000 (36% and 53%, respectively).

MORATORIUM

On January 31, 2000, Illinois governor George H. Ryan declared a moratorium on executions in his state. In March 2001, 53% of Gallup Poll respondents said they favored a moratorium on the death penalty in states with capital punishment. Such a moratorium was opposed by 40%. An ABC News/*Washington Post* poll conducted in April 2001 delivered similar results. This poll revealed that 51% of Americans favored a nationwide moratorium until a commission could study whether it was being administered fairly.

Between 2001 and 2003, however, public opinion on a nationwide moratorium apparently changed dramatically. In January 2003 an NBC News/*Wall Street Journal* survey found that 34% of Americans believed there should be a nationwide moratorium until death penalty procedures were officially reviewed. Some 57% of Americans thought that a moratorium was not needed and that enough safeguards were in place to prevent unfair executions.

In 2004 a New York appellate court declared that the state's death penalty was unconstitutional due to a flaw in a state statute. The New York State Assembly in 2005 refused to pass a bill that would effectively fix the statute and reinstate the death penalty. By doing so, the assembly ushered in an unofficial moratorium on the death penalty in New York State. The Siena Research Institute polled registered voters in New York between February 28 and March 4, 2005, asking them if they wanted the death penalty to be reinstated. Some 46% of New Yorkers replied that they did not, while 42% said they did.

DETERRENT OR NOT?

A December 2003 Harris Poll found that about four of ten Americans (41%) believed that capital punishment deters (discourages) people from committing murders. However, about five of ten Americans (53%) believed capital punishment does not have much effect. In 1976, when the death penalty was reinstated, nearly six of ten (59%) Americans thought capital punishment was a deterrent, compared with just over three in ten (34%) who thought it had little effect.

Roughly only one-third (35%) of respondents to a May 2–4, 2004, Gallup poll thought that the death penalty acted as a deterrent to the commitment of murder. A full two-thirds (62%) maintained that the death penalty did not lower the murder rate whatsoever. As with the December 2003 Harris Poll, this represented a marked shift in sentiment from decades past. In January 1985 Gallup asked Americans if they thought the death penalty lowered the murder rate, and two-thirds (62%) said it did, versus a mere one-third (31%) who responded that it did not.

IS LETHAL INJECTION AN ACCEPTABLE METHOD OF EXECUTION?

In March 2004, in connection with arguments made before the Supreme Court that lethal injection constituted cruel and unusual punishment, the Gallup Organization undertook a survey of Americans' opinions on lethal injection as a method of execution. According to the poll results, 75% believed lethal injection ought to be allowed, while 21% thought lethal injection did constitute cruel and unusual punishment. Four percent professed no opinion on the matter. Further, men (82%) approved lethal injection at a higher rate than women (70%). White respondents (80%) were significantly more likely to support it than nonwhites (58%), and political conservatives (81%) were more likely to support lethal injection than political liberals (57%).

CHAPTER 9
CAPITAL PUNISHMENT AROUND THE WORLD

UNITED NATIONS RESOLUTIONS

Capital punishment is controversial not only in the United States but also in many other countries. The ethical arguments that fuel the debate in the United States also characterize the discussions around the world. The United Nations' position on capital punishment is a compromise among those countries that want it completely abolished, those that want it limited to very serious offenses, and those that want it left up to each country to decide. In 1946, just after the end of World War II, the United Nations (UN) General Assembly gathered to draft a bill of human rights for all UN member nations to follow. From the beginning, the death penalty was a topic of contention, and in 1948 when the assembly released the International Bill of Human Rights there was no mention of the death penalty. After nine years of debate, the General Assembly included a statement on the death penalty in the International Covenant on Civil and Political Rights, which later was added to the International Bill of Human Rights. On December 16, 1966, the General Assembly adopted the Covenant in Resolution 2200 (XXI). Article 6 of the Covenant states,

- Every human being has the inherent right to life. This right shall be protected by law. No one shall be arbitrarily deprived of his life.

- In countries that have not abolished the death penalty, sentence of death may be imposed only for the most serious crimes in accordance with the law in force at the time of the commission of the crime and not contrary to the provisions of the present Covenant and to the Convention on the Prevention and Punishment of the Crime of Genocide [systematic killing of a racial, political, or cultural group]. This penalty can only be carried out pursuant to a final judgment rendered by a competent court.

- When deprivation of life constitutes the crime of genocide, it is understood that nothing in this article

shall authorize any State Party to the present Covenant to derogate [turn away] in any way from any obligation assumed under the provisions of the Convention on the Prevention and Punishment of the Crime of Genocide.

- Anyone sentenced to death shall have the right to seek pardon or commutation of the sentence [replacement of the death sentence with a lesser sentence]. Amnesty, pardon, or commutation of the sentence of death may be granted in all cases.

- Sentence of death shall not be imposed for crimes committed by persons below eighteen years of age and shall not be carried out on pregnant women.

- Nothing in this article shall be invoked to delay or prevent the abolition of capital punishment by any State Party to the present Covenant.

The UN has dealt with the death penalty in several other documents and meetings. Among them is General Assembly Resolution 2393 (XXIII) of November 26, 1968, which specifies the following legal safeguards that should be offered to condemned prisoners by countries with capital punishment:

- A person condemned to death shall not be deprived of the right to appeal to a higher judicial authority or, as the case may be, to petition for pardon or reprieve.

- A death sentence shall not be carried out until the procedures of appeal or, as the case may be, to petition for pardon or reprieve have been terminated.

- Special attention shall be given in the case of indigent [poor] persons by the provision of adequate legal assistance at all stages of the proceedings.

Since then the UN has come out more strongly for eliminating capital punishment. General Assembly Resolution 2857 (XXVI) of December 20, 1971, observed,

In order fully to guarantee the right to life, provided for in Article 3 of the Universal Declaration of Human Rights [a section of the International Bill of Human Rights], the main objective to be pursued is that of progressively restricting the number of offenses for which capital punishment may be imposed, with a view to the desirability of abolishing this punishment in all countries.

The UN Economic and Social Council Resolution 1574 (L) of May 20, 1971, made a similar declaration. In 1984 the Economic and Social Council then adopted the *Safeguards Guaranteeing Protection of the Rights of Those Facing the Death Penalty*, including those of persons younger than age eighteen at the time the crime was committed. Over the succeeding years General Assembly and Economic and Social Council resolutions have continued to call for the abolition of the death penalty.

On December 15, 1989, the UN General Assembly, under Resolution 44/128, adopted the Second Optional Protocol to the International Covenant on Civil and Political Rights, aimed at abolishing the death penalty. This international treaty allows countries to retain the death penalty in wartime as long as they reserve the right to do so at the time they become party to the treaty. As of June 1, 2005, seven countries had endorsed the treaty by signing, indicating their intention to become parties to it at a later date. Signatories are not legally bound by the treaty but are obliged to avoid acts that would go against the treaty. Fifty-four countries became parties to the protocol by ratification or accession, which means that they were legally bound by the terms of the treaty. Accession is similar to ratification, except that it occurs after the treaty has entered into force. In 1992 the United States ratified the International Covenant on Civil and Political Rights but had not signed the Second Optional Protocol to this treaty as of June 1, 2005.

UN Initiatives since 2000

On December 18, 2000, the secretary general of the United Nations, Kofi Annan, announced that he received a petition signed by more than three million people from more than 130 countries, appealing for an end to executions. Subsequently, the secretary general called for a worldwide moratorium on the death penalty, noting that the taking of life as punishment for crime is "too absolute [and] too irreversible."

Since April 1997 the UN Commission on Human Rights has adopted resolutions calling for a moratorium on executions and an eventual abolition of the death penalty. At the commission's meeting in Geneva, Switzerland, on April 25, 2001, the United States voted against the resolution on the death penalty. According to Ambassador George E. Moose, "International law does not prohibit the death penalty when due process safeguards are respected and when capital punishment is applied only to the most serious crimes."

In its 2002 session, the commission, in Resolution 2002/77, asked countries with the death penalty "[t]o ensure that . . . the death penalty is not imposed for non-violent acts such as financial crimes, non-violent religious practice or expression of conscience and sexual relations between consenting adults." The part of the resolution referring to sexual relations between consenting adults resulted from the potential execution of a Nigerian woman, who became pregnant while divorced. She was convicted of adultery and, in March 2002, was sentenced to die by stoning. The man who fathered the child claimed innocence, brought in three men to corroborate his claim as required by law, and was released. On September 25, 2003, the woman was acquitted.

The UN Commission on Human Rights adopted Resolution 2003/67 on April 24, 2003, in Geneva, Switzerland. For the first time, the commission asked countries that retained capital punishment not to extend the application of the death penalty to offenses to which it does not currently apply. It also admonished those countries to inform the public of any scheduled execution and to abstain from holding public executions and inhuman forms of executions, such as stoning. The UN also called on death penalty countries not to impose the death sentence on mothers with dependent children. The commission made no changes to this resolution when they adopted it again in 2004.

RETENTIONIST COUNTRIES

Amnesty International (AI), a human rights organization headquartered in London, England, maintains information on capital punishment throughout the world. (AI vehemently opposes the death penalty, considering it the "ultimate form of cruel, inhuman, and degrading punishment.") The organization refers to countries that retain and use the death penalty as retentionist countries; those that no longer use the death penalty are known as abolitionist countries.

As of May 24, 2005, seventy-six countries and territories in the world retained and used the death penalty as a possible punishment for ordinary crimes. (See Table 9.1.) Ordinary crimes are crimes committed during peacetime. Ordinary crimes that could lead to the death penalty include murder, rape, and, in some countries, robbery or embezzlement of very large sums of money. Exceptional crimes, however, are military crimes committed during exceptional times, mainly wartime. Examples are treason, spying, or desertion (leaving the armed services without permission).

Although many of the retentionist countries had not executed anybody in many years, in 2004 sixty-four countries preformed 7,395 executions, according to AI's annual report *The Death Penalty Worldwide*. Less than half of these countries, twenty-five, carried out at least

TABLE 9.1

Countries and territories which retain the death penalty for ordinary crimes, May 2005

Afghanistan	Laos
Antigua and Barbuda	Lebanon
Bahamas	Lesotho
Bahrain	Liberia
Bangladesh	Libya
Barbados	Malawi
Belarus	Malaysia
Belize	Mongolia
Botswana	Nigeria
Burundi	Oman
Cameroon	Pakistan
Chad	Palestinian Authority
China	Philippines
Comoros	Qatar
Congo (Democratic Republic)	Rwanda
Cuba	Saint Christopher & Nevis
Dominica	Saint Lucia
Egypt	Saint Vincent & Grenadines
Equatorial Guinea	Saudi Arabia
Eritrea	Sierra Leone
Ethiopia	Singapore
Gabon	Somalia
Ghana	Sudan
Guatemala	Swaziland
Guinea	Syria
Guyana	Taiwan
India	Tajikistan
Indonesia	Tanzania
Iran	Thailand
Iraq	Trinidad and Tobago
Jamaica	Uganda
Japan	United Arab Emirates
Jordan	United States of America
Kazakstan	Uzbekistan
Korea (North)	Vietnam
Korea (South)	Yemen
Kuwait	Zambia
Kyrgyzstan	Zimbabwe

SOURCE: "4. Retentionist: Countries and Territories which Retain the Death Penalty for Ordinary Crimes," in *The Death Penalty: Abolitionist and Retentionist Countries*, Amnesty International, May 24, 2005, http://web.amnesty.org/pages/deathpenalty-countries-eng (accessed June 1, 2005)

3,797 death sentences. AI reported that China accounted for 46% of all executions. An estimated 3,400 persons were reportedly killed by the Chinese government, although AI estimated the actual number was larger. (Note: In 2004, AI changed its method for tallying executions in China, relying on Internet-based reports instead of trial documents. Using the Internet resulted in a higher count.) Iran had at least 159 executions, and Vietnam counted sixty-four. While fifty-nine people were put to death in the United States, this number was down from sixty-five in 2003.

United States

The United States remains the only Western country that practices capital punishment. (As of 2005, the federal government, the U.S. military, and thirty-eight states approved the death penalty.) In September 1997, UN monitor Bacre Waly Ndiaye, a lawyer from Senegal, investigated the use of the death penalty in the United States. This was the first time the UN had sent an inves-

tigator to report on the U.S. capital punishment system. In his report to the UN Commission on Human Rights, the special investigator accused the United States of unfair, arbitrary, and racist use of capital punishment. He claimed that "allegations of racial discrimination in the imposition of death sentences are particularly serious in southern states, such as Alabama, Florida, Louisiana, Mississippi, Georgia, and Texas, collectively known as the 'death penalty belt.'"

FOREIGN NATIONALS. Mark Warren of Human Rights Research (Ontario, Canada), who provided information and expertise on human rights issues to government, nongovernmental organizations, consulates, and lawyers, reported that as of May 28, 2005, 118 foreign nationals representing thirty-one nationalities were on death row in the United States. Capital punishment opponents claimed that the United States generally did not inform foreign nationals under arrest of their right to consult with the consulate of their home country as required by Article 36 of the Vienna Convention on Consular Relations. Article 36 requires local law enforcement to notify all detained foreigners "without delay" of this right. The United States ratified (formally approved and sanctioned) this international agreement in 1969. Since 1976, twenty-one foreign nationals have been executed in the United States. (See Table 9.2.)

THE UNITED STATES DEFIES THE UN'S HIGHEST COURT. Angel Francisco Breard, a Paraguayan national, was arrested on charges of capital murder and attempted rape in 1992. In 1993 Breard was sentenced to death for these crimes. Following the denial of his appeals before the Virginia Supreme Court and the U.S. Supreme Court, Breard invoked the provision of the Vienna Convention on Consular Relations. The U.S. District Court, in *Breard v. Netherland* (945 F. Supp. 1255, 1266 [E.D. Va. 1996]), rejected Breard's claim because he had "procedurally defaulted" the claim when he failed to raise it in state court during his state appeals. Without doing so, he could not raise the issue in his federal appeals. In addition, the district court concluded that Breard could not show cause and prejudice for this default.

That same year, 1996, the Republic of Paraguay brought suit against Virginia officials for violation of the Vienna Convention because they failed to notify the Paraguayan consulate of Breard's arrest. The district court dismissed the suit, a decision that the appellate court affirmed. On April 3, 1998, the Republic of Paraguay brought the case before the International Court of Justice (ICJ; the UN's highest court), which ruled, on April 9, 1998, that the United States should stay Breard's execution pending the ICJ's final decision. Paraguay had also petitioned the U.S. Supreme Court.

On April 14, 1998, the day of execution, the U.S. Supreme Court, voting 6–3, refused to intervene in the

TABLE 9.2

Confirmed foreign nationals executed in the United States since 1976

Name	VCCR claim raised	Nationality	State	Date
1. Leslie Lowenfield		Guyana	Louisiana	April 13, 1988
2. Carlos Santana	*	Dominican Republic	Texas	March 23, 1993
3. Ramon Montoya	*	Mexico	Texas	March 25, 1993
4. Pedro Medina		Cuba	Florida	March 25, 1997
5. Irineo Tristan Montoya	*	Mexico	Texas	June 18, 1997
6. Mario Murphy	* (Fourth Circuit)	Mexico	Virginia	September 18, 1997
7. Angel Breard	* (US Supreme Court)	Paraguay	Virginia	April 14, 1998
8. Jose Villafuerte	*	Honduras	Arizona	April 22, 1998
9. Tuan Nguyen		Viet Nam	Oklahoma	December 10, 1998
10. Jaturun Siripongs	*	Thailand	California	February 9, 1999
11. Karl LaGrand	* (Ninth Circuit)	Germany	Arizona	February 24, 1999
12. Walter LaGrand	* (Ninth Circuit)	Germany	Arizona	March 3, 1999
13. Alvaro Calamvro	*	Philippines	Nevada	April 5, 1999
14. Joseph Stanley Faulder	* (Fifth Circuit)	Canada	Texas	June 17, 1999
15. Miguel Angel Flores	* (Fifth Circuit)	Mexico	Texas	November 9, 2000
16. Sebastian Bridges		South Africa	Nevada	April 21, 2001
17. Sahib al-Mosawi	*	Iraq	Oklahoma	December 6, 2001
18. Javier Suarez Medina	*	Mexico	Texas	August 14, 2002
19. Rigoberto Sanchez Velasco		Cuba	Florida	October 2, 2002
20. Mir Aimal Kasi	*	Pakistan	Virginia	November 14, 2002
21. Hung Thanh Le	*	Viet Nam	Oklahoma	March 23, 2004

*Cases in which the consular notification issue was raised on appeal or in clemency proceedings (major appellate opinions on consular rights are in brackets).
Note: All indications are that none of these executed individuals were informed by U.S. authorities upon arrest of their right to have their consulate notified of their detention, as required under Article 36 of the Vienna Convention on Consular Relations (VCCR). In several instances, prisoners on this list did not learn of their right to request consular assistance for more than a decade, by which time the treaty violation was considered by the appellate courts to be a procedurally defaulted claim.

SOURCE: "Confirmed Foreign Nationals Executed Since 1976," in *Foreign Nationals, Part II*, Death Penalty Information Center, May 15, 2004, http://www .deathpenaltyinfo.org/article.php?scid=31&did=582#executed (accessed June 1, 2005)

case despite requests for a stay of execution from then–Secretary of State Madeleine Albright. In *Breard v. Greene* (523 U.S. 371, 1998), the Court stated,

> It is the rule in this country that assertions of error in criminal proceedings must first be raised in state court in order to form the basis for relief in *habeas*. . . . Claims not so raised are considered defaulted. By not asserting his Vienna Convention claim in state court, Breard failed to exercise his rights under the Vienna Convention in conformity with the laws of the United States and the Commonwealth of Virginia. Having failed to do so, he cannot raise a claim of violation of those rights now on federal *habeas* review.
>
> As for Paraguay's suits (both the original action and the case coming to us on petition for *certiorari* [a petition to the Supreme Court to review the issues brought up in the direct appeal]), neither the text nor the history of the Vienna Convention clearly provides a foreign nation a private right of action in United States courts to set aside a criminal conviction and sentence for violation of consular notification provisions. . . . Though Paraguay claims that its suit is within an exemption dealing with continuing consequences of past violations of federal rights, we do not agree. The failure to notify the Paraguayan Consul occurred long ago and has no continuing effect.

Breard was executed. In November 1998 the United States formally apologized to Paraguay for failing to inform Breard of his right to seek consular assistance. Paraguay withdrew its lawsuit following the apology.

GERMANY SUES THE UNITED STATES. In 1982 German brothers Karl and Walter LaGrand killed a bank employee during a robbery attempt in Tucson, Arizona. They were sentenced to death in 1984. In February 1999 Karl LaGrand was executed. On March 2, 1999, the day before Walter LaGrand's execution, Germany sued the United States at the ICJ. According to Germany, the United States violated Article 36 of the Vienna Convention by failing to inform the defendant without delay after the arrest of his right to contact the German consulate for help. Germany also claimed that Arizona prosecutors violated Article 36 because they knowingly failed to inform Germany of the arrest and conviction until ten years after the murder. By that time it was too late, under "procedural default," for the defendant to raise the issue of the treaty violation. The U.S. rule of procedural default requires that claims challenging conviction and/or sentence have to be presented at the state appeals stage. Walter LaGrand had not argued for his Article 36 rights in previous court proceedings and, therefore, could not raise a violation of that right in later proceedings.

The ICJ ordered the United States to stay Walter LaGrand's execution, but Arizona let the execution take place. Despite the execution, Germany proceeded with the lawsuit. During a November 2000 hearing before the ICJ, the United States argued that Article 36 does not confer personal rights to individual nationals. In other words, the United States conceded that while it violated its treaty obligations to Germany, it did not violate its obligations to the brothers. The United States added that although German authorities knew of the LaGrand case in 1992, they waited until 1999 to intervene for the brothers.

On June 27, 2001, the ICJ, in *Germany v. United States of America*, ruled 14–1 that the United States had violated its obligations to Germany and to the LaGrand brothers under the Vienna Convention on Consular Relations. The ICJ also ruled that domestic law must not prevent the review of the conviction and sentencing when a defendant's right to consular notification has been violated. In addition, the United States must provide review and remedies should a similar case arise.

MEXICO SUES THE UNITED STATES. In 2003 the International Court of Justice again was asked to settle a case involving the United States and consular notification. On January 9, 2003, Mexico sued the United States for allegedly violating the Vienna Convention on Consular Relations with respect to fifty-four Mexican nationals on U.S. death row *(Avena and other Mexican Nationals [Mexico v. United States of America]).* Mexico also asked the court, pending final judgment of the case, to issue provisional measures ordering the United States to abstain from executing any Mexican national or schedule any such execution. The United States argued that Mexico's request for provisional measures should be rejected by the court because they were equivalent to "a sweeping prohibition on capital punishment for Mexican nationals in the United States, regardless of United States law."

On February 5, 2003, the court unanimously issued an order directing the United States to take all necessary measures to ensure that three Mexican nationals, who faced possible execution in the coming months or even weeks, not be executed pending its final decision. The court, however, noted that the other fifty-one death row inmates were not included in the provisional measures order because they were not in the same situation as the other three men.

Although Judge Shigeru Oda (Japan) voted with the other fourteen court members regarding the order for provisional measures, he expressed his doubts about the court's definition of "disputes arising out of the interpretation or application" of the Vienna Convention. He had expressed the same doubts in the *Breard* and *LaGrand* cases. Judge Oda stated that since the United States had admitted its failure to abide by the Vienna Convention, no dispute concerning consular notification existed. He believed the current lawsuit "is in essence an attempt by Mexico to save the lives of its nationals sentenced to death by domestic courts in the United States." Judge Oda observed that the International Court of Justice cannot act as a court of criminal appeal, adding that "if the rights of the accused as they relate to human-

itarian issues are to be respected then, in parallel, the matter of the rights of victims of violent crime (a point which has often been overlooked) should be taken into consideration."

The ICJ handed down its decision on March 31, 2004. The court found that the United States had violated sections of the Vienna Convention by not informing the fifty-four Mexicans on death row of their right to notify their government about their detention. The court did not annul the convictions and sentences as Mexico had requested, but it did rule that the United States must review and reconsider the Mexican nationals' convictions and sentences.

THE UNITED STATES' RESPONSE TO THE INTER-NATIONAL COURT OF JUSTICE RULINGS. Jose Medellin was one of the fifty-four Mexicans on death row. Texas jurors sentenced him to death for participating in the rape and murder of two teenage girls in 1993. The Mexican consular did not learn of or have the opportunity to help Medellin with his legal defense until 1997 after Medellin had exhausted most of his appeals. When the ICJ decision regarding Mexican nationals was handed down, Medellin appealed once again to the U.S. Court of Appeals for the Fifth Circuit, claiming that he did not receive adequate counsel and that he was not allowed to contact the Mexican consulate after his indictment. The federal appellate court ruled against Medellin. The court cited *Breard v. Greene*, which stated that the issues addressed by the Vienna Convention had to be considered in the state courts before they could be addressed in federal court. Since Medellin had already gone through his appeals on the state level, he had no recourse. Medellin appealed to the U.S. Supreme Court and on December 10, 2004, the Court agreed to hear his case and to reassess its position on Vienna Convention and the International Court of Justice's rulings.

Just prior to the oral arguments in the Medellin case, President George W. Bush signed an Executive Order on February 28, 2005, demanding that the appropriate U.S. state courts review the sentences and convictions of the fifty-four Mexicans on death row without applying the procedural default rule discussed in *Breard v. Greene*. By issuing this order, the president in essence forced the courts to comply to the ICJ ruling regarding the Mexicans. In light of the Executive Order, the U.S. Supreme Court dismissed Medellin's case, and it was sent back to the state courts for review.

On March, 9, 2005, President Bush pulled the United States out of the Optional Protocol to the Vienna Convention on Consular Relations, which had been in place for thirty years. The administration no longer wanted the U.S. court system to be compelled by the International Court of Justice with regard to executing foreign nationals. According to *Washington Post* staff writer Charles Lane in "U.S. Quits Pact Used in Capital Cases" (March 10, 2005), the United States removal from the international pact may put U.S. nationals in danger of being executed abroad in countries such as China.

China

Human rights groups have found that China executes more people each year than all other nations combined. In October 1999 the Chinese government passed a law allowing the imposition of the death sentence on leaders of the Falun Gong religious movement charged with murder and endangering national security. The government claimed the movement has caused the death of more than one thousand followers by dissuading them from seeking medical help.

According to Amnesty International in *Report 2002*, a massive increase in executions occurred in 2001 as a result of a nationwide anticrime campaign called Strike Hard. Chinese officials had allegedly been very inconsistent in determining which crimes warranted the death penalty. Law enforcement, under pressure to achieve results, sped up the criminal process, reportedly subjecting defendants to torture to extract confessions. It was reported that the general public approves of the death penalty.

People convicted of nonviolent offenses, such as tax fraud, bribery, embezzlement, and counterfeiting, have been put to death in China. In its *Report 2005*, AI estimated that approximately 3,400 people had been executed and 6,000 had been sentenced to death in the previous year. However, the organization reported that a Chinese government official had announced that the country executes about 10,000 people per year.

Australian journalist Hamish McDonald reported in "Chinese Try Mobile Death Vans" (*The Age*, March 13, 2003) that eighteen mobile execution buses had been outfitted for use in Yunnan province in the southwest region of China. The buses were equipped with a bed and automatic syringe to facilitate lethal injections. Amnesty International, publicizing the same development in March 2003, reported that four government officials participate in the executions—the executor, a court representative, a doctor, and an official from the procuratorate (legal supervisory organ of the state). In addition to the vans being less costly for the government, according to McDonald, one official told *Chinese Life Weekly* that the condemned prisoners prefer lethal injection to the former method, which was being shot in the head. "When they know they can't be pardoned," McDonald quoted, "they accept this method calmly, and have less fear."

Japan

In *Report 2005*, Amnesty International estimated that at least sixty-one people were under sentence of death in Japan during 2004, and two executions took place that year, both by hanging. According to Charles Lane, in "Why Japan Still Has the Death Penalty" (*Washington Post*, January 16, 2005), an estimated sixty people on death row in Japan had seen their sentences finalized (as of September 15, 2004) and could be executed at any time.

The number of prisoners sentenced to death had declined, from twelve in 1988 to five in 1992. Thirteen inmates were executed from 1982 to 1989. No executions occurred from November 1989 to March 1993 because two Ministers of Justice, who opposed capital punishment, refused to issue execution orders. Executions resumed in March 1993. Between 1993 and 2004, forty-six prisoners were put to death by hanging.

Death row inmates are forbidden from meeting with journalists and researchers collecting data on the death penalty. Any information gathered by these persons usually results from significant investigations of their own. Families have limited access to the inmates, many of whom spend their days in solitary confinement.

Japan is also known for its drawn-out process of appeals. A case that drew worldwide attention involved a prisoner who, in 1997, after having been on death row for thirty years, was executed in secrecy. The inmate had committed multiple murders at age nineteen (a minor under Japanese law) but was convicted as an adult. The law requires the Justice Ministry to carry out an execution within six months after appeals are finalized. According to human rights organizations, the ministry, nonetheless, arbitrarily sets the execution date.

The Japanese government does not announce impending executions or notify families and lawyers of death row inmates about scheduled executions. Even the inmate who is being put to death learns of his or her fate only about two hours before the execution. The government has been known to carry out executions when the Diet (parliament) is not in session or during holidays in order to avoid parliamentary debate, as reported by AI.

According to AI, many inmates have been on death row for more than thirty years, never knowing which day might be their last. In 1987 ninety-five-year-old Sadamichi Hirasawa died while awaiting execution. He had been on death row for thirty-two years. In September 2003 eighty-six-year-old Tsuneki Tomiyama died of kidney failure after having been on death row for about thirty-nine years. His death sentence was finalized in 1976. As of August 2005 sixty-nine-year old Hakamada Iwao had been on death row for thirty-six years.

"Japan Hanging on to Death Penalty" (*Human Rights Features* 6, no. 3, March 31–April 6, 2003) noted that Japanese law does not provide judges with the criteria needed to impose the death penalty. For example, homicide may be punishable by execution, life imprisonment, or a prison term of not less than three years.

Forum 90 is an abolitionist group that monitors capital punishment in Japan. In *The Hidden Death Penalty in Japan* (Sachiho Takahashi and Thomas Mariadason, eds., Tokyo, Japan, June 2001), Forum 90 reported that in addition to the other secret elements of the death penalty in Japan, the general public is not informed of the identities of those executed. Since Japan has no jury system, ordinary citizens find out about an execution only after the Ministry of Justice announces that it has occurred.

The government of Japan claims that the public, as shown by a 1999 opinion poll, approves of the death penalty. Experts, however, point out that this percentage resulted from a problematic polling question. The people were asked whether they agreed that the death penalty system should be abolished in any case or whether the death penalty is necessary through unavoidable circumstances. A majority (79.3%) chose the second response. According to Lane in the *Washington Post*, street crime had been on the rise in Japan, and this may have influenced support for the death penalty.

Initiatives toward abolishing the death penalty in Japan have not prevailed. In November 2002 the Japan Federation of Bar Associations called unsuccessfully for a moratorium on the death penalty and a public debate on the issues of the death penalty system. In July 2003 the Japan Parliamentary League against the Death Penalty planned to introduce a bill to suspend executions while a commission was formed to discuss capital punishment. The opposition blocked that effort.

ABOLITIONISM IN PRACTICE

As of May 24, 2005, Amnesty International considered twenty-four countries as abolitionist in practice. (See Table 9.3.) These countries have death penalty laws for such crimes as murder but have not carried out an execution for the past ten years or more. Some of these nations have not executed anyone for the past fifty years or more. Others have made an international commitment not to impose the death sentence.

Roger Hood, in *The Death Penalty—A Worldwide Perspective* (New York: Oxford University Press, Inc., 2002), noted that just as countries that are abolitionist in practice have eventually outlawed capital punishment, some countries that have not carried out executions for at least ten years might resume executions at some time in the future. The author gave as examples

TABLE 9.3

Countries that are abolitionist in practice, March 2005

Country	Date of last execution
Algeria	1993
Benin	1987
Brunei Darussalam	1957 (date of last known execution)
Burkina Faso	1988
Central African Republic	1981
Congo (Republic)	1982
Gambia	1981
Grenada	1978
Kenya	
Madagascar	1958 (date of last known execution)
Maldives	1952 (date of last known execution)
Mali	1980
	1987
Mauritania	
Morocco	1993
Myanmar	1993
Nauru	No executions since independence
Niger	1976 (date of last known execution)
Papua New Guinea	1950
Russian Federation	1999
Sri Lanka	1976
Suriname	1982
Togo	
Tongo	1982
Tunisia	1991

Note: Countries that retain the death penalty for ordinary crimes such as murder but can be considered abolitionist in practice in that they have not executed anyone during the past 10 years and are believed to have a policy or established practice of not carrying out executions. The list also includes countries which have made an international commitment not to use the death penalty.

SOURCE: "3. Abolitionist in Practice," in *The Death Penalty: Abolitionist and Retentionist Countries*, Amnesty International, March 21, 2005, http://web.amnesty.org/pages/deathpenalty-countries-eng (accessed June 1, 2005)

ten countries that had resumed executions since 1994: the Bahamas, Bahrain, Burundi, Guinea, Guatemala, the Philippines, St. Christopher and Nevis, Trinidad and Tobago, Qatar, and the United States, where the federal government resumed executions in 2001 after thirty-eight years.

ABOLITIONIST COUNTRIES

In 1863 Venezuela became the first nation to outlaw the death penalty. Since that time many countries have abolished capital punishment. Several countries, however, including Argentina, Brazil, and Spain, restored it after previously rejecting it. Argentina revoked the death penalty in 1921 and then again in 1972, reinstating it in 1976 after a military takeover. Then, in 1984 it abolished capital punishment again for ordinary crimes. Brazil abolished the death penalty in 1882, restored it in 1969, and revoked it again in 1979 for ordinary crimes.

Similarly, Spain repealed the death penalty in 1932, brought it back for certain crimes in 1934, totally restored it in 1938, and then abolished it again in 1978 for ordinary crimes. Finally, in 1985, Spain outlawed the death penalty for all crimes. Such swings between banning and imposing capital punishment often reflect shifts in national government between democracy and dictatorship.

As of May 24, 2005, eighty-five countries had abolished the death penalty for all crimes. (See Table 9.4.) Since 1976, when the United States reinstated the death penalty after a nine-year moratorium, many countries have stopped imposing capital punishment. Belgium, the United Kingdom, and Greece, the last three Western European democracies to have the death sentence, abolished it for all crimes in 1996, 1998, and 2004, respectively. In reality, Belgium has not executed any prisoner since 1950. The last two executions in the United Kingdom occurred in 1964. Hong Kong returned to Chinese jurisdiction in July 1997. Having abolished capital punishment in 1993, the former British colony remains abolitionist. In 2002 Yugoslavia (now Serbia and Montenegro) and Cyprus abolished the death penalty for all crimes. Armenia shut down their death penalty system in 2003. The governments of Bhutan, Greece, Samoa, Senegal, and Turkey all announced that they abolished the death penalty for all crimes in 2004. Mexico abolished the death penalty for all crimes in 2005. (See Table 9.5 for a list of the countries that have abolished the death penalty since 1976.)

Abolitionist Countries for Ordinary Crimes Only

Eleven countries do not impose the death penalty for ordinary crimes committed during peacetime, although they may impose it for exceptional crimes. (See Table 9.6.) Since 1997 four countries—Bolivia (1997), Latvia (1999), Albania (2000), and Chile (2001)—have joined this group.

Capital Punishment Is Seldom Reintroduced

Amnesty International notes that once a country abolishes capital punishment, it seldom brings it back. Between 1985 and January 1, 2005, more than fifty countries either enacted laws abolishing the death penalty or, having revoked it for ordinary crimes, eventually outlawed it for all crimes. During this period just four abolitionist countries reimposed the death penalty— Nepal, the Philippines, Gambia, and Papua New Guinea. Nepal, which reinstated the death penalty for murder, abolished it for all crimes in 1997. Gambia and Papua New Guinea remained abolitionist in practice. Although they retained the death penalty for ordinary crimes, Gambia last carried out an execution in 1981, and Papua New Guinea last put an offender to death in 1950.

After banning capital punishment in 1987, the Philippines reintroduced it in 1993. In February 1999 the first execution since 1976 took place, followed by six others. In March 2000 then-President Joseph Estrada suspended all executions in honor of the Christian Jubilee year. In October 2001 newly elected President Gloria

TABLE 9.4

Countries whose laws do not provide for the death penalty for any crime, May 2005

Country	Date of abolition for all crimes	Date of abolition for ordinary crimes	Date of last execution
Andorra	1990		1943
Angola	1992		
Armenia	2003		
Australia	1985	1984	1967
Austria	1968	1950	1950
Azerbaijan	1998		1993
Belgium	1996		1950
Bhutan	2004		1964 (Date of last known execution)
Bosnia-Herzegovina	2001	1997	
Bulgaria	1998		1989
Cambodia	1989		
Canada	1998	1976	1962
Cape Verde	1981		1835
Colombia	1910		1909
Costa Rica	1877		
Cote D'Ivoire	2000		
Croatia	1990		
Cyprus	2002	1983	1962
Czech Republic	1990		
Denmark	1978	1933	1950
Djibouti	1995		No executions since independence
Dominican Republic	1966		
Ecuador	1906		
Estonia	1998		1991
Finland	1972	1949	1944
France	1981		1977
Georgia	1997		1994 (Date of last known execution)
Germany	1987		
Greece	2004	1993	1972
Guinea-Bissau	1993		1986 (Date of last known execution)
Haiti	1987		1972 (Date of last known execution)
Honduras	1956		1940
Hungary	1990		1988
Iceland	1928		1830
Ireland	1990		1954
Italy	1994	1947	1947
Kiribati			No executions since independence
Liechtenstein	1987		1785
Lithuania	1998		1995
Luxwmbourg	1979		1949
Macedibua (former Yugoslav Rep.)	1991		
Malta	2000	1971	1943
Marshall Islands			No executions since independence
Mauritius	1995		1987
Mexico	2005		1937
Micronesia (Federated States)			No executions since independence
Moldova	1995		
Monaco	1962		1847
Mozambique	1990		1986
Namibia	1990		1988 (Date of last known execution)
Nepal	1997	1990	1979
Netherlands	1982	1870	1952
New Zealand	1989	1961	1957
Nicaragua	1979		1930
Niue			

TABLE 9.4

TABLE 9.5

Countries whose laws do not provide for the death penalty for any crime, May 2005 [CONTINUED]

Country	Date of abolition for all crimes	Date of abolition for ordinary crimes	Date of last execution
Norway	1979	1905	1948
Palau			
Panama			1903 (Date of last known execution)
Paraguay	1992		1928
Poland	1997		1988
Portugal	1976	1867	1849 (Date of last known execution)
Romania	1989		1989
Samoa	2004		No executions since independence
San Marino	1865	1848	1468 (Date of last known execution)
Sao Tome and Principe	1990		No executions since independence
Senegal	2004		1967
Serbia and Montenegro	2002		
Seychelles	1993		No executions since independence
Slovak Republic	1990		
Slovenia	1989		
Solomon Islands		1966	No executions since independence
South Africa	1997	1995	1991
Spain	1995	1978	1975
Sweden	1972	1921	1910
Switzerland	1992	1942	1944
Timor-Leste	1999		
Turkey	2004	2002	1984
Turkmenistan	1999		
Tuvalu			Ind.
Ukraine	1999		
United Kingdom	1998	1973	1964
Uruguay	1907		
Vanuatu			Ind.
Vatican City State	1969		
Venezuela	1863		

SOURCE: "1. Abolitionist for All Crimes," in *The Death Penalty: Abolitionist and Retentionist Countries*, Amnesty International, May 24, 2005, http://web.amnesty.org/pages/dcathpenalty-abolitionist1-eng (accessed June 1, 2005)

Countries which have abolished the death penalty since 1976

1976: **PORTUGAL** abolished the death penalty for all crimes.
1978: **DENMARK** abolished the death penalty for all crimes.
1979: **LUXEMBOURG, NICARAGUA** and **NORWAY** abolished the death penalty for all crimes. **BRAZIL, FIJI** and **PERU** abolished the death penalty for ordinary crimes.
1981: **FRANCE** and **CAPE VERDE** abolished the death penalty for all crimes.
1982: The **NETHERLANDS** abolished the death penalty for all crimes.
1983: **CYPRUS** and **EL SALVADOR** abolished the death penalty for ordinary crimes.
1984: **ARGENTINA** abolished the death penalty for ordinary crimes.
1985: **AUSTRALIA** abolished the death penalty for all crimes.
1987: **HAITI, LIECHTENSTEIN** and the **GERMAN DEMOCRATIC REPUBLIC**ᵃ abolished the death penalty for all crimes.
1989: **CAMBODIA, NEW ZEALAND, ROMANIA** and **SLOVENIA**ᵇ abolished the death penalty for all crimes.
1990: **ANDORRA, CROATIA**ᵇ, the **CZECH AND SLOVAK FEDERAL REPUBLIC**ᶜ, **HUNGARY, IRELAND, MOZAMBIQUE, NAMIBIA** and **SAO TOMÉ AND PRÍNCIPE** abolished the death penalty for all crimes.
1992: **ANGOLA, PARAGUAY** and **SWITZERLAND** abolished the death penalty for all crimes.
1993: **GUINEA-BISSAU, HONG KONG**ᵈ and **SEYCHELLES** abolished the death penalty for all crimes.
1994: **ITALY** abolished the death penalty for all crimes.
1995: **DJIBOUTI, MAURITIUS, MOLDOVA** and **SPAIN** abolished the death penalty for all crimes.
1996: **BELGIUM** abolished the death penalty for all crimes.
1997: **GEORGIA, NEPAL, POLAND** and **SOUTH AFRICA** abolished the death penalty for all crimes. **BOLIVIA** abolished the death penalty for ordinary crimes.
1998: **AZERBAIJAN, BULGARIA, CANADA, ESTONIA, LITHUANIA** and the **UNITED KINGDOM** abolished the death penalty for all crimes.
1999: **EAST TIMOR, TURKMENISTAN** and **UKRAINE** abolished the death penalty for all crimes. **LATVIA**ᵉ abolished the death penalty for ordinary crimes
2000 : **COTE D'IVOIRE** and **MALTA** abolished the death penalty for all crimes. **ALBANIA**ᶠ abolished the death penalty for ordinary crimes.
2001: **BOSNIA-HEZEGOVINA**ᵍ abolished the death penalty for all crimes. **CHILE** abolished the death penalty for ordinary crimes.
2002: **CYPRUS** and **YUGOSLAVIA** (later **SERBIA AND MONTENEGRO**) abolished the death penalty for all crimes.
2003: **ARMENIA** abolished the death penalty for all crimes.
2004: **BHUTAN, GREECE, SAMOA, SENEGAL** and **TURKEY** abolished the death penalty for all crimes.
2005: **MEXICO** abolished the death penalty for all crimes.

Notes:
ᵃIn 1990 the German Democratic Republic became unified with the Federal Republic of Germany, where the death penalty had been abolished in 1949.
ᵇSlovenia and Croatia abolished the death penalty while they were still republics of the Socialist Federal Republic of Yugoslavia. The two republics became independent in 1991.
ᶜIn 1993 the Czech and Slovak Federal Republic divided into two states, the Czech Republic and Slovakia.
ᵈIn 1997 Hong Kong was returned to Chinese rule as a special administrative region of China. Since then Hong Kong has remained abolitionist.
ᵉIn 1999 the Latvian parliament voted to ratify Protocol No. 6 to the European Convention on Human Rights, abolishing the death penalty for peacetime offences.
ᶠIn 2000 Albania ratified Protocol No. 6 to the European Convention on Human Rights, abolishing the death penalty for peacetime offences.
ᵍIn 2001 Bosnia-Herzegovina ratified the Second Optional Protocol to the International Covenant on Civil and Political Rights, abolishing the death penalty for all crimes.

SOURCE: "Countries which Have Abolished the Death Penalty since 1976," in *The Death Penalty: Abolitionist and Retentionist Countries*, Amnesty International, May 24, 2005, http://web.amnesty.org/pages/deathpenalty-countries-eng (accessed June 1, 2005)

Macapagal-Arroyo lifted the moratorium on the death penalty in light of the rising numbers of kidnapping cases for ransom money. The president restored the moratorium in late 2003, saying she might commute the death sentence to life imprisonment and then she lifted it again in early 2005, specifically for drug traffickers and kidnappers. More than 1,005 persons were under sentence of death as of June 1, 2005, according to Hands Off Cain, a European organization working to end the death penalty worldwide.

DEATH PENALTY AGAINST MINORS

The International Covenant on Civil and Political Rights, the UN Convention on the Rights of the Child, the African Charter on the Rights and Welfare of the Child, and the American Convention on Human Rights all ban the imposition of the death sentence on persons who were less than eighteen years old at the time of their crime. In addition, the UN Convention on the Rights of the Child further prohibits the sentence of life without the possibility of parole for those younger than eighteen. Today virtually all countries in the world either have statutes prohibiting the execution of minors or are believed to be abiding by the provisions of one or another of the aforementioned treaties.

TABLE 9.6

Countries that are abolitionist for ordinary crimes only, May 2005

Country	Date of abolition for ordinary crimes	Date of last execution
Albania	2000	
Argentina	1984	
Bolivia	1997	1974
Brazil	1979	1855
Chile	2001	1985
Cook Islands		
El Salvador	1983	1973 (date of last known execution)
Fiji	1979	1964
Israel	1954	1962
Latvia	1999	1996
Peru	1979	1979

Note: Countries whose laws provide for the death penalty only for exceptional crimes such as crimes under military law or crimes committed in exceptional circumstances, such as wartime crimes.

SOURCE: "2. Abolitionist for Ordinary Crimes Only," in *The Death Penalty: Abolitionist and Retentionist Countries*, Amnesty International, May 24, 2005, http://web.amnesty.org/pages/deathpenalty abolitionist2-eng (accessed June 1, 2005)

According to Amnesty International, between 1990 and 2004 seven countries—the Democratic Republic of Congo, Iran, Nigeria, Pakistan, Saudi Arabia, the United States, and Yemen—had executed thirty-eight offenders who were under the age of eighteen when they committed their crimes. Of these, nineteen executions occurred in the United States. Between 2000 and March 2005 only three states—Oklahoma, Texas, and Virginia—had executed people who were minors when they committed their crimes.

Several of the countries on the AI list, including the United States, had increased the age for imposition of the death penalty to eighteen since 1990. Pakistan raised the minimum age in 2000, and Yemen followed suit in 2001. In March 2005 the U.S. Supreme Court ruled in *Roper v. Simmons* (543 U.S. 633) that executing people who committed their crimes under the age of eighteen constituted "cruel and unusual punishment." With this ruling, all states were required to stop executing minors. (See Chapter 4.)

CHAPTER 10
THE DEBATE—CAPITAL PUNISHMENT SHOULD BE MAINTAINED

TESTIMONY OF JOSHUA MARQUIS, DISTRICT ATTORNEY, CLATSOP COUNTY, OREGON, BEFORE THE UNITED STATES HOUSE OF REPRESENTATIVES JUDICIARY COMMITTEE, SUBCOMMITTEE ON CRIME AND TERRORISM, JUNE 30, 2005

Popular culture . . . has created an entire alternate universe that nurtures a legal system that regularly hurls doe-eyed innocents onto death row through the malevolent machinations of corrupt cops and district attorneys who either earn bonuses for the innocent people they convict or are so intent on advancing their careers that they disregard the truth and conceal evidence that might clear the defendant. . . .

Since the death penalty was re-authorized in 1976 by the Supreme Court, there have been upwards of 500,000 murders. About 7,000 murderers were sentenced to death and about 3,700 remain on death row today. Seven hundred and fifty have been executed. Appellate courts at the state and federal levels have imposed what one justice called "super due process" for convicted capital murderers, overturning almost two-thirds of all death sentences, a rate far exceeding that in other cases. Virtually none have been overturned because of "actual innocence."

Some claim that a civilized society must be prepared to allow ten guilty men to walk free in order to spare one innocent. But the well-organized and even better-funded abolitionists cannot point to a single case of a demonstrably innocent person executed in the modern era of American capital punishment. Instead, let's tally the additional victims of the freed:

Nine, killed by Kenneth McDuff, who had been sentenced to die for child murder in Texas and then was freed on parole after the death penalty laws at the time were overturned.

One, by Robert Massie of California, also sentenced to die and also paroled. Massie rewarded the man who gave him a job on parole by murdering him less than a year after getting out of prison.

One, by Richard Marquette, in Oregon, sentenced to "life" (which until 1994 meant about eight years in Oregon) for abducting and then dismembering women. He did so well in a woman-free environment (prison) that he was released—only to abduct, kill, and dismember women again.

Two, by Carl Cletus Bowles, in Idaho, guilty of kidnapping nine people and the murder of a police officer. Bowles escaped during a conjugal visit with a girlfriend, only to abduct and murder an elderly couple.

The victims of these men didn't have "close calls" with death. They are dead. Murdered. Without saying goodbye to their loved ones. Without appeal to the state or the media or Hollywood or anyone's heartstrings. . . .

OPEN FLOOR SPEECH BY SENATOR JOHN CORNYN (R-TX), BEFORE THE UNITED STATES SENATE, 109TH CONGRESS, APRIL 4, 2005

I am troubled when I read decisions such as *Roper v. Simmons*. This is a recent decision from March 1, 2005. Let me state what that case was about. This was a case involving Christopher Simmons. Christopher Simmons was seven months shy of his eighteenth birthday when he murdered Shirley Crook. This is a murder that he planned to commit. He told his coconspirators before committing the crime, this seventeen-year-old who was seven months shy of his eighteenth birthday, he encouraged his friends to join him, assuring them that they could "get away with it," because they were minors. Christopher Simmons and his cohorts broke into the home of an innocent woman, bound her with duct tape and electrical wire, and then threw her off a bridge, alive and conscious, resulting in her subsequent death.

Those facts led a jury in Missouri, using the law in Missouri that the people of Missouri had chosen for themselves through their elected representatives, to convict him of capital murder and to sentence him to death.

Well, this seventeen-year-old boy, or young man I guess is what I would call him, Christopher Simmons, challenged that jury verdict and that conviction all the way through the State courts of Missouri and all the way to the U.S. Supreme Court. And the United States Supreme Court, on March 1, 2005, held that Christopher Simmons or any other person in the United States of America who is under the age of eighteen who commits such a heinous and premeditated and calculated murder, cannot be given the death penalty because it violates the U.S. Constitution.

In so holding, the U.S. Supreme Court said: We are no longer going to leave this in the hands of jurors. We do not trust jurors. We are no longer going to leave this up to the elected representatives of the people of the respective States, even though twenty States, including Missouri, have the possibility at least of the death penalty being assessed in the most aggravated types of cases, involving the most heinous crimes, against someone who is not yet eighteen.

This is how the Court decided to do that. First, it might be of interest to my colleagues that fifteen years earlier the same U.S. Supreme Court, sitting in Washington, across the street from this Capitol where we are standing here today, held just the opposite. Fifteen years ago, the U.S. Supreme Court held that under appropriate circumstances, given the proper safeguards, in the worst cases involving the most depraved and premeditated conduct, a jury could constitutionally convict someone of capital murder and sentence them to the death penalty. But, fifteen years later, on March 1, they said what was constitutional the day before was no longer constitutional, wiping twenty States' laws off the books and reversing this death penalty conviction for Christopher Simmons.

What I want to focus on now is the reasoning that Justice Anthony Kennedy, writing for the U.S. Supreme Court, in a 5-to-4 decision, used to reach that conclusion. First, Justice Kennedy adopted a test for determining whether this death penalty conviction was constitutional. The test—this ought to give you some indication of the problems we have with the Supreme Court as a policymaker with no fixed standards or objective standards by which to determine its decisions to make its judgments. The Court embraced a test that it had adopted earlier referring to the "evolving standards of decency that mark the progress of a maturing society." Let me repeat that. The test they used was the "evolving standards of decency that mark the progress of a maturing society."

I would think any person of reasonable intelligence, listening to what I am saying, would say: What was that? How do you determine those "evolving standards"? And if they are one way on one day, how do they evolve to be something different the next day? And what is a "maturing society"? How do we determine whether society has matured or not? I think people would be justified in asking: Isn't that fancy window dressing for a preordained conclusion? I will let them decide.

Well, it does not get much better because then the Court, in order to determine whether the facts met that standard, such as that this death penalty could not stand, or these laws in twenty States cannot stand, looked to what they called an "emerging consensus." Well, any student of high school civics knows we have a Federal system, and the national Government does not dictate to the State governments all aspects of criminal law. In fact, most criminal law is decided in State courts in the first place. But, nevertheless, the Supreme Court of the United States, in a 5-to-4 decision, looked for an "emerging consensus," and in the process wiped twenty States' laws off the books. I will not go into the details of how they found a consensus, but suffice it to say it ought to be that in a nation comprised of fifty separate sovereign State governments, where twenty States disagree with the Court on its decision that wipes those twenty States' courts laws off the books, it can hardly be called a consensus, if language is to have any meaning.

Secondly, the Court said: We will also look to our own decisions, our own judgment over the propriety of this law. In other words, they are going to decide because they can, because basically their decisions are not appealable, and there is nowhere else to go if they decide this law is unconstitutional. The American people, the people of Missouri, the people who support, under limited circumstances, under appropriate checks and balances, the death penalty for people who commit heinous crimes under the age of eighteen are simply out of luck; this is the end of the line.

Well, finally—and this is the part I want to conclude on and speak on for a few minutes—the Court demonstrated a disconcerting tendency to rely on the laws of foreign governments and even treaties in the application and enforcement of U.S. law. This is a trend that did not start with the Roper case, but I did want to mention it in that connection.

But if the U.S. Supreme Court is not going to look to the laws of the United States, including the fundamental law of the United States which is the Constitution, but interpreting what is and is not constitutional under the U.S. Constitution by looking at what foreign governments and foreign laws have to say about that same issue, I fear that bit by bit and case by case the American people are slowly losing control over the meaning of our laws and the Constitution itself. If this trend continues, foreign governments may have a say in what our laws and our Constitution mean and what our policies in America should be.

PORTIONS OF THE MINORITY VIEWS BY SENATOR ORRIN HATCH (R-UT) INCLUDED IN THE REPORT ON THE INNOCENCE PROTECTION ACT OF 2002 (S. 486) BY SENATOR PATRICK LEAHY (D-VT) TO THE SENATE, 107TH CONGRESS, OCTOBER 16, 2002

S. 486 is presented by the Majority as a bill to ensure access to DNA testing and competent counsel in capital proceedings. While such goals are laudable, the Majority Report raises broader issues relating to the overall fairness of the death penalty system in this country, the need for a national moratorium, and the need to address other "defects of capital punishment systems nationwide. . . ." Some who have injected these larger concerns into the debate over S. 486 are simply attempting to frustrate the administration of the death penalty in our country by alleging, without any credible evidence, that there is a significant risk that innocent persons have been or will be executed. By attaching itself to this claim, the Majority has lent credence to a minority of activist groups that has little concern for the overall safety of the public and the significant benefits to our society of a swift, accurate, and fair death penalty system.

Contrary to the Majority's view, we submit that the death penalty system in our country is accurate. Suggestions to the contrary are contradicted by the fact that no credible evidence has been provided to suggest that a single innocent person has been executed since the Supreme Court imposed the heightened protections in 1976. The death penalty system now includes numerous layers of court review, which ensure that errors are identified and corrected. In fact, the death penalty system saves lives by incapacitating dangerous offenders who, if freed, would pose a significant risk that they will kill again. Moreover, there is substantial evidence that the death penalty is a significant deterrent; states that impose the death penalty have reduced murder rates, while states that do not impose the death penalty have experienced increases in murder rates. For convicted murderers who are already serving life without parole sentences, the death penalty is a critical deterrent to the murder of prison guards, nurses, and other inmates. Moreover, the possibility of the death penalty has served a vital national security interest by encouraging those guilty of espionage against the United States, like Aldrich Ames and Robert Hanssen, to cooperate and provide full disclosure of the damage they caused. . . .

. . . We disagree with the underlying premise for much of S. 486—that the death penalty system in our country is "broken" and needs to be fixed. In our view, the death penalty system in our country continues to play a vital role in protecting the public from vicious criminals by deterring and punishing murderers. Moreover, aside from the protection of the public and the just punishment of the guilty, our death penalty system vindicates the right of victims and their families to see that justice is done. All too often, the value of a swift, certain, and reliable death penalty is challenged by a vocal minority of special interest groups seeking to advance their own anti–death penalty agenda by proffering unreliable studies and generalizations based on isolated incidents. Death penalty opponents pursue their cause without even considering the public benefits of the death penalty. . . .

The death penalty system in our country has been built on "super due process," a term used by former Supreme Court Justice Lewis Powell to describe the procedural system for imposing and reviewing death penalty cases. We have an elaborate system of appeals in capital cases, which typically involves multiple levels of state and federal review, ultimately landing at the United States Supreme Court. Over the past twenty-five years, procedural protections have been adopted to reduce as much as possible the likelihood that error will be committed or, if committed, that it will go undetected. Neither the Majority nor any death penalty opponents has cited any credible evidence that any innocent person has been executed since the Supreme Court reinstated the death penalty in 1976. . . .

The likely explanation for the absence of errors in capital cases during the past quarter century is the greater care taken by the courts to assure the correct resolution of such cases and, particularly, the painstaking reviews that occur in cases in which the death sentence is actually imposed.

More significantly, death penalty opponents undervalue the important benefit of the death penalty—it saves lives. Through a combination of deterrence, incapacitation, and the imposition of just punishment, a swift, certain and accurate death penalty system protects a significant number of innocent lives.

. . . Death penalty opponents attack capital punishment by focusing on the alleged risk that we will execute an innocent person or that we already have executed an innocent person. While there is no credible evidence to support these claims, there is overwhelming evidence that capital punishment saves a substantial number of innocent lives, deterring probably thousands of murders in the United States every year. The recent and most comprehensive academic studies, our nation's historical experience, and criminals' own account of their motives and behavior all point in the same direction: that the death penalty is a substantial deterrent to homicide. . . .

TESTIMONY OF KENT SCHEIDEGGER, LEGAL DIRECTOR, CRIMINAL JUSTICE LEGAL FOUNDATION, BEFORE THE UNITED STATES SENATE COMMITTEE ON THE HEARING ON "REDUCING THE RISK OF EXECUTING THE INNOCENT: THE REPORT OF THE ILLINOIS GOVERNOR'S COMMISSION ON CAPITAL PUNISHMENT," JUNE 12, 2002

. . . The correct identification and sufficient punishment of murderers is a matter of the greatest importance. Indeed, there is no more important function of the state governments than the protection of their citizens from murder. The performance of this function, while also protecting the wrongly accused, deserves the closest attention and greatest care. Regrettably, there has been a great deal of misleading information circulating on the subject of capital punishment, so I welcome the opportunity to make at least a start at getting the truth out today.

The focus of today's hearing is on the actual guilt or innocence of the defendant. This change of focus is most welcome and long overdue. For three decades, the American people have suffered inordinate delays and exorbitant expense in extended litigation over issues which have nothing to do with guilt, which are not in the Constitution as originally enacted and understood, and which often involve sentencing policy decisions of dubious merit. Congress should certainly be concerned with further reducing the already small possibility of conviction of the innocent, whether the penalty be death or life in prison. At the same time, it should take care not to exacerbate, and if possible to reduce, the interminable delays and erroneous reversals that are presently the norm in that vast majority of capital cases that involve no question whatever of the identity of the perpetrator. I suggest that the Congress set a national goal of reducing to four years the median time from sentence to execution and establish a standing commission to periodically review the system and recommend changes to achieve that goal. Four years is more than sufficient to weed out the very few cases of real doubt of identity, but short enough that the American people would finally have the benefits of [an] effective death penalty system: justice for the worst murders, certainty the murderer will not kill again, and the life-saving deterrent effect of such a system.

The specific topic of today's hearing is the Report of the [Illinois] Governor's Commission on Capital Punishment. Regrettably, that report shows little of the balance needed for this important topic. Particularly disturbing is the summary manner in which the report dismisses deterrence. While the subject has long been controversial and will likely remain so, the flurry of recent studies finding a deterrent effect cannot be brushed off. A sophisticated econometric analysis at Emory University estimated that each execution saves eighteen innocent lives. Another study at the University of Colorado estimated a lower but still very substantial five to six fewer homicides for each execution. Even using the lowest of these figures, a national moratorium would kill hundreds of innocent people each year. Indeed, a study at the University of Houston estimated that a temporary halt in executions in Texas to resolve a legal question cost over two hundred lives in a single state. There are, of course, other studies to the contrary. Even so, any public official considering a halt to or severe restriction of capital punishment must consider the very substantial possibility that such an action will result in the deaths of a great many innocent people.

One of the commission's recommendations is to narrow the scope of offenses eligible for capital punishment. Some amount of narrowing is indeed in order, but the drastic limitations in the report are not justified by any concerns with actual innocence. In particular, the recommendation that murder of the rape victim by a rapist no longer be a capital offense should be rejected out of hand. This is the kind of case where the deterrent effect is most needed, since without capital punishment the rapist is looking at a long prison sentence whether he kills the victim or not. It is also the kind of case where DNA is most likely to eliminate any doubt of identity.

On a positive note, the report does acknowledge that many of the reversed judgments in capital cases are "based on legal issues that had little to do with the trial itself," and are often the result of new rules created by the state and federal supreme courts after the trial. This is an important fact for the Congress to consider when it is confronted with misleading statistics of the so-called "error rate" in capital cases. . . .

STATEMENT OF FRANK KEATING, GOVERNOR OF OKLAHOMA, AT THE CONFERENCE OF THE PEW FORUM ON RELIGION & PUBLIC LIFE (A CALL FOR RECKONING: RELIGION AND THE DEATH PENALTY), HELD AT THE UNIVERSITY OF CHICAGO DIVINITY SCHOOL, CHICAGO, ILLINOIS, JANUARY 25, 2002

. . . I had never been to the Republic of Ireland and I arrived as a guest to participate in a debate on the subject of capital punishment. . . .

. . . [S]everal of the things I said came as somewhat of a surprise to my Irish listeners. The impression they had was that the United States is a killing field, that we execute everyone for everything, and that it is a killing field largely focused on minorities. When I explained to them that the United States' problem is its incredible violence, our problem as a country is that we—in many cities and in many rural areas—treat life cheaply. For example, the big shock was when the prime minister of Ireland said that the year previously they had had forty homicides in Ireland. We had sixty in Oklahoma City; they had forty homicides in the entire country the year previous.

When some who were Catholics pointed out that the pope felt that capital punishment should be rare if non-existent, I said, "Well, in the United States, believe it or not, that is practically true." Between 1977 and the time of my speech—and it's changed somewhat obviously unfortunately on the high side of homicides since then—we had something like 480,000 homicides and 629 executions. So for 480,000 deaths, we executed 629 people, something like 1/12th of 1% of the killings resulting in executions. If you applied that same standard to the Republic of Ireland, they wouldn't execute any-body either, because 1/12th of 1% of forty people is zero. There is no one out there.

In the state of Oklahoma in the heartland of America, right in the middle of the United States we had 8,000 homicides since 1977 and thirty executions, something like 1/2 of 1% of the killings in our state resulting in executions.

Thirdly, the Irish listeners were surprised that there was anguish on the part of those of us who consider ourselves conservative. I'm a pro-life conservative. I believe in the quality of each individual life, in the goodness of every human being and the right of everyone to stand tall, to do that which he or she can do in this magnificent free society in which we live. But they were surprised that there was anguish and debate—and in our many different religioned environment (only 3% of the people in my state are Catholic)—that we have a very vigorous debate on capital punishment. . . .

My friends were also surprised that in my state the average time between conviction and execution was ten years. They thought that if somebody committed a crime, somebody was quickly executed. They were also sur-prised to learn that nationally that statistic was a little bit less than ten years, but it's nearly double digits the number of years that pass between the time a killing results in a conviction to the time of execution.

Yes, it is true, I said, that we have offenses certainly at the federal level for trafficking large amounts of nar-cotics, treason, where the death sentence can be applied, but for all practical purposes certainly at the state level capital punishment is reserved for people who kill other human beings.

They also were surprised that a life sentence was not a life sentence. In my life I have been an FBI agent, I've been a state prosecutor, I've been a United States Attorney, I supervised all the federal prosecutions in the United States and many of the law enforcement agencies, most federal law enforcement agencies in the country, including the U.S. Bureau of Prisons. It came as a surprise to them that we had situations where people were sentenced to life in prison without parole and it didn't mean that, that people were released, people escaped, people killed other people while in prison, and that happens, by the way, far more frequently than we think.

. . . I must confess that probably some of the most ardent capital punishment advocates are people like me who have seen up close and [sic] person the flotsam, the jetsam of those who horribly, cruelly treat other people. . . .

Timothy McVeigh killed 168 of our neighbors and friends in Oklahoma City, including nineteen children. Now, people say when you debate the death penalty you shouldn't get into emotions, you shouldn't talk about individuals, but you have to because that's what it is all about, people doing horrible incredibly sick, evil things to other people.

And to have someone like Timothy McVeigh making a political statement, knowing that there was a daycare center in a building and blowing it up and seeing the wreckage, the carnage that resulted, the anguish, the agony, the destruction of lives and livelihoods and happi-ness and future that resulted, I am unforgiving.

I think, of course, that we want to make sure we have the right person. I think, of course, that that individual has the rights and the full panoply of the criminal justice system, including a first-rate defense. But when it is over, in my judgment, the law should be carried out, if that is what a judge or a jury decides. That does not cause me much disquiet. I don't have a sleepless night.

Now, for those to say, "But isn't there a chance that you would execute the innocent," there's no evidence of that. Even Barry Scheck [of the Innocence Project] admitted that that, as far as he knows, has never occurred; there's no evidence of it. But, yes, that is something that all of us have to be very concerned about. I would like to think that it's enough that ten to twelve years pass between conviction and execution, that the average num-ber of appeals is something like twelve in both the state and the federal system, that no governor, no pardon or parole board wants to execute an innocent person. Why? Because the guilty person would be free.

. . . What we have done in Oklahoma is to require that every felony case and certainly every capital case have, at our expense, DNA testing. And I think that's very sound. Now, many cases don't have DNA testing available because there is no evidence in the case that would be subject to such testing.

Secondly, I have said that if the Pardon and Parole Board recommends to me clemency, and I have granted clemency in some cases, I think "proof beyond a reason-able doubt" with respect to capital cases is too low a standard. I've said that publicly at home and I apply it in my own case. If the governor is asked to determine yes or no on a particular capital event, then what is my burden? Basically, whatever burden I seek to establish, there is nothing written.

As Justice Scalia notes, in the federal system we define "proof beyond a reasonable doubt." State systems generally don't. In Oklahoma we don't. But in the federal system, it is defined as proof of such a convincing character that you would rely [upon] it unhesitatingly in the most important of your affairs.

Is that a high enough standard when you're taking another person's life? I think there should be a moral certainty standard, which I apply to myself. If I don't have in these cases a confession or physical evidence, if I don't have that even higher standard than proof beyond a reasonable doubt, I'm willing and do commute.

But once that standard is established in my own mind—and this is not easy, because you're dealing with another human being—if that standard is applied, I with no hesitation can deny clemency, because I believe if we love and elevate human life—that means innocent human life—for those who would intentionally, with malice, with violence, take another human being's life, that person has forfeited the right to live. . . .

STATEMENT OF STEVEN D. STEWART, PROSECUTOR, CLARK COUNTY, INDIANA, NOVEMBER 7, 2001

Along with two-thirds of the public, I believe in capital punishment. I believe that there are some defendants who have earned the ultimate punishment our society has to offer by committing murder with aggravating circumstances present. I believe life is sacred. It cheapens the life of an innocent murder victim to say that society has no right to keep the murderer from ever killing again. In my view, society has not only the right, but the duty to act in self defense to protect the innocent.

Nevertheless, the value of the death penalty in our current system of justice is a limited one and should not be overstated. Because the death sentence is so rarely carried out, whatever deterrent value that exists is lessened in years of appeals and due process. Because of the unlimited power of judges, juries, and prosecutors to show mercy, the difference between those who receive the death penalty and those who do not is minimal. Finally, because the system allows it, the financial costs to state and local governments can be staggering.

In spite of these shortcomings, it is my view that pursuing a death sentence in appropriate cases is the right thing to do. There is no adequate and acceptable alternative. Life Without Parole does not eliminate the risk that the prisoner will murder a guard, a visitor, or another

inmate, and we should not be compelled to take that risk. It is also not unheard of for inmates to escape from prison. The prisoner will not be eligible for parole until the next legislative session, when the parole laws can be changed. Considering that a defendant sentenced to "life imprisonment" across the country actually serves on the average less than eight years in prison, it is a good bet that "life without parole" will not have the meaning intended as years go by.

No system of justice can produce results which are 100% certain all the time. Mistakes will be made in any system, which relies upon human testimony for proof. We should be vigilant to uncover and avoid such mistakes. Nevertheless, the risk of making a mistake with the extraordinary due process applied in death penalty cases is very small, and there is no credible evidence to show that any innocent persons have been executed at least since the death penalty was reactivated in 1976. The estimated fifty to eighty-five inmates "exonerated" and released from death row, as trumpeted by anti–death penalty activists, should be considered in context of over 7,000 death sentences handed down since 1973. The inevitability of a mistake should not serve as grounds to eliminate the death penalty any more than the risk of having a wreck should make automobiles illegal. At the same time, we should never ignore the risks of allowing the inmate to kill again. Our "system" was created by legislators and judges. In order for the death penalty to remain a meaningful and effective punishment, those same legislators and judges need to make necessary changes to reflect the will of the people in a democratic society.

STATEMENT OF PRESIDENT GEORGE W. BUSH ABOUT THE EXECUTION OF TIMOTHY MCVEIGH, JUNE 11, 2001

This morning, the United States of America carried out the severest sentence for the gravest of crimes. The victims of the Oklahoma City bombing have been given not vengeance, but justice. And one young man met the fate he chose for himself six years ago. For the survivors of the crime and for the families of the dead, the pain goes on. The final punishment of the guilty cannot alone bring peace to the innocent. It cannot recover the loss or balance the scales, and it is not meant to do so.

Today, every living person who was hurt by the evil done in Oklahoma City can rest in the knowledge that there has been a reckoning. At every point from the morning of April 19, 1995, to this hour, we have seen the good that overcomes evil. We saw it in the rescuers who saved and suffered with the victims. We have seen it in a community that has grieved and held close the memory of the lost. We have seen it in the work of detectives, marshals, and police. And we have seen it in the courts. Due process ruled. The case was proved. The verdict was calmly reached. And the rights of the accused were protected and observed to the full, and to the end. Under the laws of our country, the matter is concluded. Life and history bring tragedies, and often they cannot be explained. But they can be redeemed. They are redeemed by dispensing justice, though eternal justice is not ours to deliver.

By remembering those who grieve, including Timothy McVeigh's mother, father, and sisters, and by trusting in purposes greater than our own, may God in his mercy grant peace to all, to the lives that were taken six years ago, to the lives that go on, and to the life that ended today.

STATEMENT OF REPRESENTATIVE HENRY J. HYDE (R-IL), CHAIRMAN, HOUSE REPRESENTATIVES JUDICIARY COMMITTEE, DECEMBER 10, 1997

With regard to the issue of capital punishment, it is my view that the death penalty, if imposed fairly and without undue delay, can serve a deterrent purpose in our criminal justice system. There are some cases of murder that are so heinous and brutal that society must impose its ultimate penalty. These cases would include terrorism, treason, hijacking resulting in the death of a hostage, or the killing of a police [officer] or prison guard acting in the line of duty. If, under careful deliberation, it is determined that such a crime has occurred and the defendant in the crime has been proven guilty beyond a reasonable doubt, then I would support the imposition of capital punishment.

Society has a right to impose whatever punishment it collectively determines befits the violation of its laws. Denying society the ability to impose the death penalty on those convicted of murder devalues the lives of its citizens.

STATEMENT OF REPRESENTATIVE ROBERT K. DORNAN (R-CA), DECEMBER 4, 1995

As a U.S. congressman, one of my primary concerns is the rule of law. Over the last thirty years, our nation has experienced a crippling decline in effective law enforcement resulting from the erosion of the concept of swift and sure punishment for law breakers. This has resulted from multiple causes, including a politicized judiciary, which all too often has been more sympathetic to the criminal than the victim, and as well, to a general judicial philosophy which has become more concerned with questions of procedure than the search for truth. . . .

As a conservative, I believe there are certain crimes for which the death penalty is justified. Some individuals commit crimes so reprehensible that they forfeit their right to live in society. And some commit crimes so heinous that they do not deserve to be supported for life by the society they injured. These are the people who should be sentenced to death. The death penalty should remain our most severe punishment and should be used only in extraordinary cases. But as has always been the standard in our justice system, the punishment should fit the crime.

STATEMENT OF REPRESENTATIVE SAM JOHNSON (R-TX), NOVEMBER 8, 1995

Regarding capital punishment, I continue to believe that the best way to prevent crime is to target repeat offenders. Criminals must understand the consequences of their actions. We should make prisoners serve out their entire sentences and enforce stiffer penalties, such as capital punishment against felons convicted of heinous crimes, such as rape, murder, and drug-related deaths. I am aware of the need for individual responsibility in determining the death penalty's applicability, and we must always be diligent not to punish the innocent. However, in spite of these risks, I believe that capital punishment is a morally justifiable, necessary, and effective punishment.

Thirty-six states currently administer capital punishment. Texas alone has executed ninety-nine criminals in the past seven years. The people of Texas have made it known that violent crime will not be tolerated.

STATEMENT OF SENATOR JESSE HELMS (R-NC), NOVEMBER 6, 1995

Although I wish that the death penalty was never necessary, I do believe that it should be available to our courts to punish those responsible for especially violent crimes. I believe that the death penalty protects society from further harm by the offender. I also think that it is useful in deterring others from committing similar crimes.

American society will be increasingly plagued by violent crime without the use of the death penalty. In order to combat crime, we must give our police officers and judges the support and encouragement necessary to get tough with criminals. The death penalty is one step in the *right* direction.

EXCERPTS FROM JUSTICE ANTONIN SCALIA'S CONCURRING OPINION IN THE SUPREME COURT DECISION *CALLINS V. COLLINS* (510 U.S. 1141, 1994), DENYING REVIEW OF THE DEATH PENALTY CASE (IN RESPONSE TO JUSTICE HARRY A. BLACKMUN'S DISSENT)

The Fifth Amendment provides that "no person shall be held to answer for a capital crime, unless on a presentment or indictment of a Grand Jury . . . nor be deprived of life . . . without due process of law." This clearly permits the death penalty to be imposed and establishes beyond doubt that the death penalty is not one of the "cruel and unusual punishments" prohibited by the Eighth Amendment. . . .

Convictions in opposition to the death penalty are often passionate and deeply held. That would be no excuse for reading them into a Constitution that does not contain them, even if they represented the convictions of a majority of Americans. Much less is there any excuse for using that course to thrust a minority's views upon the people. Justice Blackmun . . . describ[es] with poignancy the death of a convicted murderer by lethal injection. He chooses . . . one of the less brutal of the murders—the murder of a man ripped by a bullet suddenly and unexpectedly, with no opportunity to prepare himself and his affairs, and left to bleed to death on the floor of a tavern. The death-by-injection, which Justice Blackmun describes, looks pretty desirable next to that. It looks even better next to some of the other cases currently before us, which Justice Blackmun did not select as the vehicle for his announcement that the death penalty is always unconstitutional—for example, the case of the eleven-year-old girl raped by four men and then killed. . . . How enviable a quiet death by lethal injection compared with that! If the people conclude . . . that . . . brutal deaths may be deterred by capital punishment, indeed, if they merely conclude that justice requires such brutal deaths to be avenged by capital punishment, the creation of false, untextual, and unhistorical contradictions within the "Court's Eighth Amendment jurisprudence" should not prevent them.

STATEMENT OF PAUL G. CASSELL, ASSOCIATE PROFESSOR OF LAW, UNIVERSITY OF UTAH, SALT LAKE CITY, BEFORE THE SENATE JUDICIARY COMMITTEE, APRIL 1, 1993

The paucity of examples of innocent defendants who have been executed provides compelling evidence that the risk of mistaken execution is virtually non-existent. If opponents of the death penalty are able to produce no better examples of mistaken executions [in the testimony], then the overwhelming majority of Americans who support capital punishment can rest assured that the criminal justice system is doing an admirable, if not indeed perfect, job of preventing the execution of innocent defendants. . . .

Capital sentences, when carried out, save innocent lives by permanently incapacitating murderers. Some persons who commit capital homicide will slay other innocent persons if given the opportunity to do so. The death penalty is the most effective means of preventing such killers from repeating their crimes. The next most serious penalty, life imprisonment without possibility of parole, prevents murderers from committing some crimes but does not prevent them from murdering in prison.

At least five federal prison officers have been killed since December 1982, and the inmates in at least three of the incidents were already serving life sentences for murder. . . .

While the innocent lives saved through the incapacitative effect of capital punishment are important, the penalty also saves far more innocent lives through its general deterrent effect. . . .

Logic supports the conclusion that the death penalty is the most effective deterrent for some kinds of murders—those that require reflection and forethought by persons of reasonable intelligence and unimpaired mental facilities. Many capital offenses are quintessential contemplative offenses. Murder for hire, treason, and terrorist bombings all require extensive planning. It stands to reason that capital punishment deters such persons more than the next most serious penalty, life imprisonment without parole.

Anecdotal evidence in support of the deterrent value of capital sentences comes from examples of persons who have been deterred from murdering, or risking a murder, because of the death penalty. For instance, Justice McComb of the California Supreme Court collected from the files of the Los Angeles Police Department fourteen examples within a four-year period of defendants who, in explaining their refusal to take a life or carry a weapon, pointed to the presence of the death penalty. . . .

Statistical studies support the proposition that capital sentences, like other criminal sanctions, have a deterrent effect. To be sure, some statistical surveys, often conducted by opponents of the death penalty, have found no such effect. . . .

One of the most recent substantial econometric studies [applying statistical methods to economics to study problems] was performed by Professor Stephen K. Layson of the University of North Carolina at Greensboro, who analyzed data for the United States from 1936 to 1977. Layson concluded that increases in the probability of execution reduced the homicide rate. Specifically, Layson found that, on average, each execution deterred approximately eighteen murders. . . .

Through the imposition of just punishment, civilized society expresses its outrage and sense of revulsion toward those who, by contravening its laws, have not only inflicted injury upon discrete individuals, but also weakened the bonds that hold communities together. Certain crimes constitute such outrageous violation of human and moral values that they demand retribution. It was to control the natural human impulse to seek revenge and, more broadly, to give expression to deeply held views that some conduct deserves punishment, that criminal laws, administered by the state, were established.

The rule of law does not eliminate feelings of outrage but does provide controlled channels for expressing such feelings. People can rely on society to sanction criminal conduct and to carry out deserved punishments. . . .

The death penalty's retributive function thus vindicates the fundamental moral principle that a criminal should receive his or her just deserts. Through the provision of just punishment, capital punishment affirms the sanctity of human life and thereby protects it.

. . . The system imposes a vast array of due process protections to assure that no innocent person is convicted of a crime.

STATEMENT OF MIRIAM SHEHANE, STATE PRESIDENT, VICTIMS OF CRIME AND LENIENCY, MONTGOMERY, ALABAMA, BEFORE THE SENATE JUDICIARY COMMITTEE, APRIL 1, 1993

My daughter, Quenette, was brutally murdered in 1976. . . .

Time will not permit nor will I burden you with the gory details of how one of the defendants described her hours of torture and final death, but the memory is imprinted in my mind permanently. The three men who killed her were arrested and brought to trial—literally seven trials over a period of six years. . . . The frustrations the families go through when they think justice will soon prevail, only to receive jolt after jolt as they learn the case is going back for trial due to technicalities, [are] enough to cause fatal health problems.

. . . As you know, thirty-six states have determined that the death penalty is the most appropriate punishment for certain brutal and vicious murders. As the parent of a murder victim, I feel this punishment is not only fair, it is essential. What is not fair is when this punishment is prolonged by extensive appeals, stays, and postponements. We victims need a closure to our grief. I did not rejoice when Wallace Norrell was executed July 13, 1990, for murdering Quenette, but I certainly felt relief. I could not have a sense of completion and finally put my dear Quenette to rest if I didn't [sic] have to worry about two others being released at some point. . . .

I can assure you that the system, as it now operates, gives far more consideration to death row inmates than it affords the victims and their families. What are the safeguards for the victim when a murderer is tried, acquitted by a jury, but can never be retried no matter how much evidence is produced in the future? Are the scales of justice earnestly balanced when a convicted murderer is not executed for thirteen and a half years? Lest we forget, in addition to the extensive appeals of the courts, every state with a capital punishment statute has a procedure for executive clemency.

STATEMENT OF BRUCE FEIN, PRIVATE ATTORNEY SPECIALIZING IN CONSTITUTIONAL AND COMMUNICATIONS LAW, BEFORE THE HOUSE JUDICIARY COMMITTEE, MAY 23, 1990

Although the death penalty certainly is not the answer to the worrisome . . . levels of crime today, it is an important tool, I think, in creating a right kind of moral climate that suggests there are certain standards of behavior that must be accepted in order to avoid degeneration of society, anarchy, and a level of bestiality. . . .

We must recognize that death laws have tongues. They speak to a moral universe that places some kind of conduct simply beyond the level of decent mankind. . . .

It seems to me as well that certainly when you speak of the need for a death penalty for [killing] prison wardens, that would not threaten somebody who is already in prison under a life term with no possibility of parole, and who has very little incentive to do anything to control his conduct, to try to escape, to kill to escape because there isn't any further punishment that is available if death is not an option.

I think we owe a certain decency toward our prison wardens who undertake very dangerous positions to have that death penalty option there.

STATEMENT OF JOHN C. SCULLY, COUNSEL, WASHINGTON LEGAL FOUNDATION, WASHINGTON, D.C., BEFORE THE HOUSE JUDICIARY COMMITTEE, MAY 3, 1990

The overwhelming majority of Americans, black and white, support the death penalty. The Supreme Court has consistently upheld the constitutionality of the death penalty. The drug-war killings and the other murders that occur daily in our country demonstrate the need for the death penalty. The death penalty is a deterrent to future murders. Finally, some murders are so shocking that it is evident that there is no other punishment that fits the crime.

Yet, the will of the majority of the people is regularly frustrated by the opponents of the death penalty who repeatedly devise new and often bizarre forms of lethal attacks upon the death penalty. The rejection by the U.S. Supreme Court of the statistical disparity-death-by-racial-quota theory has led the anti–death penalty advocates to seek a legislative vehicle to attack the death penalty. . . .

WLF [Washington Legal Foundation] strongly opposes racial discrimination in the justice system. Individuals sentenced to death should and do have the right and opportunity to challenge any act of racial discrimination in the justice system.

. . . The BJS [Bureau of Justice Statistics] report showed that for every 1,000 whites arrested on homicide charges, approximately sixteen were given a death sentence, while fewer than twelve blacks were sent to death row for every 1,000 blacks arrested for homicide. This means that white murderers are 36% more likely to be sentenced to death than their black counterparts.

Does that mean that white murderers are the victims of racial discrimination? Of course not. There are numerous individual circumstances that comprise each murder case; those circumstances make it impossible to use statistics to prove discrimination in a manner similar to that utilized in employment discrimination cases.

. . . Studies, unable to show racial discrimination against blacks by examining the race of the defendant, also examined the race of the victim. The Baldus study concluded that for some types of murders, if the victim of the crime was white, then the murderer was more likely to receive a death sentence than if the victim was black.

The race-of-the-victim theory, if accepted, means that even a white murderer can level charges of racism at a jury that sent him to death row for killing a white person. . . .

The Katz study showed that the black defendant/white victim cases are the most aggravated of the four defendant–victim racial combinations. The interracial nature of this kind of homicide minimized the possibility that the killing arose due to a family dispute or fight between friends, neighbors, or relatives.

The black defendant/black victim homicides occurred most frequently and were characterized by poor defendants who kill family members, friends, or other acquaintances during a fight or argument. Those types of murders generally have the most mitigating circumstances.

The white defendant/white victim homicides reflected a mix between killings precipitated by a dispute similar to those precipitating black-on-black homicides, but with a substantial percent (about one-third) of the killings comparable to the black-on-white homicides.

Only twenty-seven of the 1,082 cases were characterized as white defendant/black victim homicides. The relatively small number of such homicides made them difficult for Katz to classify.

STATEMENT OF JAMES C. ANDERS, SOLICITOR, FIFTH JUDICIAL CIRCUIT OF SOUTH CAROLINA, BEFORE THE SENATE JUDICIARY COMMITTEE, SEPTEMBER 19, 1989

I believe that in certain cases, the death penalty can be shown to be the only rational and realistic punishment for an unspeakable crime. . . . Obviously, the most basic right a citizen has is the right to be secure in his person, the right to be safe from physical or economic harm from another. Laws to protect citizens and advance the harmony of society are founded upon these principles. To enforce these laws, created in the best interest of society as a whole, there has to be a deterrent for a breach of the law. Therefore, deterrence is the first aim of a system of punishment.

Deterrence is only one side of the punishment coin, however. An equally fundamental reason to punish lies in society's compelling desire to see justice done. Punishment expresses the emotions of the society wronged, the anger and outrage felt, and it solidifies and reinforces the goals, values, and norms of acceptable behavior in the society. . . .

The deterrent effect of the death penalty is the favorite criticism of the opponents of capital punishment. The social scientists' studies have been mixed at best, and there is no authoritative consensus on whether or not the death penalty deters anyone from committing a crime. Threats of punishment cannot and are not meant to deter everybody all of the time. They are meant to deter most people most of the time. Therefore, the death penalty can only be a deterrent if it is meted out with a reasonable degree of consistency. The deterrence effect lies in the knowledge of the citizenry that it will more likely than not be carried out if the named crime is committed.

Even if one is not fully convinced of the deterrent effect of the death penalty, he or she would surely choose the certainty of the convicted criminal's death by execution over the possibility of the deaths of new victims.

Death penalty opponents argue that if life is sacred, then the murderer's life, too, is sacred . . . and for the state to punish him by execution is barbaric and causes the state to bend to the murderer's level. The only similarity between the unjustified taking of an innocent life and the carrying out of a convicted murderer's execution is the end result—death. The death penalty is a legal sentence, enacted by the legislatures of various states, which presumably reflect their constituents' desires. It is a penalty that can finally be carried out only after a trial where the defendant is afforded all of his constitutional rights. . . .

Death penalty opponents are also troubled by the studies that purport to show that the death penalty is applied capriciously, that it discriminates racially and economically. . . . Assuming that premise for the sake of argument, is that a rational reason to abolish the death penalty? Is the fact that some guilty persons escape punishment sufficient to let all guilty persons escape it?

. . . If the death penalty can deter one murder of an innocent life or if it can make a statement to the community about what will and will not be tolerated, then it is justified.

Opponents of the death penalty advocate the life sentence in prison as a viable alternative to execution. . . . Early release programs, furloughs, and escape combine to place a shockingly high number of convicted murderers back on the streets in record time.

The life without parole sentence is no solution either. First, the possibility of escape cannot be completely eliminated, even in the most secure of institutions. . . . Second, the life without parole sentence places a tremendous burden on prison administrators. Faced with controlling inmates who have already received the worst punishment society can mete out, they can only throw their hands up in frustration. Lastly, the true lifer is not only capable of continuing to murder, but may actually be more likely to do so. Every prison in the country has its own stories of the lifer who killed another inmate over a cigarette or a piece of chicken.

STATEMENT OF ROBERT B. KLIESMET, PRESIDENT, INTERNATIONAL UNION OF POLICE ASSOCIATIONS, BEFORE THE SENATE JUDICIARY COMMITTEE, SEPTEMBER 19, 1989

Street cops, in their pragmatic view, believe, as does 86% of the public, that the death penalty is a viable deterrent for persons convicted of certain crimes. A search of the literature shows there are a number of studies and articles that show a direct deterrent effect by imposing and carrying out the death penalty. One study goes as far as to point out that for each execution for a homicide, up to fifteen lives can be saved through the deterrent effect. The safety of society, which is the real goal of the criminal justice system, is being compromised by saving the life of a convicted offender. This compromise is a needless sacrifice of a blameless victim's life.

STATEMENT OF SENATOR JOHN P. EAST (R-NC), JANUARY 16, 1986

With the tougher attitude towards crime that we have taken in the past five years, the murder rate has gone down, but day after day we still read newspaper accounts of murders, many of which are carried out with chilling cruelty and detachment. The American people deserve continued protection from this wave of killing, protection often denied them by a system that often still gives lenient penalties to the most vicious criminals.

Death is the only suitable penalty for reprehensible crimes, such as premeditated murder. Murder does not simply differ in magnitude from extortion or theft. It differs in kind as well, and its punishment also should differ in kind. Murderers have not simply injured their victims, but they have weakened the most important bond that holds communities together—respect for life. By imposing the supreme penalty in cases of murder, society

expresses its moral outrage at such a crime; it sends a signal that innocent human life is precious; and it declares that such life cannot be violated without a like consequence to the killer. By imposing the death penalty, it also deters other would-be murderers, and it prevents the murderer from killing again.

I am convinced that there needs to be a federal death penalty statute. In particular, we need to be able to impose the death penalty for the assassination of high government officials. We also need to provide for capital punishment in cases where convicted killers, already confined in a federal prison and serving life sentences, commit murder again. At present, such people have no incentive not to kill because they are already suffering the severest penalty that federal law has to offer. As a result, the number of gruesome murders at federal correctional institutions is on the rise.

TESTIMONY OF ERNEST VAN DEN HAAG, ADJUNCT PROFESSOR OF SOCIAL PHILOSOPHY, NEW YORK UNIVERSITY, BEFORE THE SUBCOMMITTEE ON CRIMINAL LAW AND PROCEDURES OF THE SENATE JUDICIARY COMMITTEE, MARCH 15, 1972

It is suggested that the death penalty discriminates against the poor and the black. . . . If true, . . . the suggestion would be nonetheless wholly irrelevant. It concerns the unfair way in which the penalty is distributed, not the fairness or unfairness of the penalty.

Any penalty . . . could be unfairly or unjustly applied. The vice is not in the penalty, but in the process by which it is inflicted. It is unfair to inflict unequal penalties on equally guilty parties, or on any innocent parties, regardless of what the penalty is. . . . You should try to correct the judicial processes by which, it is alleged, the penalties are unfairly inflicted. . . .

All penalties—including fines, prison sentences, and the death penalty—are deterrent roughly in proportion to their severity . . . . Were that not the case, we would certainly not have varied penalties, but might impose a uniform penalty of $5 for any crime whatsoever. We impose penalties roughly differentiated because we feel that crimes of different gravity deserve different punishment.

On the basis of the statistics available, no logical conclusion one way or the other can be reached. It cannot be proven that the death penalty is additionally deterrent; it cannot be proven either that it is not.

No penalty can deter the irrational, perhaps. But penalties do influence those who are rational enough to be influenced. In this respect the data suggest the death penalty has been very effective, precisely because very few murders are committed by rational persons.

CHAPTER 11
THE DEBATE—CAPITAL PUNISHMENT SHOULD BE ABOLISHED

TESTIMONY OF RICHARD C. DIETER, EXECUTIVE DIRECTOR, DEATH PENALTY INFORMATION CENTER, BEFORE THE NEW YORK STATE ASSEMBLY, STANDING COMMITTEES ON CODES, JUDICIARY, AND CORRECTION, JANUARY 25, 2005

. . . In broad terms, the death penalty is about a *search for justice and the safety of the community*. There are many ways to make the community safer, and most of these have costs associated with them. There is no bottomless pot of government money to be spent on things that might help the community. The more you spend on one project, the less there is available for other worthwhile endeavors.

All of the studies regarding the cost of the death penalty have concluded that it amounts to a *net expense* to the state and the taxpayers. As a recent article on this very subject in the *Wall Street Journal* put it: "Nothing is certain except the death penalty and higher taxes." The extra money spent on the death penalty could be spent on other means of achieving justice and making the community safer: compensation for victims, better lighting in crime areas, more police on the streets, even longer periods of incarceration for certain offenders, or projects to reduce unemployment. Quite a few jurisdictions with the death penalty have recently had to cut back on other vital services. In some states, people are being released from prison early as a cost saving measure. Other states are closing libraries and other vital services. The costs of the death penalty have a direct bearing on these issues.

A second reason why the costs of the death penalty are so central is that they play a key role in how the death penalty is implemented. Supporters and opponents of the death penalty agree that the capital punishment system should not take unnecessary risks with innocent lives and should be applied with a strict fairness. As with many things, the death penalty on the cheap is really no bargain. There is no abstract dollar figure for

the cost of the death penalty—it depends on the quality of the system you demand. In Illinois, their system was fraught with error. Over a twenty-year period, they freed more innocent people from death row than they executed. As a result, a blue-ribbon commission there recommended eighty-five changes to make the death penalty more reliable; most of these changes will now cost the state even more money.

There is little dispute that the death penalty is expensive. Of course, sentencing someone to life in prison is also very expensive. But death penalty costs are accrued upfront, especially at trial and for the early appeals, while life-in-prison costs are spread out over many decades. A million dollars spent today is a lot more costly to the state than a million dollars that can be paid gradually over forty years.

But the most expensive system is one that combines the costliest parts of both punishments: lengthy and complicated death penalty trials followed by incarceration for life. Surprisingly, research has shown that that is exactly what you can expect from the death penalty. In most cases where the prosecution announces that the death penalty will be sought, it is never imposed. And even when it is imposed, it is rarely carried out. New York's experience bears this out.

Death penalty cases are clearly more expensive at every stage of the judicial process than similar non-death cases. Everything that is needed for an ordinary trial is needed for a death penalty case, only more so:

- more pre-trial time will be needed to prepare: cases typically take a year to come to trial
- more pre-trial motions will be filed and answered
- more experts will be hired
- twice as many attorneys will be appointed for the defense, and a comparable team for the prosecution

- jurors will have to be individually quizzed on their views about the death penalty

- they are more likely to be sequestered

- two trials instead of one will be conducted: one for guilt and one for punishment

- the trial will be longer: a cost study at Duke University estimated that death penalty trials take three to five times longer than typical murder trials

- and then will come a series of appeals during which the inmates are held in the high security of death row.

These individual expenses result in a substantial net cost to the taxpayer to maintain a death penalty system as compared to a system with a life sentence as the most severe punishment. It is certainly true that after an execution the death row inmate no longer has to be incarcerated while the life-sentence prisoner remains under state care. But that partial saving is overwhelmed by the earlier death penalty costs, especially because relatively few cases result in an execution, and, even those that do occur, happen many years after the sentence is pronounced. A recent study at Columbia University Law School demonstrated how few capital cases actually result in an execution: the study found that 68% of death penalty sentences or convictions are overturned on appeal. The serious errors that are discovered require that at least the sentencing phase be done over. When these death penalty cases are re-tried, approximately 82% result in a life sentence. Thus, the typical death penalty case has all the expenses of its early stages and appeal; it is then overturned, and a life sentence is imposed, resulting in all the costs of a lifetime of incarceration. Nationally, only about 12% of people who have been sentenced to death have been executed. . . .

STATEMENT OF SENATOR RUSSELL FEINGOLD (D-WI) ON THE FEDERAL DEATH PENALTY ABOLITION ACT FROM THE SENATE FLOOR, JANUARY 24, 2005

[T]oday I introduce the Federal Death Penalty Abolition Act of 2005. This bill would abolish the death penalty at the Federal level. It would put an immediate halt to executions and forbid the imposition of the death penalty as a sentence for violations of Federal law.

Since 1976, when the death penalty was reinstated by the Supreme Court, there have been almost one thousand executions across the country, including three at the Federal level. At the same time, over one hundred people on death row were later found innocent and released from death row. Exonerated inmates are not only removed from death row, but they are usually released from prison altogether. Apparently, these people never should have been convicted in the first place. While death penalty proponents claim that the death penalty is fair, efficient, and a deterrent, the fact remains that our criminal justice system has failed and has resulted in at least 117 very grave mistakes.

Nine hundred and forty-four executions, and 117 exonerations in the modern death penalty era. That is an embarrassing statistic, one that should have us all questioning the use of capital punishment in this country. And we continue to learn about more cases in which our justice system has failed. Since I first introduced this bill in November of 1999, thirty-six death row inmates have been exonerated throughout the country, twelve since I introduced this bill in the last Congress in February 2003. Since I last introduced this bill, 115 people have been executed nationwide. How many innocents are among them? We may never know.

While executions continue and the death row population grows, the national debate on the death penalty intensifies and has become even more vigorous. The number of voices joining in to express doubt about the use of capital punishment in America is growing. As evidence of the flaws in our system mounts, it has created an awareness that has not escaped the attention of the American people. Layer after layer of confidence in the death penalty system has been gradually peeling away, and the voices of those questioning its fairness are growing louder and louder. . . . We must not ignore them.

That our modern society relies on killing as punishment is disturbing enough. Even more disturbing, however, is that our States' and Federal Government's use of the death penalty is often not consistent with principles of due process, fairness, and justice. These principles are the foundation of our criminal justice system. It is clearer than ever before that we have put innocent people on death row. In addition, statistics show that those States that have the death penalty are more likely to put people to death for killing white victims than for killing black victims. . . .

I am certain that not one of my colleagues here in the Senate, not a single one, would defend racial discrimination in this ultimate punishment. The most fundamental guarantee of our Constitution is equal justice under law, and equal protection of the laws. Yet we have a system in place today that raises grave questions about whether that guarantee is being met.

At the beginning of 2005, I cannot help but believe that our progress has been tarnished by our Nation's not only continuing, but increasing use of the death penalty. We are a Nation that prides itself on the fundamental principles of justice, liberty, equality and due process. We are a Nation that scrutinizes the human rights records of other nations. Historically, we are one of the first nations to speak out against torture and killings by foreign governments. We should hold our own system of justice to the highest standard.

Over the last few years, some prominent voices in our country have done just that. And they are not just voices of liberals, or of the faith community. They are the voices of Justice Sandra Day O'Connor, Reverend Pat Robertson, George Will, former FBI Director William Sessions, Republican Governor George Ryan, and Democratic Governor Parris Glendening. The voices of those questioning our application of the death penalty are growing in number, and they are growing louder.

And while we examine the flaws in our death penalty system, we cannot help but note that our use of the death penalty stands in stark contrast to the majority of nations, which have abolished the death penalty in law or practice. There are now 117 countries that have abolished the death penalty in law or in practice. The European Union denies membership in the alliance to those nations that use the death penalty. In fact, it passed a resolution calling for the immediate and unconditional global abolition of the death penalty, and it specifically called on all States within the United States to abolish the death penalty. This is significant because it reflects the unanimous view of a group of nations with which the United States enjoys the closest of relationships and shares the deepest common values. . . .

As we begin a new year and another Congress, our society is still far from fully just. The continued use of the death penalty shames us. The penalty is at odds with our best traditions. It is wrong and it is immoral. The adage "two wrongs do not make a right," applies here in the most fundamental way. Our Nation has long ago done away with other barbaric punishments like whipping and cutting off the ears of criminals. Just as our Nation did away with these punishments as contrary to our humanity and ideals, it is time to abolish the death penalty as we seek justice in this new century. And it is not just a matter of morality. The continued viability of our justice system as a truly just system that deserves the respect of our own people and the world requires that we do so. Our Nation's striving to remain the leading defender of freedom, liberty and equality demands that we do so.

Abolishing the death penalty will not be an easy task. It will take patience, persistence, and courage. As we work to move forward in a rapidly changing world, let us leave this archaic practice behind.

TESTIMONY OF ROBERT M. MORGENTHAU, DISTRICT ATTORNEY, MANHATTAN, NEW YORK, BEFORE THE NEW YORK STATE ASSEMBLY, STANDING COMMITTEES ON CODES, JUDICIARY, AND CORRECTION, DECEMBER 15, 2004

. . . The public and their elected officials have short memories, and capital punishment has always had its supporters, who see it as a response to fears of rise in violent crime. In 1994 Congress enacted a new Violent Crime Control and Law Enforcement Act which increased the number from two to sixty federal offenses for which someone may be sentenced to death and created more than sixty new federal crimes for conduct already harshly punished under state law. Legislators who think these measures will reduce violent crimes fool themselves and the public. Such provisions may be good politics, but they are not good law enforcement. They divert our attention from present needs. I know of no law enforcement professional who believes that the death penalty provisions and all the new crimes covered by the act have affected public safety in the slightest. The criminal laws we needed were already on the books. What was missing was the commitment to enforce them. . . .

There is no correlation between executions and low homicide rates. For example, Texas, which has the highest number of executions in the nation, with 336 executions since 1976, also has one of the highest murder rates. In fact, FBI statistics show that the homicide rate in states that have the death penalty are 44% higher than in non–death penalty states. Here in the Northeast, in nearby Philadelphia, the District Attorney has been an avid proponent of the death penalty; there are 124 inmates on death row in Philadelphia County, the third highest total for any county in the nation. Nonetheless, in 2003, Philadelphia, which has population roughly equal to Manhattan's, had nearly four times as many murders as we did—348 versus 93.

To serve as an effective deterrent, punishment must be prompt and certain. The death penalty is neither. According to the Columbia University study, the review process in capital cases takes an average of nine years to complete—and, as the Florida case shows, the process can take a great deal longer. As a result of the seemingly endless litigation in these cases, there are now 3,490 inmates awaiting execution in the United States. In addition, the imposition of the death penalty varies so greatly depending on geography, race, gender, and other factors that receiving it is somewhat akin to being struck by lightning. The arbitrary manner in which the death penalty is applied, can only deepen cynicism and disrespect for the law among those who are disposed to commit violent criminal acts.

Some crimes are so depraved that execution might seem a just penalty. But even in the virtually impossible event that a statute could be crafted and applied so wisely that it would reach only those cases, the price would be too high. When the state kills, it sends the wrong message. The death penalty is an endorsement for violent solutions, and violence begets violence. In the words of George Bernard Shaw "it is the deed that teaches, not the name we give it."

Executions waste scarce law enforcement, financial, and personnel resources. Cost estimates vary from state to state, but all are high. A 2003 study by the State of Kansas found that the median cost of a capital case in that state, since the death penalty was reinstated in 1994, was $1.26 million, but the study included no cases in which a defendant had actually been executed. A study authorized by Duke University in 1993 found that for each person executed in North Carolina the State paid over $2 million more than it would have cost to imprison him for life, in part because of court proceedings. The costs per case in New York are no doubt much higher than in these other states, even though no case has yet resulted in an execution. The *New York Law Journal* reported in April 2002 that, since the death penalty was restored in 1995, the state had paid $68.4 million to defense lawyers representing defendants charged with crimes that might warrant the death penalty; in one case, in which the defendant was sentenced to death but not executed, defense costs alone totaled $1.7 million. Defense costs are, of course, only one component of the total costs involved in a capital case, which require extraordinary expenditures on the part of the police, the prosecution, the courts and corrections. A 1989 study by the Department of Correctional Services estimated that the death penalty would cost the state $118 million a year.

There are far better methods of reducing murders and other violent crimes than imposition of the death penalty. When I first took office, in 1975, Manhattan led the city with 648 murders, 39% of the total citywide. In 2003, by contrast, there were ninety-three murders in Manhattan, the lowest number in any of the four major boroughs and only 16% of the city total. That is an 86% reduction in the number of murders; today, only Staten Island has fewer murders than Manhattan. Thus far in 2004, the number of murders in Manhattan is eighty-eight. If this trend continues through the end of the year, Manhattan will have had, in each of the last three years, fewer murders than in any year since 1937, the first year for which we have reliable statistics, In fact, we have now less than half as many murders in Manhattan as in 1937, when, incidentally, the death penalty was in regular use.

This was accomplished, in large part, by rigorously enforcing the law, assigning experienced and well-trained prosecutors to homicides and other serious cases early on in the process, and concentrating resources on drug gangs and violent recidivists. From 1975 to 2003, 115,00 defendants were sentenced to state prison from New York County and nearly three times that number were sentenced to terms of one year or less in city jails. Of course, there are many other aspects to crime reduction, including specialized bureaus for sex crimes, domestic violence, and other areas that require particular expertise, drug treatment programs as an alternative to incarceration and close working relations between prosecutors, the police and the community. But those are topics that go beyond the scope of this hearing.

I have pointed out that the death penalty does not deter crime, that it is far more expensive than life imprisonment, that the wrong person can be executed, and that in its application, it most closely resembles a lottery where the winners are losers. The only honest justification for the death penalty is vengence. But the Lord saith "vengeance is mine." It is wrong for secular governments to usurp that role.

Capital punishment merely allows proponents to convince themselves that they have done something to fight crime. It is a mirage that distracts society from more fruitful, less facile answers. The death penalty exacts a terrible price in dollars, lives, and human decency. Rather than tamping down the flames of violence, it fuels them while draining millions of dollars from more promising efforts to restore safety to our lives. For all these reasons, I urge all of our lawmakers, in the strongest terms, not to reinstate the death penalty in New York.

STATEMENT OF MARYLAND ATTORNEY GENERAL J. JOSEPH CURRAN, JR., NEWS CONFERENCE AT LAWYERS MALL, ANNAPOLIS, MARYLAND, JANUARY 30, 2003

Over the past forty years, there have been three executions in our State. Over the next few months, seven men are poised to be executed. In the fractured history of the death penalty in Maryland, this is a watershed moment.

I have long opposed human executions on moral grounds, and I stand today with clergy and others from many different faiths who share this view. I believe that we should hold ourselves to a higher moral standard than those who commit these unspeakable wrongs. Serious questions are also being raised about racial and geographic disparities in our application of the death penalty.

But I am here to talk today about what I believe is the most compelling issue: the inevitability of mistake.

We are blessed in Maryland with dedicated police officers, prosecutors, judges, and lawyers, all who labor every day to make our criminal justice system work. But despite our best efforts, this system makes mistakes. It is a human institution, and humans are not infallible. Any trial judge and any trial lawyer will tell you—mistakes happen. People are imperfect, the system is imperfect. Mistakes are inevitable.

With appeals and reviews, we catch many of them. We hope to catch most of them. But we do not catch all of them.

Since the Supreme Court reinstated capital punishment in 1976, 821 people have been executed. During the same time period, 103 people have been exonerated, the most recent just this week in Florida. Those 103 were lucky. The mistake that led to their wrongful death sentence was found and corrected. Others are not so lucky. We will never know how many mistakes were not caught in time.

I support with the strongest conviction the need to severely punish those who have committed these unspeakable wrongs. They have taken a life. They have caused incomprehensible suffering for the victims' families. They have forfeited the right to live among us.

We now have a way to punish them which we lacked when we reinstated the death penalty. Life without parole puts people away for the rest of their lives, with no hope or possibility of ever getting out. Let me be absolutely clear: they die in prison.

But, there is one pivotal difference between death in prison and the death penalty. That is the chance to correct a mistake. It is a terrible injustice to wrongfully incarcerate an innocent person. We have just witnessed such an injustice with Bernard Webster, who was recently exonerated from a rape conviction after serving twenty years in prison. But at least we were able to set him free, to correct the mistake. The death penalty allows no such possibility.

So let me say it again: Capital punishment comes only at the intolerable risk of killing an innocent person. This is unworthy of us.

Therefore, today I call for abolition of the death penalty.

A JOINT STATEMENT, *TO END THE DEATH PENALTY*, BY THE NATIONAL JEWISH/ CATHOLIC CONSULTATION (COSPONSORED BY THE NATIONAL COUNCIL OF SYNAGOGUES AND THE BISHOPS' COMMITTEE FOR ECUMENICAL AND INTERRELIGIOUS AFFAIRS OF THE NATIONAL CONFERENCE OF CATHOLIC BISHOPS, DECEMBER 3, 1999

"A Sanhedrin [Jewish court of law] that puts one person to death once in seven years is called destructive. Rabbi Eliezer ben Azariah says: Or even once in seventy years. Rabbi Tarfon and Rabbi Akiba say: Had we been the Sanhedrin, none would ever have been put to death." *Mishnah Makkot, 1:10 (2nd Century, C.E.)*

"A sign of hope is the increasing recognition that the dignity of human life must never be taken away, even in the case of someone who has done great evil. Modern society has the means of protecting itself, without definitively denying criminals the chance to reform. I renew the appeal for a consensus to end the death penalty, which is both cruel and unnecessary." *Pope John Paul II, January 27, 1999, St. Louis, Missouri*

Almost two millennia separate these two statements, which together embody the collective wisdom and moral insights of our two ancient religious traditions, Rabbinic Judaism and Roman Catholicism, on a burning issue of our time, capital punishment. At our meeting of March 23, 1999, we religious leaders, Catholic and Jewish, probed and shared our own traditions with each other. The result was a remarkable confluence of witness on how best in our time to interpret the eternal word of God.

Both traditions begin with an affirmation of the sanctity of human life. Both, as the above statements imply, acknowledge the theoretical possibility of a justifiable death penalty, since the Scriptures mandate it for certain offenses. Yet both have, over the centuries, narrowed those grounds until, today, we would say together that it is time to cease the practice altogether. To achieve this consensus, we analyzed the statements of our respective bodies going back to the late 1970s and we agree that in them we found a growing conviction that the arguments offered in defense of the death penalty are less than persuasive in the face of the overwhelming mandate in both Jewish and Catholic traditions to respect the sanctity of human life.

Some would argue that the death penalty is needed as a means of retributive justice [exacting punishment for offense done] to balance out the crime with the punishment. This reflects a natural concern of society, and especially of victims and their families. Yet we believe that we are called to seek a higher road even while punishing the guilty, for example through long and in some cases life-long incarceration, so that the healing of all can ultimately take place.

Some would argue that the death penalty is needed as a deterrent to crime. Yet the studies that lie behind our statements over the years have yet to reveal any objective evidence to justify this conclusion. Criminals tend to believe they will escape any consequences for their behavior, or simply do not think of consequences at all, so an escalation of consequences is usually irrelevant to their state of mind at the time of the crime.

Some would argue that the death penalty will teach society at large the seriousness of crime. Yet we say that teaching people to respond to violence with violence will, again, only breed more violence.

Some would argue that our system of justice, trial by jury, can ensure that capital punishment will be meted out equitably to various groups in society and that the innocent will never be convicted. This is the least persuasive argument of all. Statistics, however weighted, indicate that errors are made in judgment and convictions. Recent scientific advances, such as DNA testing, may reveal that persons on death row, despite seemingly "overwhelming" circumstantial evidence, may in fact be innocent of the charges against them. Likewise, suspiciously high percentages of those on death row are poor or people of color. Our legal system is a very good one, but it is a human institution. Even a small percentage of irreversible errors is increasingly seen as intolerable. God alone is the author of life.

The strongest argument of all is the deep pain and grief of the families of victims and their quite natural desire to see punishment meted out to those who have plunged them into such agony. Yet it is the clear teaching of our traditions that this pain and suffering cannot be healed simply through the retribution of capital punishment or by vengeance. It is a difficult and long process of healing, which comes about through personal growth and God's grace. We agree that much more must be done by the religious community and by society at large to solace and care for the grieving families of the victims of violent crime.

. . . We affirm that we came to these conclusions because of our shared understanding of the sanctity of human life. We have committed ourselves to work together, and each within our own communities, toward ending the death penalty.

STATEMENT OF SAMUEL JORDAN, DIRECTOR, PROGRAM TO ABOLISH THE DEATH PENALTY, AMNESTY INTERNATIONAL U.S.A., MARCH 4, 1998

The death penalty as imposed in the United States has the power to mislead even the most attentive social observer. Despite its fatal brutality, the death penalty is permitted by the Constitution, honored by custom, and upheld by the courts—as was slavery. Beneath the veneer, the practice of executions is accompanied by a resolute defiance of internationally accepted standards of human rights and fairness.

Repeatedly, studies have shown that capital punishment is imposed arbitrarily with disproportionate weight given to race—of the victim. Although African-Americans account for 50% of the homicide victims in the nation, 82% of death row offenders have been convicted for the murder of whites. Poverty as well as race often determines the allocation of the death sentence. Inadequate, inexperienced representation for indigent defendants characterizes most capital litigation. In addition, imposition of the death penalty often costs as much as three times the expense of lifetime incarceration. The system of executions has also sought to lower the age of offenders against whom it may be applied, thus ensnaring juveniles. And sadly, there are no reliable statistics on the numbers of mentally deficient victims of the executioner.

Many organizations have begun to support the call for a moratorium on the death penalty. They argue that the same conditions persist today, which led the U.S.

Supreme Court to order a moratorium on executions in 1972 in the landmark case, *Furman v. Georgia*. The resumption of executions after *Gregg v. Georgia* in 1976 has not been marked by the abatement of racial disparities, arbitrariness, and substandard representation in the judicial process leading to the death sentence.

While the moratorium effort draws attention to the shortcomings of the judicial process, we must not rely upon the courts alone to settle matters of public morality and human rights. The role of the abolitionist in the struggle to rid our nation of the death penalty is not unlike the task that confronted abolitionists in the era of chattel slavery in the United States. The answer will not be found in the law. Laws which permit executions must be changed. They must reflect instead an attempt by our society to respect and enhance the dignity of human life without regard to race, wealth, and prestige.

The first challenge for the modern abolitionist is to topple the death penalty from its pedestal of broad, popular acceptance and to expose it for what it is, a brutal and dehumanizing rationale for legal murder. Next, we must demand that all sectors of the society, especially religious organizations, take command of the moral and humanitarian dimensions of this issue. In the end, to be successful, we must drive a wedge between those who promote capital punishment for selfish reasons, including vote totals and public image, and those who might honestly believe that there is a connection between the death penalty and fairness.

Meeting these challenges will release enormous social energies which can be employed to change the laws. Only then will we join the 101 of the 194 nations of the world which have abandoned the practice of state-sanctioned killing. We deserve a criminal justice system free of the ritual of human sacrifice.

STATEMENT OF REPRESENTATIVE HENRY B. GONZALEZ (D-TX) IN THE HOUSE OF REPRESENTATIVES, JUNE 30, 1995

I believe that the death penalty is an act of vengeance veiled as an instrument of justice. Not only do I believe that there are independently sufficient moral objections to the principle of capital punishment to warrant its abolition, but I also know that the death penalty is meted out to the poor, to a disproportionate number of minorities, and does not either deter crime or advance justice.

Violent crimes have unfortunately become a constant in our society. . . . The sight of any brutal homicide excites a passion within us that demands retributive justice. . . . We cannot allow ourselves to punish an irrational action with an equally irrational retaliation—murder is wrong, whether it is committed by an individual or by the state.

. . . The United Nations Universal Declaration of Human Rights states, "No one shall be subjected to torture or to cruel, inhuman, or degrading treatment or punishment." The death penalty is torture, and numerous examples exist, emphasizing the cruelty of the execution. . . .

. . . Studies fail to establish that the death penalty either has a unique value as a deterrent or is a more effective deterrent than life imprisonment. We assume that perpetrators will give greater consideration to the consequences of their actions if the penalty is death, but the problem is that we are not always dealing with rational actions. Those who commit violent crimes often do so in moments of passion, rage, and fear—times when irrationality reigns.

. . . Proponents advocate that some crimes simply deserve death. This argument is ludicrous. If a murderer deserves death, I ask why then do we not burn the arsonist or rape the rapist? Our justice system does not provide for such punishments because society comprehends that it must be founded on principles different from those it condemns. How can we condemn killing while condoning execution?

. . . In practice, capital punishment has become a kind of grotesque lottery. It is more likely to be carried out in some states than in others. . . . The death penalty is far more likely to be imposed against blacks than whites. . . . It is most likely to be imposed upon the poor and uneducated—60% of death row inmates never finished high school. . . .

. . . There are moves in Congress to speed up the execution process by limiting and streamlining the appeals process. But when the statistics show how arbitrarily the death penalty is applied, how can we make any changes without first assuring fairness? . . . There are no do-overs in this business when mistakes are made.

EXCERPTS FROM JUSTICE HARRY A. BLACKMUN'S DISSENTING OPINION IN THE SUPREME COURT DECISION *CALLINS V. COLLINS* (510 U.S. 1141, 1994), DENYING REVIEW OF THE DEATH PENALTY CASE

Twenty years have passed since this Court declared that the death penalty must be imposed fairly, and with reasonable consistency, or not at all, and, . . . despite the effort of the states and courts to devise legal formulas and procedural rules to meet this daunting challenge, the death penalty remains fraught with arbitrariness, discrimination, caprice, and mistake. . . . Experience has taught us that the constitutional goal of eliminating arbitrariness and discrimination from the administration of death . . . can never be achieved without compromising an equally essential component of fundamental fairness—individualized sentencing. . . .

From this day forward, I no longer shall tinker with the machinery of death. For more than twenty years, I have endeavored—indeed, I have struggled—along with a majority of this Court, to develop procedural and substantive rules that would lend more than the mere appearance of fairness to the death penalty endeavor. Rather than continue to coddle the Court's delusions that the desired level of fairness has been achieved and the need for regulation eviscerated, I feel morally and intellectually obligated simply to concede that the death penalty experiment has failed. It is virtually self-evident to me now that no combination of procedural rules or substantive regulations ever can save the death penalty from its inherent constitutional deficiencies. . . . The problem is that the inevitability of factual, legal, and moral error gives us a system that we know must wrongly kill some defendants, a system that fails to deliver the fair, consistent, and reliable sentence of death required by the Constitution. . . .

There is little doubt now that *Furman*'s essential holding was correct. Although most of the public seems to desire, and the Constitution appears to permit, the penalty of death, it surely is beyond dispute that, if the death penalty cannot be administered consistently and rationally, it may not be administered at all.

Delivering on the *Furman* promise, however, has proved to be another matter. *Furman* aspired to eliminate the vestiges of racism and the effects of poverty in capital sentencing; it deplored the "wanton" and "random" infliction of death by a government with constitutionally limited power. *Furman* demanded that the sentencer's discretion be directed and limited by procedural rules and objective standards in order to minimize the risk of arbitrary and capricious sentences of death.

. . . It soon became apparent that discretion could not be eliminated from capital sentencing without threatening the fundamental fairness due a defendant when life is at stake. Just as contemporary society was no longer tolerant of the random or discriminatory infliction of the penalty of death, . . . evolving standards of decency required due consideration of the uniqueness of each individual defendant when imposing society's ultimate penalty. . . .

. . . While one might hope that providing the sentencer with as much relevant mitigating evidence as possible will lead to more rational and consistent sentences, experience has taught otherwise. It seems that the decision whether a human being should live or die is so inherently subjective—rife with all of life's understandings, experiences, prejudices, and passions—that it inevitably defies the rationality and consistency required by the Constitution. . . .

STATEMENT OF SENATOR CAROL MOSELEY-BRAUN (D-IL) BEFORE THE SENATE JUDICIARY COMMITTEE, APRIL 1, 1993

The Supreme Court's recent holding in the *Herrera* case, that a death row inmate's claim of actual innocence does not entitle him to *habeas* relief (a prisoner's petition to be heard in federal court), is deeply troubling in an era when Congress and state legislatures are rushing to make more and more crimes punishable by death yet simultaneously curtailing the right to appeal at both the state and federal levels. . . .

When human judgment becomes infallible, our system will be infallible. Until then, those who would strip the system of vital safeguards lead us ever closer to the day when, in the name of the state, we will execute an innocent man. And that, in the word of Justice Brennan's dissent in the *Herrera* case, "comes perilously close to simple murder."

STATEMENT OF WALTER MCMILLIAN, MONROEVILLE, ALABAMA, BEFORE THE SENATE JUDICIARY COMMITTEE, APRIL 1, 1993

My name is Walter McMillian. I was sentenced to die in the electric chair and spent nearly six years on death row in Alabama awaiting execution for a murder that I did not commit, a murder that I knew nothing about, a murder that I had nothing to do with. Today, the state of Alabama has acknowledged that I am an innocent man and that I was wrongfully convicted. What happened to me could have happened to you, or to anyone else. I was convicted and sentenced to death on the false testimony of one man. I am here today to urge you to do all that is in your power to prevent what happened to me from happening to anyone else.

TESTIMONY OF JULIUS L. CHAMBERS, DIRECTOR-COUNSEL, NAACP LEGAL DEFENSE AND EDUCATIONAL FUND, INC., BEFORE THE HOUSE JUDICIARY COMMITTEE, MARCH 14, 1990

Passage of the proposed death penalty bills would not advance—but would instead retard—resolution of the vexing problems associated with urban crime. While holding up the mirage of fighting and deterring crime, these death penalty bills would surely result in furthering the historical and well-documented racial disparities in the imposition of capital punishment in the United States.

Our concern is squarely grounded in the stark reality, which black people have traditionally faced. For more than three centuries, the weight of the death penalty in this country has been borne far more heavily by blacks than by whites. . . .

. . . There is no question that the financial cost of sentencing a single person to death is astronomical. . . .

For example, the GAO [General Accounting Office] noted that one study done on "death penalty costs in New York estimated it would cost at least $1.8 million to defend and prosecute a capital case." By contrast, the cost of feeding and housing the defendant convicted in that same case for a period of forty years would only be $602,000. The proposed statutes are absolutely silent as to where the millions of dollars would come from to "foot the bill. . . ."

Perhaps the true purpose of the bills is to divert the public's attention away from considering measures which could truly serve to fight crime. One commentator correctly observed that . . . "the death penalty debate enables public officials and legislators to falsely assert that they are being tough on crime because they favor the death penalty." More emphasis should be placed on the less glamorous side of fighting crime. Most major cities in the country, for example, cannot afford to offer adequate treatment to young offenders who have become ensnared with the drug world.

TESTIMONY OF HENRY SCHWARZSCHILD, DIRECTOR, AMERICAN CIVIL LIBERTIES UNION CAPITAL PUNISHMENT PROJECT, BEFORE THE HOUSE JUDICIARY COMMITTEE, MARCH 14, 1990

The American Civil Liberties Union . . . hold[s] capital punishment to be inherently cruel and unusual punishment, barred by the Eighth Amendment of the Constitution. We conclude, furthermore, that in its application, the death penalty violates the due-process-of-law clause of the Fifth Amendment and the equal-protection-of-the-law clause of the Fourteenth. These judgments are grounded in the evidence that the retention of the death penalty in no way contributes to a lessening of the incidence of violent crime, that executions are a barbaric spectacle inflicted upon isolated individual criminal offenders in circumstances redolent with arbitrariness, racial and sex discrimination, as well as status bigotry, that entirely innocent persons are unavoidably executed on occasion, and that the death penalty is not only staggeringly expensive to administer but radically distorts the entire scheme of criminal sentencing.

No one—I want to emphasize—opposes the death penalty because we think that violent crime is not so terrible or that punishment for it should not be proportionately severe. It is the *limits* of severity that is in controversy, not deep anguish about violent crime; that latter, we all, of course, share. When two hundred years ago Western countries, including ours, abolished medieval forms of criminal punishment—drawing and quartering, boiling in oil, burning at the stake, gibbeting [hanging], and their like—we did so not because crimes were no longer thought to be so bad or because criminals had become nicer people: Those brutal forms of execution were abolished because we had come to think of *ourselves* as too civilized to do that sort of thing to another human being, no matter who he or she was or what [he or she] had done. *That*, and not the baseless claim that execution makes for less crime, is the issue.

THE REVEREND GUILLERMO CHAVEZ, CHAIRMAN, NATIONAL INTERRELIGIOUS TASK FORCE ON CRIMINAL JUSTICE, BEFORE THE HOUSE JUDICIARY COMMITTEE, NOVEMBER 7, 1985

I question the notion of "standards of decency" as an accepted rationale upon which to base public policy. We need to remember that, about two hundred years ago, slaveholding was not considered offensive to the then-current "standards of decency."

. . . As people of religious and ethical conscience, we seek the restoration and the renewal of wrongdoers, not their deaths. Capital punishment makes it possible for human error or prejudice to send innocent persons to their death. It eliminates forever the healing possibilities of human love and respect. Penal history provides us with prominent examples of innocent persons falsely condemned. Our Judeo-Christian heritage affirms that for the state to assume the power of absolute judgment is to assume a power that belongs only to God.

Another issue that concerns us is that the value of life, when confronted with the death penalty, is cheapened. In this regard, we are especially concerned with what the death penalty does to a society that inflicts it.

As the United Presbyterian Church has declared, "The use of the death penalty tends to brutalize the society that condones it." In denying the humanity of those we put to death, even those guilty of the most terrible crimes, including espionage or treason, we deny our own humanity, and life is further cheapened. Nothing is achieved by taking one more life or adding one more victim.

REMARKS OF SUPREME COURT JUSTICE THURGOOD MARSHALL AT A JUDICIAL CONFERENCE OF THE SECOND CIRCUIT IN HERSHEY, PENNSYLVANIA, SEPTEMBER 6, 1985

Capital defendants frequently suffer the consequences of having trial counsel who are ill-equipped to handle capital cases. Death penalty litigation has become a specialized field of practice, and even the most well-intentioned attorneys often are unable to recognize, preserve, and defend their client's rights. Often trial counsel simply are unfamiliar with the special rules that apply in capital cases. Counsel—whether appointed or retained—often are handling their first criminal cases, or their first murder cases, when confronted with the prospect of a death penalty. Though acting in good faith, they inevitably make very serious mistakes. . . . The federal reports are filled with stories of counsel who presented *no* evidence in mitigation [lessening of the gravity of the crime] of their client's sentences because they did not know what to offer or how to offer it, or had not read the state's sentencing statute.

. . . The Court has not yet recognized that the right of effective assistance must encompass a right to counsel familiar with death penalty jurisprudence at the trial stage. Instead, in all but the most egregious case, a court cannot or will not make a finding of ineffective assistance of counsel, because counsel has met what the Supreme Court has defined as a minimal standard of competence for criminal lawyers. As a consequence, many capital defendants find that errors by their lawyers preclude presentation of substantial constitutional claims, but that such errors—with the resulting forfeitures of rights—are not sufficient in themselves to constitute ineffective assistance.

Contrary to popular perceptions, all capital defendants have *not* spent years filing frivolous claims in federal courts. Many of these defendants have not yet filed *any* federal claims when their execution dates are set. We simply cannot allow this inaccurate view to blind us to reality or to accept the hasty review process on the ground that defendants already have had the benefits of an untruncated [lengthy] review process. Until an execution date is set and the situation becomes urgent, capital defendants simply have been unable to secure counsel.

Once the execution date is set, the race is on. Prisoners who have not yet sought state or federal *habeas corpus* relief have roughly one month to do so. . . . But the new attorney often has no knowledge of the record, has not met the client, and has only a few days to read hundreds of pages of transcripts and prepare a petition. This petition, hastily prepared, must include all claims that the defendant might raise, because subsequent petitions will likely be declared abusive of the process if they entertain collateral attacks.

IMPORTANT NAMES AND ADDRESSES

American Bar Association
Criminal Justice Section
740 15th St., NW
10th Fl.
Washington, DC 20005-1009
(202) 662-1500
FAX: (202) 662-1501
E-mail: crimjustice@abanet.org
URL: http://www.abanet.org/crimjust/
home.html

American Civil Liberties Union
Capital Punishment Project
122 Maryland Ave., NE
Washington, DC 20002
(202) 675-2319
E-mail: cappunaclu@aol.com
URL: http://www.aclu.org/DeathPenalty

Amnesty International U.S.A.
National Office
5 Penn Plaza
14th Fl.
New York, NY 10001
(212) 807-8400
FAX: (212) 627-1451
E-mail: aimember@aiusa.org
URL: http://www.amnestyusa.org

Amnesty International U.S.A.
The Program to Abolish the
Death Penalty
600 Pennsylvania Ave., SE
5th Fl.
Washington, DC 20003
(202) 544-0200
FAX: (202) 546-7142
E-mail: padp@aiusa.org
URL: http://www.aiusa.org/abolish

Bureau of Justice Statistics
U.S. Department of Justice
810 Seventh St., NW
Washington, DC 20531

(202) 307-0765
E-mail: askbjs@ojp.usdoj.gov
URL: http://www.ojp.usdoj.gov/bjs

Criminal Justice Legal Foundation
P.O. Box 1199
Sacramento, CA 95812
(916) 446-0345
E-mail: cjlf@cjlf.org
URL: http://www.cjlf.org/

Death Penalty Information Center
1101 Vermont Ave., NW
Suite 701
Washington, DC 20005
(202) 289-2275
FAX: (202) 289-7336
E-mail: dpic@deathpenaltyinfo.org
URL: http://www.deathpenaltyinfo.org/

Federal Bureau of Investigation
J. Edgar Hoover Building
935 Pennsylvania Ave., NW
Washington, DC 20535-0001
(202) 324-3000
URL: http://www.fbi.gov/

Federal Bureau of Prisons
320 First St., NW
Washington, DC 20534
(202) 307-3198
E-mail: info@bop.gov
URL: http://www.bop.gov/

Innocence Project
Benjamin N. Cardozo School of Law
100 Fifth Ave.
3rd Fl.
New York, NY 10011
(212) 364-5340
E-mail: info@innocenceproject.org
URL: http://www.innocenceproject.org/

International Association of Chiefs of Police
515 North Washington St.

Alexandria, VA 22314
(703) 836-6767
1-800-THE-IACP (843-4227)
FAX: (703) 836-4543
E-mail: information@theiacp.org
URL: http://www.theiacp.org/

Justice for All
Houston, TX
(713) 935-9300
E-mail: info@jfa.net
URL: http://www.jfa.net/

Justice Research and Statistics
Association
777 North Capitol St., NE
Suite 801
Washington, DC 20002
(202) 842-9330
FAX: (202) 842-9329
E-mail: cjinfo@jrsa.org
URL: http://www.jrsa.org/

The Moratorium Campaign
P.O. Box 13727
New Orleans, LA 70185-3727
E-mail: info@moratoriumcampaign.org
E-mail: hprejean@earthlink.net
(Sister Helen Prejean)
URL: http://www.moratoriumcampaign.org/

Murder Victims' Families for
Reconciliation, Inc.
6911 Richmond Highway
Suite 205
Alexandria, VA 22306
(703) 721-1888
E-mail: info@mvfr.org
URL: http://www.mvfr.org/

NAACP Legal Defense and
Educational Fund, Inc.
99 Hudson St.
Suite 1600
New York, NY 10013

(212) 965-2200
E-mail: dfins@naacpldf.org
URL: http://www.naacpldf.org/

**National Association of Criminal
Defense Lawyers**
1150 18th St., NW
Suite 950
Washington, DC 20036
(202) 872-8600
FAX: (202) 872-8690
E-mail: assist@nacdl.com
URL: http://www.nacdl.org/

National Center for Victims of Crime
2000 M St., NW
Suite 480
Washington, DC 20036-3398
(202) 467-8700
FAX: (202) 467-8701
URL: http://www.ncvc.org/

**National Coalition to Abolish
the Death Penalty**
920 Pennsylvania Ave., SE
Washington, DC 20003
(202) 543-9577
FAX: (202) 543-7798
E-mail: info@ncadp.org
URL: http://www.ncadp.org/

National Criminal Justice Reference Service
P.O. Box 6000
Rockville, MD 20849-6000

(301) 519-5500
1-800-851-3420
FAX: (301) 519-5212
URL: http://www.ncjrs.org/

**National District Attorneys
Association**
99 Canal Center Plaza
Suite 510
Alexandria, VA 22314
(703) 549-9222
FAX: (703) 836-3195
URL: http://www.ndaa.org

Pro-Death Penalty.com
E-mail: info@prodeathpenalty.com
URL: http://www.prodeathpenalty.com/

The Sentencing Project
514 10th St., NW
Suite 1000
Washington, DC 20004
(202) 628-0871
FAX: (202) 628-1091
URL: http://www.sentencingproject.org/

U.S. Commission on Civil Rights
624 9th St., NW
Washington, DC 20425
(202) 376-7700
URL: http://www.usccr.gov/

U.S. Department of Justice
950 Pennsylvania Ave., NW

Washington, DC 20530-0001
(202) 514-2000
E-mail: askdoj@usdoj.gov
URL: http://www.usdoj.gov/

**U.S. House Committee on the
Judiciary**
2138 Rayburn House Office Bldg.
Washington, DC 20515
(202) 225-3951
E-mail: judiciary@mail.house.gov
URL: http://judiciary.house.gov/

**U.S. Senate Committee on the
Judiciary**
224 Dirksen Senate Office Bldg.
Washington, DC 20510
(202) 224-5225
FAX: (202) 224-9102
URL: http://judiciary.senate.gov/

**U.S. Sentencing Commission
Office of Public Affairs**
1 Columbus Circle, NE
Washington, DC 20002-8002
(202) 502-4500
E-mail: pubaffairs@ussc.gov
URL: http://www.ussc.gov

U.S. Supreme Court
1 First St., NE
Washington, DC 20543
(202) 479-3211
URL: http://www.supremecourtus.gov/

RESOURCES

The U.S. Department of Justice collects statistics on death row inmates as part of its National Prisoner Statistics (NPS) program. Based on voluntary reporting, the NPS program collects and interprets data on state and federal prisoners. Begun by the U.S. Bureau of the Census in 1926, the program was transferred to the Federal Bureau of Prisons in 1950, to the now-defunct Law Enforcement Assistance Administration (LEAA), and then to the Bureau of Justice Statistics (BJS) in 1979.

Since 1972 the Bureau of the Census, as the collecting agent for the LEAA and the BJS, has been responsible for compiling the relevant data. The BJS annually prepares a bulletin titled *Capital Punishment*, which provides an overview of capital punishment in the United States. The BJS *Sourcebook of Criminal Justice Statistics*, prepared by the Hindelang Criminal Justice Research Center of the University at Albany, State University of New York, is the most complete compilation of criminal justice statistics.

The Department of Justice released *The Federal Death Penalty System: A Statistical Survey (1988–2000)* (2000) and *The Federal Death Penalty System: Supplementary Data, Analysis and Revised Protocols for Capital Case Review* (2001). *The Report to the Attorney General on Delays in Forensic DNA Analysis* (2003) and *Postconviction DNA Testing: Recommendations for Handling Requests* (1999), both by the National Institute of Justice, were helpful in the preparation of this book. *Federal Death Penalty Cases: Recommendations Concerning the Cost and Quality of Defense Representation*, prepared by the Subcommittee on Death Penalty Cases of the Committee on Defender Services of the Judicial Conference of the United States (1998), provides information on the cost of federal death penalty cases.

The NAACP Legal Defense and Educational Fund, Inc. (LDF), is a New York–based, private institution that maintains statistics on capital punishment. LDF is strongly opposed to the death penalty. Despite its name, LDF is not part of the National Association for the Advancement of Colored People (NAACP), although it was founded by that organization. Since 1957 LDF has had a separate board of directors, program, staff, office, and budget. LDF publishes *Death Row U.S.A.*, a periodic compilation of capital punishment statistics and information, including the names of all those currently on death row. Data from this quarterly release were helpful in preparing this book.

The Death Penalty Information Center (DPIC) is a nonprofit organization based in Washington, D.C., that provides the media and the general public with information and analysis regarding capital punishment. The DPIC, which is against the death penalty, serves as a resource to those working on this issue. Its reports and charts on capital punishment were used in preparing this book. The National Coalition Against the Death Penalty (NCADP), also located in Washington, D.C., maintains an up-to-date list of news stories from the media regarding the death penalty.

Amnesty International is the Nobel Prize–winning human rights organization headquartered in London, England. It strongly opposes the death penalty. Amnesty International maintains information on the death penalty and torture throughout the world and periodically publishes its findings. Its publication *The Death Penalty: List of Abolitionist and Retentionist Countries (24 January 2005)* provided data on the status of capital punishment worldwide.

Charts and data from *Death Penalty for Female Offenders: January 1, 1973, through June 30, 2005* (2005) and *The Juvenile Death Penalty Today: Death Sentences and Executions for Juvenile Crimes: January 1, 1973–December 31, 2004* (2005), by Professor Victor L. Streib of the Claude W. Pettit College of Law at Ohio Northern University (Ada, OH), were used in the preparation of this book.

Other studies used in this book include *Innocence and the Crisis in the American Death Penalty* by Richard C. Dieter (Death Penalty Information Center, 2004); "Explaining Death Row's Population and Racial Composition" by John Blume, Theodore Eisenberg, and Martin T. Wells (*Journal of Empirical Legal Studies* 1, no. 1, March 2004); *Performance Audit Report: Costs Incurred for Death Penalty Cases* (Kansas Legislative Division on Post Audit, 2003); *Study Pursuant to Public Act No. 01-151 of the Imposition of the Death Penalty in Connecticut* (State of Connecticut Commission on the Death Penalty, 2003); *Critique of DPIC List "Innocence: Freed from Death Row,"* by Ward A. Campbell (http://www.prodeathpenalty.com/DPIC.htm, 2002); *Case Histories: A Review of 23 Individuals Released from Death Row* (Florida Commission on Capital Cases, 2002); "Capital Punishment Proves to be Expensive" by Daniel Wise (*New York Law Journal* 227, April 30, 2002); *Race and the Death Penalty in North Carolina, an Empirical Analysis: 1993–1997, Initial Findings* by Isaac Unah and John Charles Boger (Chapel Hill: University of North Carolina and the Common Sense Foundation, 2001); *The Disposition of Nebraska Capital and Non-Capital Homicide Cases (1973–1999): A Legal and Empirical Analysis* by David C. Baldus, George Woodworth, Gary L. Young, and Aaron M. Christ (2001); *A Broken System: Error Rates in Capital Cases, 1973–1995* by James S. Liebman, Jeffrey Fagan, and Valerie West (2000); "Capital Appeals Revisited" by Barry Latzer and James N. G. Cauthen (*Judicature* 84, no. 2, September–October 2000); and *The Fair Defense Report: Analysis of Indigent Defense Practices in Texas* (Texas Appleseed Fair Defense Project, 2000).

David G. Chardavoyne's *A Hanging in Detroit: Stephen Gifford Simmons and the Last Execution under Michigan Law* (Detroit, MI: Wayne State University Press, 2003) provided, among other things, information on the rituals of public executions. *Executions in the United States, 1608–2002: The ESPY File* by M. Watt Espy and John Ortiz Smykla (Inter-university Consortium for Political and Social Research, 2004) lists every known execution to have occurred in the North American British colonies and the United States from 1608 to 2002. The third edition of Roger Hood's *The Death Penalty—A Worldwide Perspective* (Oxford University Press, Inc., New York, 2002) provided a wealth of information about the scope and application of the death penalty in different countries.

The news feature service, Human Rights Features (New Delhi, India), and Forum 90, an abolitionist group that monitors capital punishment in Japan, provided information on the imposition of the death penalty in Japan ("Japan Hanging on to Death Penalty" [2003] and "The Hidden Death Penalty in Japan" [2001], respectively).

In *FYI: Rights of Survivors of Homicide* (1999) the National Center for Victims of Crimes (Washington, D.C.), a nonprofit organization that supports victims' rights and promotes victim assistance, describes some state statutes and policies that allow victims' families to witness executions. Other information about victims' families as execution witnesses comes from *Who Owns Death? Capital Punishment, the American Conscience, and the End of Executions* (New York: William Morrow, 2000) by Robert Jay Lifton and Greg Mitchell.

Polls taken by the Gallup Organization (Princeton, NJ) and Harris Interactive (New York, NY) were also used in preparing this book.

INDEX